7/20

Party Reform

Party Reform

William Crotty
Northwestern University

Longman
New York & London

Party Reform

Longman Inc., 1560 Broadway, New York, N.Y. 10036
Associated companies, branches, and representatives
throughout the world.

Developmental Editor: Irving E. Rockwood
Editorial and Design Supervisor: Joan Matthews
Production Supervisor: Ferne Y. Kawahara
Manufacturing Supervisor: Marion Hess
Composition: Kingsport Press
Printing and Binding: Fairfield Graphics

The excerpt on page 118 is from "Democracy," by Langston
Hughes, copyright 1948 by Alfred A. Knopf, Inc. Reprinted from
SELECTED POEMS OF LANGSTON HUGHES, by Langston Hughes,
by permission of the publisher.

Library of Congress Cataloging in Publication Data

Crotty, William J.
  Party reform.

  Includes index.
  1. Political parties—United States. I. Title.
JK2261.C843 1983   324.273   82–20836
ISBN 0–582–28177–6

MANUFACTURED IN THE UNITED STATES OF AMERICA
Printing: 9 8 7 6 5 4 3 2 1   Year: 91 90 89 88 87 86 85 84 83

Contents

v

Preface

Political parties are undergoing uncertain times. Much in the contemporary political and social environment appears hostile to the continuing functioning of the political parties in anything resembling the way in which they used to operate in the past. The political parties are changing, although whether quickly enough or in the directions needed to satisfy the demand of a social order in transition is open to debate.

One response of the party system has been to attempt "reform." In the present context, this means a turn toward more open, participant-oriented, and representative party structures intended to revitalize parties along a more policy-oriented base. The movement has been controversial; in fact, it has been resisted with varying degrees of success by party professionals within both of the political parties. Yet reform has left its mark on the political parties. In particular, the presidential nominating procedures and power distributions have been significantly and, more than likely, permanently transformed. The impact of the reform movement on other aspects of political party operations is less certain.

This book reviews and assesses the reform era, from its earliest days in the late 1960s to the present. It analyzes the contributions of various reform bodies and the issues in contention between those wishing to move toward a new party system and those committed to preserving what they can of the old ways. The book is written from the perspective of one sympathetic to the reform objectives of openness, representativeness, and political accountability.

In writing a book such as this, I owe a debt of gratitude to a number of people. I would like to thank Irv Rockwood of Longman, in particular, for his continued assistance, Edward Artinian, Joan Matthews, David Estrin, and all the others who contributed to the book's appearance.

William Crotty

Party Reform

PART ONE

The Basis for Reform

ONE

Why Reform?

American political parties are in serious trouble. The evidence is everywhere. One of the two major parties intersperses impressive, but short-run, electoral successes with a long-running flirtation with extinction. The other has been rocked by internal divisions and a hardheaded unwillingness or inability to adapt to a radically changing political environment. Factional bickering and attitudinal intransigence towards adaptation has resulted in electoral defeats severe enough to question the party's ability to govern and its self-proclaimed role as the champion, and representative, of the majority of subgroups within the diverse American electorate. The twilight of the American party system, at least in the form in which it has been known since the time of Washington, Jefferson, and Jackson, may be at hand.

Yet the crisis in party operations comes at a curious time. For once, and perhaps for the only time in their long and tumultuous history, the value of political parties within a democratic society is almost universally appreciated. In truth, the contributions of political parties to a representative democracy has been—at least among academicians of the last generation—virtually universally celebrated; an obsession that has closed many eyes to their faults and may, in part, contribute to their present difficulties.

The argument—dogma?—in favor of political parties runs something like this: Political parties are critically significant agencies for any democratic society. They perform a variety of services for a democracy, from nominating and helping to elect its leadership to representing and, in their own way, resolving the diverse sets of group pressures, policy demands, and festering social problems that beset the society, as well as join and divide their diverse constituencies. And most importantly, the political party executes its responsibilities better and more democratically than any comparable agency devised by man. Political parties, in short, are and have been indispensible to a functioning democratic society of any size.

So be it. If parties are as crucial as this argument suggests, then

3

society (as well as the parties) may be in for a period of uncertainty and rapid and uncharted change. For while the indispensibility of parties to democratic governing is broadly agreed upon, the quality of the contributions the parties make, what it is or could or should be, is a matter of continuing dispute. Since the 1950s, a period of stability for the parties and one that gave birth to much of the currently accepted theorizing as to their utility and functioning, political party influence has been on the wane. By any objective indicator, the parties are in difficulty. Participation in elections is down to one-half of the eligible electorate in presidential contests and even less (30–40%) in many congressional, senatorial, statewide, and mayoral races. The number of people claiming identification with one of the two parties has been in steady decline, and the end of the attrition in partisanship is nowhere in sight. The continual erosion of the past several generations in Republican partisanship (to where it now wavers between 15 and 25 percent of the American electorate) has led forecasters to predict the party's eventual demise, a prognosis that periodic victories at the presidential level (Reagan, Nixon, Eisenhower) tends to mute. The Republican successes may be as much a product of the Democratic party's weaknesses and chronic divisiveness as they are of any positive Republican appeal.

Both parties have fared poorly in attracting younger voters, a trend that indicates the demographics of change favor an increasingly anti-party evolution. Among those just entering the electorate, slightly better than one-half claim no party identification. As a consequence, the proportion of political independents has about doubled over the last three decades. Independents appear to be the wave of the future.

As the numbers affiliated with the parties, and the strength of partisanship more generally, has eroded, the parties themselves appear unable to offer coherent party programs, designed to seriously address the most pressing issues facing the nation. They appear incapable of even disciplining their own members once in office on issues of fundamental concern. The inability of the Democratic party in the Congress to fashion reasonably attractive alternatives to Republican policies or to deliver their vote as a bloc on the most crucial issues separating the parties is one indication of the vacuity and potential obsolescence of present party arrangements.

Third parties give promise of future challenge, a sure sign of the declining appeal of the major parties. Corporate, labor, ideological, and single issue PACs (political action committees) push their policy ends, fund campaigns and even recruit, and help nominate and elect, candidates. They have become parties within parties, an additional contributor to the fragmentation of the American two-party system.

The events of the last two decades indicate that the major parties

are, at least partially, aware of their problems. The extent of their ✓
awareness and of their willingness to do something of consequence
about their problems is questionable. Both parties have attempted "reform"; change designed to quiet critics within the party's ranks and
to ameliorate, on a short-term basis, the internal clashes and mini-
crises that perpetually threaten party consensus. The efforts of the
parties to reform themselves has led to some surprising results. How
effective these changes have been in arresting the decline in American
parties is open to debate.

This is, in effect, what this book is all about. The chapters that
follow will take a look at the reform movements within the two parties
and evaluate what they attempted and what they accomplished. Included in the assessment will be an examination of several of the unanticipated consequences of reform and the problems that these in turn
have raised for the parties. It also includes a case study of party reform
at the local level, linking the national party with its base constituency,
an uneasy alliance that produces problems for both. Reform exacer-
bated these tensions. The book reviews the strengths and weaknesses
of the reform era and analyzes the current state and possible future
orientation of the party enterprise.

First, however, it is necessary to develop two areas that lend perspective to the events of recent years. While many social scientists ✓
have tended to venerate the political parties and their accomplishments, the general public has been considerably less enthusiastic about
the parties and their contributions to modern society. In fact, the public
has been highly critical of party operations and appears to tolerate
them as a necessary evil. This attitude has provided a fertile ground
for reform. The public's perception of political parties and the constant
efforts, and their consequences, to mold parties into more acceptable
social institutions ("reform") are covered in the next several chapters.

TWO

A Party System under Siege

Political parties have been with us for so long and have served for such a lengthy period as objects of derision that it is often difficult to think of them in any positive sense. Yet they are a vitally important ingredient in the democratic enterprise.

A Brief in Defense of Parties

It is important to begin by recognizing that political parties grew out of a need. In effect, they were created to fill a void in the democratic system; they evolved because no other agency could as effectively serve as a force upon government acting in the name of a democratic mass. The American constitution ignored the possibility of parties, and the nation's early leadership was antagonistic to them. The Founding Fathers were frightened of the divisiveness and polarization parties, or factions as they referred to them, would create in political life. The distaste for parties, if anything, grew over the years. The excesses of democratic government—at least, as seen from the vantage point of the ruling elites—during the Age of Jackson and the inauguration of mass democratic institutions; the inability of a floundering party system to deal with secession or the issue of slavery; the association of parties with the evolving urban machine and its (and the ethnic groups it represented) threat to the established social order; the corruption synonymous with the "age of boodle" and the misuse of public monies; continuing on up to the present and the ineffectiveness of the parties in checking the worst of the Watergate abuses have all contributed to the negative associations made with the institution.

Yet there is no denying their contribution to democratic government. Many have made the point. Political parties allow a sublimation of the once bloody conflicts between ins and outs over succession to power. They permit a legitimate, organized resistance to authority, and they provide a vehicle through which officials in disfavor can be replaced. They represent the views of their constituent masses and they try to bring these to bear on government policies. The parties select through their nominating systems the finalists for the nation's major offices, and they attempt to establish some criteria to judge officials once in office. Ideally, they are agencies intended to express the democratic will; the bridge between the citizen and government. Political parties, it would seem, are indispensable to democratic government.

This certainly has been a theme among the more serious students of party developments. A knowledge of political parties, as Avery Leiserson has said, "is virtually a prerequisite to a realistic understanding of the problems of democracy, both in theory and in action."[1] E. E. Schattschneider goes further. Political parties, he contends, "created democracy, or perhaps more accurately, modern democracy is a byproduct of party competition."[2] As Schattschneider indicates, their contribution to American democracy has been substantial:

> American parties . . . have transformed the American constitution. They have substantially abolished the electoral college, created a plebiscitary president, and contributed powerfully to the extraconstitutional growth of that office. . . . The parties have greatly simplified the most complex system of government in the world. . . . More important than all other changes the parties have wrought in the system of government is the fact that they have democratized it. They took over an eighteenth-century constitution and made it function to satisfy the needs of modern democracy in ways not contemplated by the authors. . . . these parties have presided over the transformation of the government of the United States from a small experiment in republicanism to the most powerful regime on earth, vastly more liberal and democratic than it was in 1789.[3]

Their contribution to an organized, representative, and accountable democratic polity then would appear critical. "Political parties," concludes Schattschneider, "created democracy and . . . modern democracy is unthinkable save in terms of the parties."[4] Schattschneider's defense of political parties is a categorical one. It leaves little room for dispute.

Most students of American parties would more than likely agree in principle with his contentions. V. O. Key, Jr., the most influential modern analyst of party behavior, might take exception to Schattschneider's sweeping declaration as to the absolute necessity of parties, but he would argue that political parties have been one of the few institutions essential to the democratic experiment and that the functions they perform are vital to the preservation of orderly democratic government. Apparently, they represent the only effective agency that democracies of any size have been able to devise "for handling the problem of succession to authority more or less peacefully."[5]

More recently, Walter Dean Burnham has raised the spectre of what a democracy without political parties might be like. Burnham is concerned with tracing the electoral disaggregation of the parties' coalitions and the resulting "decomposition" (an unpleasant term) of the party-in-the-electorate, the party that coalesces and represents on different levels the policy views of relatively like-minded people. Burnham prophesizes: "the old-style American major party-in-the-electorate may very well be on its way out as a channel through which the collective power of the many can at least occasionally control the behavior of the elites who run this political system."[6] Should the party system continue to deteriorate, "a true crisis of the regime will emerge—perhaps sooner than later. If 'partisan decomposition' continues under . . . conditions of pervasive public discontent, democracy will be progressively emptied of any operational meaning."[7]

Schattschneider may well have been correct: democracy without a vital party system may be unthinkable. The outcome sketched by Burnham is not the only possible one of course. It is, however, a frightening prospect, made less unimaginable by a full appreciation of the implications of the Watergate episode and the internal repressions and civil disobedience of the Vietnam period. It does speak to the need for a strong and representative party system.

Two things most close observers of political parties would agree on then are:

1. Political parties are, at a minimum, extremely important to the American democratic enterprise.
2. Political parties are, as noted in the introduction to this book, in trouble.

At Best, an Uncertain Tradition

Americans could never be said to have had a love affair with their political parties. Rather, they have tended to view these institutions with suspicion. Their existence has been seen as a necessary evil. George Washington would not have gone this far. During the period of their birth, he cautioned against institutions and leaders that would divide a nation and a people. James Madison, himself a party tactician of the first rank, shared Washington's concern. Writing in *Federalist No. 10*, Madison warned against the "instability, injustice, and confusion" parties introduced into the public's business. "The public good is disregarded in the conflicts of rival parties; and that measures are too often decided, not according to the rules of justice and the rights of the minor party, but by the superior force of an interested and overbearing majority."[8]

Washington and Madison were among the first of many. As the party system evolved in concert with a developing nation, experimental political arrangements, and a changing social order, others came to view them in much the same light. Alexis de Tocqueville drew attention to the lack of principles in the parties he encountered in the 1830s. Their squabbling and materialism he believed would "threaten the future of the Union."[9] James Byrce, writing a half-century later, was equally critical:

> Neither party has anything definite to say on . . . issues; neither party has any principles, any distinctive tenets. . . . [their] interests are in the main the interests of getting or keeping the patronage of the government. Tenets and policies, points of political doctrine and points of political practice, have all but vanished. . . . All has been lost, except office or the hope of it.[10]

M. I. Ostrogorski, Russian émigré and student of democratic institutions, would agree. After extensively studying the American parties near the turn of the century, he concluded that "God takes care of drunkards, of little children, and of the United States."[11]

Political parties had come to be identified with corruption, weak candidates, the exploitation of the public trust, graft, bossism, crime, rowdyism, and about everything else that was held in disrepute. Equally odious, political parties were seen as ties to the immigrant masses, the unlettered newcomers to city life that made up the bulk of the urban work force and the political base for the machine. These newer groups had a different perception of government and what it should do that, along with their strange customs and the political bosses they spawned, unsettled the older immigrants.

Reform in the early twentieth century

A school of journalism, the Muckrakers, made their reputations to a large extent at the expense of the parties of their day. One consequence was the reform wave—the Progressive Era—of the period roughly from the late 1890s to 1920. A serious attempt was mounted during these years to reconstruct the economic and political priorities of the nation. Politically, the chief targets were the parties and their abuses. The objective was to incapacitate the parties and destroy the boss while returning power to the hands of the citizenry. Toward these ends, the "good government" advocates pressed for such reforms as nonpartisan elections; city manager or council forms of government (with policy areas supervised by those with the necessary professional expertise); registration laws and other safeguards against a fraudulent vote; the secret ballot; primaries to destroy the boss's control over nominations for elective office; the statutory regulation of party finances, party activities, and party structures; the initiative, referendum, and recall to give citizens a direct voice in creating legislation and some control over legislators once elected; and an expansion of civil service protections to minimize the evils of patronage.

The intentions of these earlier reformers appear commendable. They attack citadels of power and abuse: the plutocracy of wealth (the Rockefellers, Morgans, and Mellons), who disproportionately controlled the nation's economic resources; and the parties and their bosses that managed the country's politics. Their goal was to give the individual a direct voice in their political and economic destiny.

The people who were to benefit the most from these reforms were, interestingly, remarkably similar in economic status and civic values to the reformers themselves. They were the middle class burgers, professionals, and academicians with the desired interest, skills, and disposition to conduct governmental affairs in the impersonal manner the Progressives thought proper. If political parties were to be destroyed in the process of achieving broader aims, so much the better. They were considered to be of little value, barriers to honest and effective government.

The reformers succeeded to a large extent in getting the changes they wanted adopted. But they failed in their major objectives. Political parties and the party boss were not destroyed. After a period of readjustment to the new political environment, the boss continued to exercise power much as he did in days gone by. There is a lesson here. The Progressives did not understand politics or the value or functions of a political party. Reform is best understood as change and change that: (1) adapts to current political realities, and (2) rewards some groups and emphasizes some values at the expense of others. The boss (and the political party) survived, despite their profiteering and marked abuse of authority, because he (and it) performed a number of crucial (if less obvious) political services. The Progressives wanted a political arrangement that nicely rewarded the virtues upon which they had been weaned and the talents they had developed. Their "reforms" held little attraction for the groups that supported the boss and de-pended upon him, whatever the price, for a toehold in the new society. The Progressives, the established, could offer the economic classes just beginning to climb the social ladder nothing beyond the promise of good government as they defined it, one that was scrupulously clean and aboveboard in its formal dealings. Theirs was a defensive concep-tion of politics basically irrelevant to the needs of the immigrants and workers that provided the lifeblood of the machine.

It could be argued that something of a role reversal would take place in the more recent reform period, with the reformers promoting changes they believed responsive to a developing social context and party regulars and anti-reformers more generally blindly opposing any threat to established political arrangements which they found to be both comfortable and personally rewarding. It is fair to question which group best read the temper of the times and the manner in which democratic government could be made to work most effectively in the late twentieth century. Finally in this regard, some judgment would have to be rendered on the extent to which the institutional arrange-ments being proposed, or defended, could effectively realize the oppos-ing conceptions of democratic performance being advanced.

Political parties survived the onslaught of the Progressives but they were markedly less successful in another regard. What they failed to overcome was the disrepute in which they were held. The American people continued to distrust the parties.

A Contemporary View of Public Perceptions

Professor Jack Dennis has been concerned about the levels of public support for the party system in recent decades. Immediately following the 1964 presidential election, Dennis polled a representative sample of Wisconsin's adult population on their views of political parties. He did not find strong popular support for the parties.[12] Overall, the results of his survey were mixed. The public seemed to approve of some aspects of the parties' performance while disapproving of others. For example, respondents rejected the contention that elections would be improved if ballots carried no party labels. An impressive majority of the Wisconsin sample expressed the belief that strong party competi-tion helped democracy and that the people who worked for parties during campaigns performed a public service. On the other hand, a plurality of those interviewed agreed that parties actually created dis-sension (shades of Washington and Madison); that they confused rather than clarified issues; that controversies between the parties hurt the nation; and that the country would be better off if we could get rid of the conflict between parties.

Not unlike previous periods in American history, there appears to be a lack of understanding of exactly what the parties do of consequence for the political system. While the attitudes toward the parties are ambivalent, the weight of the responses ran to the negative. Dennis was cautious. He admitted that the "mass endorsement is infirm and narrow," but he saw grounds for hope in that the "younger, more active, better educated" support the party system more enthusiastically than other groups and he found a continued high level of identification with the parties among voters.[13] As noted, this was in the mid-sixties.

Dennis repeated his study twice in the 1970s, sampling both the adult populations of Wisconsin and the nation. The findings from the 1970s reemphasize Dennis's contention that "the political party system has indeed suffered a long-term erosion of positive public feeling" and that "at the most basic level the parties have been subject to deinstitutionalization."[14] Virtually all indices of party support were down, and most declined precipitously. One indicator did remain stable however: In comparison with the Congress, the presidency and the Supreme Court, political parties ranked as the least trusted major institution in American political life. Dennis's conclusion that the parties continue as a "diseased organ of the body politic" appears warranted.[15]

A "Diseased Organ"?

Continuing public support for the contemporary party system has been weak. In addition, the strains engendered by the Vietnam era, Watergate, and the economic ills of the sixties, seventies, and eighties have all had their impact. The result has been a party system that, within this context, appeared unable to offer relative policy alternatives powerful enough to resolve the most critical problems of the day; was incapable of guiding or restraining, in the name of a broader public or party good, the actions of its leaders once in office; and that remained largely unaccountable to its membership. Given these conditions, it is not difficult to understand why the parties were ripe for reform. Nonetheless, it takes specific, and highly publicized, abuses of political institutions—critical and unignorable demonstrations of need—before the broad public constituency necessary for reform can be built.[16] The events of the late 1960s (and more specifically the election year of 1968) were to provide such a catalyst.

THREE

The Roots of Reform

The Specific Events Leading to Reform

The year 1968 will go down in history for many reasons. It was one of the most tumultuous years of the modern era. War, assassinations, cities on fire, race riots, federal troops in the streets, the withdrawal of a president, the Chicago convention, and the election of Richard Nixon constitute some of the guideposts along the way. The year was a watershed in American history.

In retrospect, it is difficult to capture the frenzy of events and the intensity of feelings unleashed. Yet these help explain the major efforts at institutional change that followed.

A Nation in Turmoil

The 1968 election year actually began on November 30, 1967, when a little-known senator from Minnesota, Eugene McCarthy, announced his intention to challenge the renomination of the incumbent president, Lyndon Johnson. The move was supported by a small group of liberals and anti-war activists within the Democratic party. It was widely considered to be futile.

Vietnam and popular discontent

Seemingly, the Vietnam War was destined to dominate the election year activities. In late January of the new year, the Viet Cong and the North Vietnamese launched their most ambitious assault, the Tet, or lunar new year, offensive. The results were staggering. The offensive was aimed at thirty provincial capitals in South Vietnam. Before it concluded, the North Vietnamese had overrun much of the more populated areas of the South; captured and held for twenty-five days, despite massive American and South Vietnamese counterattacks, Hue, the

13

traditional capital of Vietnam; launched a serious attack on Saigon; and enemy troops had even managed to enter the U.S. Embassy. This despite an American troop level in Vietnam (474,300) that exceeded that in Korea at any point during the Korean War and an American financial and material investment estimated by President Johnson in his State-of-the-Union address two weeks before the assault to be in the neighborhood of $25 billion per year.

These events were particularly galling to the anti-war activists. They came on the heels of repeated assurances by the military and the president that victory was in sight. The point was made by McCarthy in a speech on the campaign trail in New Hampshire:

> In 1963, we were told we were winning the war. In 1964, we were told the corner was being turned. In 1965, in 1967, and now again in 1968, we hear the same hollow claims of programs and victory. For the fact is that the enemy is bolder than ever, while we must steadily enlarge our own commitment. The Democratic Party in 1964 promised "no wider war." Yet the war is getting wider every month. Only a few months ago we were told that sixty-five percent of the population [of South Vietnam] was secure. Now we know that even the American Embassy is not secure.[1]

Lyndon Johnson had campaigned against the presumably more hawkish Barry Goldwater in 1964 promising, as he phrased it in his much-quoted September speech, that no American boys would die in an Asian land war. Despite Johnson's assurances, in the immediate aftermath of his election the war against North Vietnam was intensified. The Administration pushed for, and won, from the Congress the "Gulf of Tonkin" resolution, following the alleged attack on two U.S. destroyers by enemy torpedo boats. The resolution signified congressional support for the extraordinary measures needed to sustain the American effort in Indochina. The American troop level in Vietnam was drastically and continuously increased, as were the materiel and other commitments to the South Vietnamese government. In due course, bombings of North Vietnam were authorized, including as targets the population centers of Hanoi and Haiphong and extending from the demilitarized zones separating North from South to within ten miles of the Chinese border (and later, of course, the war was extended to Cambodia).

The commander of the American troops in Vietnam, General William Westmoreland, found cause for optimism. "We are winning a war of attrition," declared Westmoreland in November 1967, that should lead in two years or less to a "phase down [of] the level of our military effort."[2] Others were less convinced. From January 1964, when Johnson assumed the presidency in his own right, until January 1968 and the Tet offensive, American forces had increased from 23,000 to just under 500,000. Before his term was over, the number would rise to 536,000. The American casualties list kept pace, rising from a total of 267 killed and 783 wounded in the pre-1965 period to 30,347 killed and 99,004 wounded during the years 1965–1968. Before the war was over, more than forty-six thousand American soldiers would die and fifty-three thousand would be wounded severely enough to require hospitalization. The war was to become the longest in American history and the most unpopular. Its financial costs ($111.6 billion) would rank second only to that of World War II.

Many found the bloodshed senseless. To them, the American government had involved itself in a civil war in a remote Asian nation on the dubious premise that such intervention was needed to contain an advancing communism that theoretically, at least, would eventually threaten the United States. For Lyndon Johnson, the war in Vietnam was being fought to prevent World War III. For others, American and Asian lives were being wasted to prop up a corrupt dictatorship in a fight in which the United States had no legitimate stake. As the fighting and casualties escalated, so did the number and intensity of the anti-war protests. All of these served as a backdrop to the events surrounding the Tet offensive.

The government's reaction was predictable. Government spokesmen claimed that the offensive had, in reality, proven to be a victory for the United States. The North Vietnamese had failed to capture control of South Vietnam and, in fact, had actually been beaten back. According to the Defense Department, the media had misinterpreted the results and given the American public the wrong picture of what had happened. All that was needed to secure final victory was rededication of effort on the part of the American people. In accordance with these views and past responses, the American commander in Vietnam requested an additional complement of 206,000 American troops.

The military implications of the North Vietnamese assault might be disputed. Its effect on domestic policies cannot be. The public appeared shocked and, although the polls assessing opinions on Vietnam were confused, increasingly skeptical of administration claims and unsympathetic to the war. The Congress appeared more reluctant to continue an open-ended military commitment to South Vietnam. And the intensity of the anti-war opposition continued to escalate.

The New Hampshire primary

The New Hampshire primary followed in the wake of the renewed debate over American objectives in Southeast Asia. It was unusually nasty. While McCarthy campaigned on a theme "Let Us Begin Anew" and directed his attacks against the administration's Vietnam policies, the White House attempted to make the contest a vote of confidence in the soldiers fighting in Asia. The emphasis was on patriotism and, by implication, the loyalty of New Hampshire voters.

The Democratic State Committee took out newspaper advertisements urging the state's voters "to support our fighting men in Vietnam" by writing-in Johnson's name on the primary ballot. The president's supporters passed out ticket stubs which the voters were asked to sign pledging their support to the president. Each ticket was numbered and divided into three stubs: one for the voter, one to be filed with the Democratic State Committee, and one to be sent to the White House.

A few days before the primary, the President's campaign manager in the state argued that any "significant vote" for McCarthy, in his words, "will be greeted with great cheers in Hanoi." It would be, he added, a "sign that the American people are ready to quit." The election would be seen as "a measure of the will and resolve of the people of New Hampshire."[3]

The day before the election, a radio commercial featuring the state's Democratic U.S. senator received wide play:

> Senator McCarthy said Saturday he would ask for laws which would allow American draft dodgers, men who have fled to Canada or Sweden to avoid fighting in Vietnam, to return home scot free without punishment. This is a cruel affront to those who have answered their country's call to duty. To honor draft dodgers and deserters will destroy the very fabric of our national devotion. This is fuzzy-thinking about principles that have made our nation great. Support the loyal men who *do* serve this country by writing the name of President Johnson on your ballot.[4]

Going into the election, Johnson's campaign director claimed that 25,000 pledge cards had been forwarded to the White House and he predicted the president would be a three-to-one victor. He added that if McCarthy received as much as 25 percent of the vote, "I will be disappointed with the voters of New Hampshire."[5]

It is within this context that the New Hampshire outcome takes its meaning. Despite what they admitted to be a "hard sell" campaign and an all-out effort by the Democratic party on behalf of the president and despite the attempt to equate support of McCarthy with disloyalty to the troops in Asia and possibly to the nation, Johnson had not done well.

McCarthy had secured an impressive "victory." In actuality, the Minnesota senator did not win the popular vote in the Democratic primary. He fell a little over four thousand votes short of Johnson, with 41.9 percent of the votes cast to the president's 49.6 percent. But he accomplished this in a state with a conservative electorate. He did it with a volunteer army of amatuers and against the full apparatus of the state's Democratic party and in spite of the resources of the White House. With the votes that Johnson and McCarthy received in both the Republican and Democratic primaries lumped together, the president was able to edge out a relatively unknown senator by only about five hundred votes.

The pressure served to dramatize the unpopularity of the administration and its policies generally and the softness of its popular support. It effectively knocked Johnson out of the presidency.

Johnson withdraws

Others were aware of the implications. On March 16, Robert Kennedy announced his intentions to seek the Democratic party's presidential nomination. Kennedy was a far more formidable candidate than McCarthy. Basically a traditional politician, Kennedy had fashioned a constituency of the disaffected—blacks, those opposed to the war, the poor, and youth—while still holding appeal for blue collar workers and the more traditional sources of support for Democratic candidacies. Unlike McCarthy, and despite his opposition to the administration, Kennedy was acceptable to many party regulars. He was also a candidate that Johnson intensely disliked and, to a degree, feared. The Kennedy candidacy was a long shot but it offered the insurgents their most realistic hope of capturing the party's nomination and reversing its stand on the war.

Two weeks after Kennedy's entry into the race another bombshell came in a year filled with them. On March 31st, with the Wisconsin primary imminent, and a McCarthy victory predicted, Johnson announced his withdrawal from the race: "I shall not seek and I will not accept the nomination of my party as president."[6]

Instead, Johnson pledged to devote the remainder of his presidency to a search for peace. In the speech accompanying the statement removing himself from the presidential contest, the president suspended the bombing over most of North Vietnam and invited the communists to reciprocate in some manner. The balance of the election year witnessed the hesitant beginnings of peace talks and a number of sputtering efforts to deescalate the hostilities. Further steps would be left to the incoming Nixon administration.

Curiously perhaps, Johnson's voluntarily stepping down did not cool emotions. Matters had progressed too far and the continuing events of the election year served, if anything, to exacerbate the situation. Few of his opponents trusted Johnson and they questioned the strength of his commitment to an immediate peace. The president himself appeared to be ambivalent. Right up to the time of his unexpected decision to retire from office, Johnson continued his hawklike posturing, assuring all who would listen there would be "a total national effort to win the war."

Reflecting on those who disagreed with him and on the events leading up to his withdrawal, Johnson seemed at once confused, offended, and resentful. Speaking of the anti-war coalition that had opposed him, Johnson told a biographer:

> How is it possible . . . that all these people could be so ungrateful to me after I had given them so much? Take the Negroes. I fought for them from the first day I came into office. I spilled my guts out in getting the Civil Rights Act of 1964 through Congress. I put everything I had into that speech before the joint session in 1965. I tried to make it possible for every child of every color to grow up in a nice house, to eat a solid breakfast, to attend a decent school, and to get a good and lasting job. I asked so little in return. Just a little appreciation. That's all. But look at what I got instead. Riots in 175 cities. Looting. Burning. Shooting. It ruined everything. Then take the students. I wanted to help them, too. I fought on their behalf for scholarships and loans and grants. I fought for better teachers and better schools. And look what I got back. Young people by the thousands leaving their universities, marching in the streets, chanting that horrible song about how many kids I had killed that day. And the poor, they, too, turned against me. When Congress cut the funds for the Great Society, they made me Mr. Villain. I remember once going to visit a poor family in Appalachia. They had seven children, all skinny and sick. I promised the mother and father I would make things all better for them. I told them all my hopes for their future. They seemed real happy to talk with me, and I felt good about that. But then as I walked toward the door, I noticed two pictures on the shabby wall. One was Jesus Christ on the cross; the other was John Kennedy. I felt as if I'd been slapped in the face.[7]

A period of turmoil

With the president out of the race, Hubert Humphrey, Johnson's vice-president and the administration's heir apparent, lay claim to the nomination. He, of course, automatically became the favorite. Humphrey, however, did not wish to test his strength, or the administration's popularity, in an open contest with either Kennedy or McCarthy. Correspondingly, an awkward interregnum ensued while Humphrey delayed the formal declaration of his candidacy until the final deadline for the last of the primaries had passed. On April 27, he made the expected announcement: "Here we are, just as we ought to be, the people, here we are in a spirit of dedication, here we are the way politics ought to be in America, *the politics of happiness, the politics of purpose, and the politics of joy.* And that's the way it's going to be, all the way, from here on in!" (italics added).[8] And for Humphrey it was. The "politics of joy" was a campaign strain repeated up to and through the disasterous Chicago Convention. The theme was repugnant to many. It seemed particularly inappropriate to the year—and, on a more limited scale, even the events that had transpired since Johnson's announcement.

On April 4th, the country had been rocked by the assassination of Martin Luther King, Jr., the nation's preeminent civil right leader. King had been in Memphis to lend moral support to a strike by predominantly black garbage workers when he had been killed. The inept and prolonged search for the killer and the confusing official announcements that followed did little to restore a sense of legitimacy, or purpose, to a nation badly in need of both.

King's murder touched off riots in Detroit, Chicago, Philadelphia, Boston, San Francisco, Toledo, and other major cities. Washington itself was in flames. The president had to call out federal troops to protect the White House and to quell the disturbances. Looting was rampant. In Chicago, Mayor Daley gave his police the infamous "shoot-to-kill" orders, an unneeded addition to a series of troubled events in a very troubled year.

Two months after King's assassination, Robert Kennedy was killed, also the victim of an assassin. Kennedy's death came in the immediate aftermath of his close but significant victory over McCarthy (and a stand-in slate for Humphrey) in California, the last of the primaries and the one with the greatest delegate prize.

For all practical purposes, the insurgent's campaign ended with Kennedy's murder. The nomination went by default to Humphrey. McCarthy was anathema to the party regulars, and he proved unable to expand his appeal beyond his original base of support. George McGovern, another virtual unknown at the time, tried in the few weeks prior to the convention to rally the Kennedy coalition behind him. It was a token effort.

Humphrey had avoided the primaries and any real chance to test his personal popularity or to allow a referendum on his, and the administration's, views. He was heir to a marred legacy and the symbol of a discredited administration. Yet his nomination was never in doubt. With the support of major interest groups (such as the AFL-CIO) within the party, and with the delegate votes commanded by the party regulars, the big city mayors, and the industrial state governors, Humphrey's claim was secure. Given the manner in which presidential delegates were selected and national conventions managed, and despite all that had occurred in the preceeding months, the vice-president could be expected to win his party's highest prize without serious opposition. This he did.

The Democratic National Convention

"Thank you, Mr. President."[9] These words were spoken by Hubert Humphrey in his speech accepting the Democratic party's presidential nomination. They were accompanied by a slight bow in the direction of the television cameras transmitting the event to the public, and of greater immediate concern to Humphrey, to the party's absentee landlord and the nation's incumbent president, Lyndon Johnson, who was watching the proceedings back in his native Texas. The words symbolized to many much of what was wrong with the way in which the party operated and its presidential nominees were selected.

Humphrey's speech came at the close of the most remarkable and discouraging national convention of the contemporary era. The convention hall had been in constant disorder. The streets outside had witnessed bloody confrontations between police and combat-equipped national guardsmen on the one side and tens of thousands of demonstrators on the other. Cries were heard on the convention floor about "the politics of shame" and reference was made from the podium to the "gestapo tactics" in the streets of Chicago.[10]

Humphrey's nomination had followed one of the bitterest series of nomination fights in either party's history. In state after state, those attempting to offer an alternative to the nomination of Humphrey had complained of being arbitrarily excluded from processes controlled by party professionals. Humphrey was backed by the party regulars who controlled the nominating machinery. Those not supporting the Humphrey candidacy felt deprived of any real voice in the selection process. Their bitterness, fueled by the nightmare developments of the election year, was largely responsible for the crowds that flocked to Chicago in August 1968 in an attempt to influence the national convention and to make their displeasure known to the Democratic party, the media, and the nation.

The Democratic party regulars, in turn, bitterly resented the actions of the insurgents within the party and the actions of the demonstrators at the Chicago convention. They found their tactics and their unremitting hostility for the Democratic party and its proposed nominee highly objectionable. The regulars held little sympathy for the views of the demonstrators. It would appear that the two groups could not have had less in common.

The most visible response in Chicago to the challenge posed by the dissidents came from city authorities. The police insisted on enforcing all ordinances, including those closing the public parks at night to demonstrations or sleep-ins. Many felt the authorities were out to teach the demonstrators a lesson. The heavy-handed approach of the police combined with the determination of the demonstrators to make their point at whatever the cost ended in a daily series of confrontations, clubbing, gassings, attacks, and counterattacks that stormed across the nation's television screens. The authorities were out to show who was in charge. They succeeded but at a fearful cost to themselves and their city and to the Democratic party and its nominee.

Mayor Daley's reaction

The response of Chicago's Mayor Daley both to the demonstrators drawn to the city for the convention and to those opposing the party regulars within the convention hall was unrestrained. The demonstrators and the mayor came to symbolize a very unhappy period. Daley appeared in Walter Cronkite's CBS-TV booth on the last day of the national convention to defend his administration's actions and to excoriate television for its role in the debacle. Referring to the demonstrators as "terrorists," the Mayor charged:

> The intention of these terrorists was openly displayed. They repeatedly stated they had come to Chicago to disrupt a national political convention and to paralyze our city. They came here equipped with plastic, with helmets, and with their own brigade of medics. They had maps locating the hotels and routes of buses for the guidance of terrorists from out of town. To protect the delegates and the people of Chicago from this planned violence the city worked with the Secret Service, the Federal Bureau of Investigation, the Department of Justice, and other agencies directly involved in the maintenance of law and order. In every instance the recommendations of both the Kerner and Austin reports were followed, that is, to use manpower instead of firepower. The newspapers stated specifically terrorists were planning to use those who were opposed to the present Vietnam policy as a front for their

violence. It was also pointed out they would attempt to assault, harass and taunt the police in reacting before television cameras. Fifty-one policemen have been injured. Sixty percent of those arrested did not live in Illinois, and 70 percent did not live in Chicago. In the last two days we have seen the strategy of these announced plans carried on in full, and the whole purpose of the city and law enforcement agencies distorted and twisted. One can understand how those who deeply believe in their cause concerning Vietnam would be deeply disappointed, but to vent their disappointment on the city and law enforcement agencies, that these dissenting groups and television should be used as a tool for their purpose of calculated disruption and rioting is inexcusable.[11]

Daley conceded that the police may have "overreacted" in the "heat of emotion" but he concluded:

This administration and the people of Chicago and particularly people from whence I come, because they have suffered this long enough, have never condoned brutality at any time, but they will never permit a lawless violent group of terrorists to menace the lives of millions of our people, destroy the purpose of this national political convention, and take over the streets of Chicago.[12]

Daley was never to change his views; not in the aftermath of the election, the continuing debate over police actions, the controversial trials of demonstrators that followed, or the negative publicity that plagued the city for years. He believed the demonstrators represented a threat to his city and to political authority in general and he felt that television had been sympathetic to the rioters. He was not one to forget.

Humphrey's views

Daley's strong emotions, however, were not out-of-line with those of other party leaders. Writing in his memoirs, Hubert Humphrey, for example, found personal and other provocations associated with the demonstrations unpardonable. Speaking for himself, the former vice-president remarked:

I was prepared to take a certain amount of verbal abuse, but the idea of embarrassment or physical harm to Muriel [his wife] and my children enraged me. The plans began with talks of dousing Muriel with red paint to symbolize the blood of the war. Then there was talk of throwing human excrement on her and the kids, and finally serious discussion of kidnapping one of the children. When you're involved in the most democratic process in the world leading to the selection of a head of state, it is unsettling, at the least, to contemplate injury or mayhem to your family as a result of your involvement.[13]

Humphrey believed that there are a few ("enough" in his words) "revolutionaries and anarchists" among those who had come to Chicago to protest the war. These provocateurs "were capable and determined to play with aroused emotions, to escalate their own war, and [to] manipulate a situation in which a sharp confrontation with the police was inevitable."[14]

Humphrey continued:

The reports [from the Secret Service, the Chicago police, etc.] kept coming. More meetings in Chicago led by professional radicals, not just American youngsters who deplored the war but others, who hated the whole system. Their intention was to organize local blacks in protest, stirring racial strife, and then to organize the students for a confrontation with the police. Expert violence was not just in the streets, but directed at the convention hall.[15]

Humphrey's views do capture the bitterness—and even hate—that characterized feelings on both sides of the controversy.

The siege mentality evidenced by Humphrey and Daley appeared to be shared by the most powerful of the party's and the nation's leaders. While they did not totally excuse the police for their conduct, they could find mitigating circumstances. As Humphrey was to put it: "The police were provoked in an environment created in large part by a few people whose threats, plotting, and determination to wreck the Democratic convention were almost as central to the havoc in Grant Park as the billy clubs."[16]

Conclusion

The demonstrations, then, were a plot. The riots were planned and had been provoked by the students, clergymen, housewives, and others assembled in Chicago to rally for an end to the war, a Democratic party commitment to peace, and possibly a more acceptable presidential nominee. The well-meaning demonstrators were led by professional radicals attempting to destroy the Democratic party and the American system of government. Such a threat to civil order had to be dealt with severely—and it was.

The emotions present and the rationalizations invoked seem bizarre in hindsight (as they did to many at the time). Yet they were powerful and they go far in explaining the official response to the challenge posed by the demonstrations and the chaos and violence that followed. They also help define the gulf that divided, on the one side, the party regulars who could boast of their operations as "the most democratic" in the world and the insurgents and protesters, on the other, who felt excluded from the system and embittered by its results. On one point, few would contest Humphrey when he wrote: "The clash [between the police and the crowds] was a microcosm of the whole year in our whole society."[17]

With Humphrey's nomination, all that remained was for the fall campaign to be played out, with the resulting election of Richard Nixon—in what turned out to be a surprisingly close race—and the planting of the seeds of Watergate.

FOUR

The Opening Shots in the Battle for Control of a Party

Abuses in the Nominating System

The much-heralded "open process" that party professionals boasted of bears close examination. The regulars' views of the nominating system contrasted pointedly with those held by the reformers. As the McGovern-Fraser Commission was later to report, "the day Eugene McCarthy announced his candidacy, nearly one third of the delegates [for the 1968 Democratic National Convention] had in effect already been selected. And, by the time Lyndon Johnson announced his intention not to seek another term, the formal delegate selection process had begun in all but twelve of the states. *By the time the issues and candidates that characterized the politics of 1968 had clearly emerged, therefore, it was impossible for rank-and-file Democrats to influence the selection of these delegates"* (emphasis added).[1] Perhaps this is as much as need be said.

For years, those who opposed administration policies had been admonished to "work within the system." Once they did, these critics—the insurgents within the Democratic party's ranks—came to believe that the system was far from the answer; in fact, they came to view it as the problem.

The insurgents misread the nature of nominating politics in the United States. They presumed that the people—in this case, the party's membership—had a significant impact on deliberations. They further assumed that by taking their case to the people, that is, the Democratic voters in the primaries and those who participated in the caucus/convention systems in the nonprimary states, they could, in effect, force

25

a referendum on the administration and its policies. They grossly miscalculated how closed and unresponsive the presidential selection processes remained and how inaccessible they were to influence from the party's base. Presidential selection was controlled from the top down. The rules governing the process, to the extent that they existed, were made and enforced by those in power, the party regulars in charge of party operations. Such things as primary victories and popular support among grassroots party elements had little effect on the choice of a presidential nominee.

The message was that the presidential nominee delegate selection ran on an internal clock of its own. It was not greatly swayed by the conditions or challenges of an election year. It was directly responsive to the wishes of the party regulars and elective officeholders that sat at the apex of the party hierarchy. The system operated in such a manner as to give these party chieftains ultimate control of the national convention and the Democratic (and for that matter, Republican) party's presidential nomination. It took the insurgents a good deal of time to fully appreciate this fact of political life, and in most cases, the lesson had to be learned and relearned in one state after another. It turned out to be a bitter experience.

The Primaries

The connection between primary results in 1968 and a state delegation's vote once at the national convention often was not clear. Hubert Humphrey took the presidential nomination on the first ballot with 67 percent of the 2,622 national convention delegate votes cast. Eugene McCarthy, with 23 percent of the convention vote, and George McGovern (the Robert Kennedy stand-in) did not provide serious competition at this stage. Humphrey won handsomely although only taking 2.2 percent of the total primary vote as a write-in candidate.

An examination of the relationship between the primary vote in selected races that were contested and a state's convention vote demonstrates the lack of association between the two. This was not true in all the primary states (California, Wisconsin, and Oregon being the most notable exceptions), but it was the case in most. At times, the discrepancies were pronounced. This was particularly true for the large, industrial states of the northeast and midwest, firmly controlled by the party professionals and responsive to such major pro-administration interest groups as organized labor.

In Pennsylvania, McCarthy received 72 percent of the primary vote. Eighty percent of Pennsylvania's delegation's vote at the Democratic National Convention went to Humphrey. In Illinois, the insurgent candidates (Kennedy and McCarthy) took two-thirds of the primary vote, while Humphrey received 95 percent of the state party's support at the national convention. The insurgents took three-fourths of the New Jersey vote in that state's primary, and Humphrey (not even on the ballot) claimed three-fourths of its vote at the national convention. Overall, in fifteen primary states Humphrey and Johnson combined won but 7 percent of the vote; yet they received 53 percent of the convention vote from these five states.

This may be one way of saying that the primary vote was virtually worthless, which may be another way of saying that the grassroots voter had little to no power in most primary states to decide who his or her state would support for the party's presidential nomination at the national convention.

Yet primaries were the only route open to candidates who opposed the choice of the party regulars. Most states (35) in 1968 (and before) employed some form of appointive system in selecting national convention delegates, a process even more hostile to grassroots influence or penetration by insurgent candidates. As the McGovern-Fraser Commission later wrote: "Secret caucuses, closed slate-making, widespread proxy voting—and a history of procedural irregularities—were all too common at precinct, county, district, and state conventions."[2]

An examination of the processes found in the states reveals how closed the system actually was.

Non-Primary States

It is difficult to establish even a rough gauge of popular sentiment in the non-primary states. The rules covering delegation selection in the twenty-six states (in 1968) employing caucus selection, party committee nominations or state convention choices, or some combination of these purer forms, were, if anything, more complex and less intelligible than those governing outcomes in the primary states. Such procedures are highly susceptible to control by party leaders. Attendance at party-sponsored meetings involved in national convention delegate selection were open to abuse and the sentiments of the participants, as well as the numbers of people involved in such processes, difficult to ascertain.

A few points are clear. Participation in presidential nomination sessions in the convention-caucus-committee states is well below that for the primary states. No figures are available for the 1968 election year, but estimates for the 1972 presidential year indicate that possibly 6 percent of the eligible Democratic voters participated in caucus/convention systems at the state level. The corresponding estimate for the primaries is about 51 percent. The figures for the primary states are necessarily rough estimates, and more than likely they are inflated guesses as to the turnout. They are also for 1972, a year in which reforms in the nominating system had been encouraged, and even forced on the state parties, on occasion, to increase participation and to make it more broadly representative of the party's electorate. If the same ratio of primary to non-primary turnout for 1972 held for 1968, it would mean that approximately three-quarters of a million Democrats participated in nominating decisions in the convention-caucus-committee states. The figure is not impressive yet, more than likely, the actual participation fell well below this mark.

Less speculative is the way in which the non-primary states voted in the national convention. Fifty-nine percent of the delegate votes were selected in non-primary states. Of these, three-fourths (76.1%) went to Humphrey; only 18 percent (18.3%) were awarded to either McCarthy or McGovern.

Even these figures, stark as they may seem, underestimate the power of the party regulars. When party regulars would later rhapso-dize about "caucus democracy" and the party-building virtues of grass-roots representation through state caucus-convention participation by the "truly interested," reformers would point to the testimony given in the McGovern-Fraser hearings of those who tried to participate.

Such examples began to suggest the nature of the problems faced by those who wished to participate in choosing their party's nominee in non-primary states. Four states selected their national convention delegates through state party committees, the least open of all party processes. In four other states, one-third to one-half of the national convention delegates were appointed by state committees. And in two states (Georgia and Louisiana), the Democratic governor appointed the entire delegation.

In most cases, the state committee members who selected the national convention delegates had been appointed to their offices one to four years before the year of the presidential election. They consisted of party regulars, little known to, or influenced by the party member-ship and insulated from the events and peculiar pressures of the presi-dential election year. Some would argue that this was a strength of the old system; for others it was one of its most glaring weaknesses.

In the better than one-half of the state Democratic parties that employed some form of state convention selection of national conven-tion delegates, the process could be as open, or closed, as party officials, state tradition and state and local party rules allowed. In such states, the party regulars in power pretty much did things as they had been doing them for generations.

Specific abuses

Overall, the presidential nominating system, as it operated in 1968, was fraught with problems. The list of abuses uncovered by the Mc-Govern-Fraser Commission is a long one. In summarizing the irregularities it found in state party nominating procedures, the commission reported:[3]

- In a minimum of twenty states the rules governing presidential delegate selection were either nonexistent or inadequate. In other states, they were unavailable. The absence of specific, easily available rules regulating the process left most decisions to the discretion of party officials.
- The forced application of majority rule and the unit rule at some or all (in the case of Texas) stages of delegate selection; a practice that denied minority contenders for the presidential nomination any support whatsoever.
- Widespread use of proxy voting, which enabled one person at a meeting to cast the votes of absentees. The practice was unregulated in most states, resulting in repeated abuses. These included proxy votes cast on behalf of nonexistent individuals and, in one case, proxy votes totaling three times the membership present cast by the chair for a presidential candidate the group opposed.
- No public notices given as the dates, time, location, or for that matter, no information at all made available to inform would-be participants that presidential delegate selection was in progress. This pattern was encountered repeatedly in caucus/convention states.
- Candidates for national delegate positions ran with no indication of which presidential contender they supported, thus not allowing the primary or caucus participant a knowledgeable choice among prospective nominees.
- In states in which the state committee selected all, or sizable portions of, the national convention delegation, voters selecting the state's committee members were *not* informed that one function of the incoming committee members was to choose national convention delegates, thus depriving these party members of even an indirect say in this aspect of presidential selection.
- Slates of delegates for national convention positions were chosen by party leaders in closed sessions and then presented to the primary voters or state convention membership for ratification on a take-it-or-leave-it basis. Such slates were given preferential treatment on the primary ballot and in convention states were protected from effective challenge by party rules.

- No uniform dates or places for delegate selection meetings were established in many states. These matters were left to the discretion of local party officials.
- No quorum provisions governing presidential delegate selection meetings existed in most states. In effect, there was no limit on how few people might select presidential delegates.
- No rules existed in most states governing the selection of alternate delegates or for providing uniform procedures to fill vacancies that might occur on a state's national convention delegation. These decisions were again left to the discretion of party leaders.
- Thirty-eight percent of the national convention delegates were selected prior to the national convention year and prior to the beginning of the prenomination campaigns.
- Ex officio (i.e., nonelected or automatic) delegate positions were reserved for party officials in many states. These could range up to 25 percent of a state's national convention.
- Appointment of national convention delegates within states was often arbitrary, involving traditional (and outdated) allocations of votes among party and/or territorial units without regard to population or party strength in an area. This "rotten borough" system ensured that some localities and some groups of voters would exercise a disproportionate influence on the state party's commitment in presidential races.
- The financial costs of participating in presidential delegate selection could be prohibitive. Filing fees for a state could be high (up to $14,000 for a slate of candidates) and "hospitality" suites and other party-related assessments frequently ran between $250 and $5,000. These were in addition to the housing, meals, and transportation expenditures involved in attending the national convention.
- The representation of blacks, women, and youth in national conventions was often negligible and always far below what their numbers in the population or their importance to the party warranted.

Overall, for a nation that believed in fair play and a free and unfettered democratic choice, the presidential nominating process provided a case study in how not to achieve such ends. The practices encountered had evolved over generations; they were arbitrary and prejudicial to the operations of an open and—in relating to the party's base—responsive party system. Individually, many of the irregularities may seem insignificant. Cumulatively however, they combined to deny full access to or participation in presidential selection by even those most strongly committed of partisans. These practices had never been investigated in depth. The state parties that employed them had never been forced to conform to any assumptions of common decency or legitimate standards of democratic operations. All of this was about to change.

An alternative approach

The procedures employed in presidential delegate selection prior to the 1970s in the old party system made meaningful representation of the concerns of the rank and file through any direct influence in the deliberations over presidential nominations extraordinarily difficult. The criticisms of the system in place at the time and a listing of its deficiencies make sense only if one believes, as the reformers did, that the selection of presidential nominees should be:

· Open to participation and influence from grassroots party members.
· Representative of the views held by party members, with candidates offering major policy choices on the issues facing the nation.
· Consistent with procedures that are fair to all who participate; neutral in application, favoring neither one side or the other; and containing safeguards for all who participate akin to those associated with "due process of the law" in judicial procedures.

If you held to such objectives, then you found a presidential nominating system objectionable. It represented the antithesis of many of these values. If, on the other hand, you felt as the party regulars did, that the real danger in party and electoral decision-making was too much democracy and if you believed that the real decisions as to presidential nominees and the issue positions and policy solutions a political party should commit itself to should be decided by those in authority, then the presidential nomination process was more than adequate.

Party regulars ("people with constituencies," as they liked to be called) felt that they knew best and, as a consequence, that they could best represent the "true interests" of party members and, consequently, best meet the needs of the nation. "Governance" and "winnability" were ends that they felt their system best achieved. Within such a frame of reference, the specific procedures for national convention delegate selection and whatever alleged shortcomings they might have were secondary. Such processes as the state primaries and caucuses fulfilled, at best, an advisory role. At worst, they were something to be tolerated to give party members the illusion of participation. The party regulars suffered through the largely ceremonial nominating season awaiting the national convention when they would make the meaningful decisions. From such a perspective, any listing of procedural "abuses" was obviously irrelevant.

There was little common ground between reformers and regulars and little room for accommodation. The two camps held starkly different views of what the presidential nominating process should be; assumptions that would sharply divide them over the coming years and ones that would provide the basis for a continuingly bitter controversy.

The Stirrings of Reform

There was one point on which both groups did agree. Party regulars and party reformers—and, in fact, anyone concerned about orderly democratic governance—were determined that the violence and disorder that characterized the Chicago debacle, and the events leading to it, should not be repeated, and could not be tolerated, by a political party seeking to represent a broad spectrum of American opinion. Such actions symbolized a breakdown of peaceful procedures for manifesting dissent, and not incidentally, the inability of a major political party to accommodate opposing points of view within its coalition. At a minimum, the price paid was the election of Richard Nixon to the presidency. More broadly seen, the very future of the Democratic party would appear to hang in the balance. Party preservation, if nothing else, dictated that something had to be done.

The immediate answer was for the national convention to pass resolutions authorizing the creation of reform commissions "to assure the fullest possible participation [in the presidential delegate selection process] and to make the Democratic Party completely representative of grass-roots sentiments"; to allow all Democratic voters a "full and timely opportunity to participate" in presidential selection; and to codify the rules for and assess the performance of the national convention.[4] Toward these ends, the reform commissions would study delegate selection processes in presidential contests and the operations of Democratic national conventions. The reform commissions, if necessary, would work with (in the case of delegate selection) the state parties in bringing about the relevant changes needed in state laws and party rules and both would report their findings and recommendations to the next national convention.

The mandates given to yet-to-be-named reform commissions looked impressive. They constituted one of the national convention's least publicized actions, ignored by party members, the media, and the public alike. In reality, the reform resolutions may well have been face-saving proposals intended to begin the process of symbolically reunifying the party. In the past (with the exception of one little-known committee), party agencies created in this manner had little authority and even less impact on the operations of the national party. The presumption was that they would meet infrequently; conduct their business quietly; and before expiring, would issue an innocuous, and largely ignored, report containing several noncontroversial recommendations. Future national conventions might, or might not, act on the proposals at their discretion. Either way, the results would be heralded as a goodwill effort to mend fences, sufficient (it was hoped) to appease critics and unite the party for the next campaign.

There was little to indicate at this early stage that this time it would be any different. Overlooked in such critiques, however, was the depth of feelings evident on both sides. The extent to which party processes had been publicly exposed as inadequate and held up to general ridicule was without parallel in the modern era. This reform effort would not be as benign as its predecessors.

The reform commissions—the Commission on Party Structure and Delegate Selection (or the McGovern-Fraser Commission, named after its successive chairs) and the Commission on Rules (O'Hara Commission)—were appointed in early 1969. With their creation, reform began in earnest.

Conclusion

The years that followed were to prove tumultuous for the parties (and for the Democrats, in particular). Party processes, from the grassroots up to and including national party operations, would be subject to an unprecedented scrutiny. Presidential selection procedures would be revolutionized and efforts would be made to modernize national conventions and to restructure the national party. Eventually, the reform period would result in the most profound reassessment of political parties since the Progressive Era of the early 1900s. The fruits of the reform labors have, for better or worse, transformed the practice of American politics. In one form or another, they will be with us for a long time to come.

PART TWO

Reform in the Democratic Party

FIVE

Overview of the Democratic Party's Reform Process

Reform got off to an explosive start. The early work of the McGovern-Fraser Commission was implemented to a degree by the later Mikulski Commission and paralleled the efforts of the O'Hara Commission and the Sanford Commission in introducing change into different areas of party concern. Much of the energy of the later reform period went into efforts to undo the earlier work of these path-breaking bodies (and especially the McGovern-Fraser Commission). The later emphasis was on accommodating interests of the party regulars and forging a closer correspondence to the pre-reform party system. This is not a totally accurate depiction: the post-1980 Platform Accountability Commission attempted to serve as a wedge toward a more policy-oriented party and many of the later reform bodies (the Winograd Commission is the most notable example in this regard) also attempted to implement rules that would advance the presidential aspirations of one candidate or faction within the party. Still, the broad characterization has merit and provides an initial grasp of a long and complex series of political processes.

Beyond this, it is difficult to place the reform era and its accomplishments in a readily manageable context. Much was attempted, and more accomplished, than had been thought possible in the previous five decades.

In explaining what has taken place, one possibility is to deal with the reform bodies chronologically, beginning with the first and proceeding through the most recent. There is a reassuring quality to such a historical approach that does have appeal. There are difficulties, however. One problem is that the various commissions, approached in this manner, have an awkward relationship to each other (Table 5.1).

TABLE 5.1   CHRONOLOGY OF DEMOCRATIC REFORM COMMISSIONS

Time Frame	Reform Commission Evolution		
1964	1964 National Convention		
	Special Equal Rights Committee		
1968 Harold Hughes Ad Hoc Committee	1968 National Convention McGovern-Fraser Commission on Delegate Selection	O'Hara Commission on Convention Reform	
	Joint party charter proposed		
1972	1972 National Convention		
	Mikulski Commission on Delegate Selection	Sanford Commission on Party Structure	
1974	Compliance Review Commission		1974 Midterm Convention
		Winograd Commission (1975)	
1976	1976 National Convention		
1978	Winograd Commission		1978 Midterm Convention
	Compliance Review Commission		
1980	1980 National Convention		
	Hunt Commission	Platform Accountability Commission	

They deal with different issues—sometimes of no direct relationship to each other—and they responded to different political environments. The end result may be confusion: a series of overlapping vignettes with no intrinsic substantive relationship.

The interactions among the commissions are not always clear. The substance of the commissions' deliberations often overlapped. At times, the commissions fought to assert both their independence and their rights to the areas in dispute (delegate allocation formulas; prescriptions for reforming party structures; enforcement of reform mandates). At other points, the commissions attempted to cooperate, tentatively, in uniting their efforts to achieve some desired goal (the party charter, for example). Each of the commissions responded to different leadership and different sets of political stimuli. The chemistry of the membership interactions and the chair–staff–member relationship varied widely. Each group had its own timetable. Some worked with a sense of urgency; others were more leisurely, hoping to evolve a working consensus over time. Some desired to accomplish specific goals by given dates; others wanted to prevent any precipitous actions or hoped that through delay, confusion, and inaction party regulars or the leadership of the Democratic party might work its will.

Under such conditions, an effort to trace the impact of one body on another and to follow the deliberations on substantive matters of various bodies that sometimes met concurrently, and other times sequentially, invites problems. As examples, the McGovern-Fraser, the first and most formidable of the reform bodies, began its work on presidential nominating procedures in earnest in early 1969. Although the O'Hara Commission formally began at the same time, it was far slower to make its recommendations. And while the O'Hara Commission's mandate to assess national convention operations implicitly overlapped with some aspects of the McGovern-Fraser mandate, the two committees had very little in common. Each went its own way, jealous of its independence and prerogatives.

Most noticeable, rather than cooperating with each other in staff work or in a division of labor in terms of the topics covered of concern to both, the commissions fought intermittently for complete authority in the one area in which they both claimed jurisdiction: reforming the national party organization. As events moved on, the commissions, exhausted by their work in their principal fields of presidential delegate selection and convention procedures, respectively, did attempt to cooperate—or more correctly, their leadership did—in developing a basis for structural reform of the national party immediately prior to the 1972 national convention. The intention was to present the agenda developed (the first of the "party charters") to the national convention as the combined work of the two reform bodies. This was done but it generated little enthusiasm and was carried over as unfinished business into the post-convention period with a new group, the Sanford Commission, appointed to look into the problem. The party charter and national party reform are best discussed within the context of the Sanford Commission's activities.

TABLE 5.2 A COMPARISON OF THE DEMOCRATIC PARTY'S REFORM COMMISSIONS

(1) Known as	(2) Formal Name	(3) Years in Operation	(4) Chairperson	(5) Size	(6) Mandating Body
McGovern-Fraser	Commission on Party Structure and Delegate Selection	1969–1972	Senator George McGovern (S.D.), 1969–1970; Cong. Donald M. Fraser (Minn.), 1971–1972[1]	28	1968 National Convention
O'Hara Commission	Commission on Rules	1969–1972	Congressman James G. O'Hara of Michigan	28	1968 National Convention
Mikulski Commission	Commission on Delegate Selection and Party Structure	1972–1973	Barbra A. Mikulski, Baltimore City Councilwoman	81	1972 National Convention
Party Charter (Sanford) Commission	Democratic Charter Commission	1972–1974	Terry Sanford, President of Duke Univ. & former governor of North Carolina (1960–1964)	103	1972 National Convention

(7) Area of Concern	(8) Major Recommendations	(9) Distinctive Features	(10) Principal Reports
Presidential selection	"Quotas"; rules for opening delegate selection to 1972 National Convention	First, most ambitious, and most important of reform groups; completely rewrote rules for presidential selection; made them mandatory for state parties and state practices; changed power distribution within Democratic party; set model other reform commissions attempted to follow.	*Mandate for Change* (1970)
National convention procedures	Rules to modernize and formalize national convention operations	Commission's life paralleled that of McGovern-Fraser's. Received little public attention. Democrats had no permanent rules governing convention deliberations. O'Hara Commission recommended such rules and new sets of procedures for dealing with disputes such as credentials challenges.	*Call to Order* (1972)
Presidential selection (revising McGovern-Fraser rules)	Modified McGovern-Fraser rules; revised quotas; provided for proportional representation of presidential candidates strength; increased role of party regulars in delegate selection	Commission had a stormy, if brief, life. Its principal recommendations were intended to placate regulars and modify most controversial aspects of McGovern-Fraser rules. Its major achievement, however, was in *not* seriously revising the McGovern-Fraser provisions. With the work of this commission, the assumption underlying the reforms became generally accepted within the party.	*Democrats All* (1973)
National party structure	Party Charter; Midterm Conferences	Only commission to deal with national party organization; adopted ambitious reform plan; expanded size of national committee; overall, relatively little long-run impact outside of policy conferences.	*Party Charter: The Democratic Party of the United States* (1974)

TABLE 5.2 (Continued)

(1) Known as	(2) Formal Name	(3) Years in Operation	(4) Chairperson	(5) Size	(6) Mandating Body
Winograd Commission	Commission on Presidential Nomination and Party Structure	1975–1976, 1976–1980[2]	Morley Winograd, former chair of Michigan Democratic Party	58	1976 National Convention
Hunt Commission	Commission on Presidential Nomination	1980–1982	Governor James B. Hunt, Jr., of North Carolina	70	1980 National Convention
Platform Accountability Commission	Platform Accountability Commission	1980–	Yvonne B. Burke, former Congresswoman from California; Terry Herndon, Executive Director, National Education Association; William Winter, Governor of Mississippi	52	1980 National Convention

The confusion is best resolved by taking each body in relation to its area of concern, then developing its operations and accomplishments within the context of the reactions and modifications introduced by succeeding bodies created specifically to assess the work of the earlier group (Table 5.2). In this manner, it is easier to deal in order with the four commissions—McGovern-Fraser, Mikulski, Winograd, and Hunt—that attempted to remodel presidential nominations. Next, the O'Hara Commission (1968–1972) and the Platform Accountability Commission (1980–   ) dealt with concerns relevant to national conventions. Finally, the Sanford Commission (1972–1974) attempted to reassess the operations of the Democratic party nationally. Its objectives were to open and reinvigorate the party and to make it more appealing to the voter. While developing out of concerns expressed, initially, in the 1968 national convention and addressed sporadically by the

(7) *Area of Concern*	(8) *Major Recommendations*	(9) *Distinctive Features*	(10) *Principal Reports*
Primaries, presidential nominations	10% "add-on" delegates for party officials; steps to close system at top	Vehicle of party regulars and Carter administration to tighten system, increase role of party regulars, and adopt rules expected to help Carter's renomination; developed complicated procedures that are heavily dependent on national party interpretation.	*Openness, Participation and Party Building: Reforms for a Stronger Democratic Party* (1978)
Presidential selection	25% quota for party officials	Expanded role of party and elected officials in national conventions.	*Report of the Commission on Presidential Nomination* (1982)
Enforcing platform commitments			

---

[1] Fraser assumed chair January 7, 1971.
[2] The original Winograd Commission was not authorized by the national convention. It was created by the national chair, Robert Strauss. The post-1976 committee membership was expanded.

McGovern-Fraser and O'Hara commissions, it is a separate entity that did important work on party structure in the early to mid-1970s.

There are still overlaps among these bodies but such an approach allows for a continuity of development that should place the major achievements of each, as well as their differences in objectives and style, in an intelligible context.

SIX

Presidential Selection I: The McGovern-Fraser Commission

The McGovern-Fraser Commission was the first, and most famous, of the reform bodies. It was, also, by all odds, the most important. This commission was characterized by a number of things.

First, it assumed importance from the substance of its concerns: the manner in which presidential nominees were selected. Presidential nominations are the single most important function the national parties perform. This area went to the heart of the political and the party system. The reformers felt that to attain real change within the society they needed to recast the methods by which presidential candidates were chosen. When they had tried and, in 1968, failed in seeking to gain party recognition and policy concessions for their stands, they felt the reason had to do with the archaic and closed party processes they had encountered.

A Matter of Tactics

Thus, the reformers took initial aim at the presidential nominating process. Would it not have been better—and less disruptive—to begin (some party regulars were to argue later) by focusing on some other less critical aspect of party affairs, capturing a majority on the national committee perhaps, or controlling local party organization and building toward an essential nationwide consensus?

Such efforts would have been wasted. The national committee—or any other national party agency outside of the national convention—was hardly worth controlling. The national committee normally met only twice a year. It was the captive of the president (if the incumbent was from the same party) or the national chairman and the national committee staff. The national chairman determined the agenda, the content of reports to reach the national committee, the time and place of meetings, and anything else of consequence relevant to the body. The national committee's only real power was the influence it exerted over presidential nominations and the power was indirect. In the pre-reform period, the states determined their own selection procedures and the credentials committee of the national convention decided on challenges to individual delegates. The national committee did issue the "Call" to the convention specifying the site and date of the gathering, the number of delegate votes to be distributed among the states, and the formula to be used in allocating the vote to the states, (the state's vote in the electoral college, the state's population, evidence of party support in the last or previous presidential election(s), for example, or some combination of these factors). A technical matter, surely, but one of great concern to the state parties and to the balance of power within the party. The national committee also had effective control of all convention arrangements, although in reality this meant the president (if of the same party) or the national chairman could exercise his will in rewarding his friends through preferential treatment or punishing his enemies, as he saw fit.

Any effort to gain control of the national committee was badly disproportionate to the power it exercised. Committee members were selected once every four years. Some were appointed by a state chairman, governor, or a state executive committee. Others were elected by the state convention or the state's delegation to the national convention. Predictably, the position went to well-known party regulars, people who had held party and elective office in the past and who had the funds to pay their own expenses in attending meetings. The position was rarely contested and committee members held office for long periods. They often exercised little power within their own state parties. It was a honorary position in many states, meant for older and less active party figures of eminence.

Why then not begin at the grassroots level, capturing party organizations in one locality after another and building eventually toward a national coalition? The reformers were not naive enough to believe that this was either possible or desirable. Party organization at the community level is minimal. Few local parties are active and even fewer exercise any influence of consequence on elections or policies. Local organizations able to match the much-publicized Chicago organization are anachronisms (if they exist at all); the political legacies of another age that for reasons peculiar to their immediate environment have continued to flourish long after their day has passed. There may be a few more Chicago organizations in other localities. If so, they go unreported. Most local elections are nonpartisan and most local parties moribund.

Exciting people to the point where they are motivated to participate in local politics is, in most cases, quite unusual. Sustaining interest in local candidacies and issues sufficient to man a political organization of any consequence over time has become the exception.

A second point is worth noting. There is no cohesion to the groupings of local party entities across the nation. The state and community party organizations, to the extent they exist, share little beside the party name. Furthermore, the ties between the state and local party organizations and the national party are tenuous. The emissaries to the national parties from the states are the national committee members. The state and local parties have little reason to call upon the national headquarters. The national staff, in turn, does little of consequence for a community party, outside of, for example, distributing campaign handbooks and holding occasional campaign seminars. The national committee is best thought of as roughly the equivalent of the Continental Congress, called to give broad direction on matters of common interest to the actions of the confederacy of independent state and local parties. Actually, the national party's power falls far short of even this weak model. Its chief function is to plan for the quadrennial convention.

The reformers then chose to focus their energies on the party's presidential nominating process. In retrospect, they had few other choices.

First of all, the 1968 national convention had defined the focus of their interest in specific response to the problems it had encountered. Once mandated by the national convention, the supreme policy-making body within either party, this could not be changed (not that anyone on either commission—or in the national party at that point in time—advocated any other approach).

Second, there were distinct advantages for the reformers in focusing on presidential selection. If they went after any other aspect of party operations—control of local or state parties, the national committees, or even more improbable, the congressional party—their efforts would have been in vain. Change would take decades at best; public interest would be hard to arouse or focus; and if victory were attained, exactly what had been achieved would be left in doubt.

Third, while already noted, this point cannot be stressed too much: presidential nominations were the single most important activity either political party engaged in. The choice of a presidential nominee with all its ramifications for leadership, policy initiatives, and economic and group rewards within both the party and the society more generally was of enormous consequence. The parties did nothing else that began to compare with their influence in this one area.

Fourth, it was the presidential nomination process—not party operations or party reform specifically—that the reformers were interested in. Most wanted to change national policy and all wanted to change the national leadership. The vehicle for accomplishing these ends was the party's choice of a presidential nominee. A general election that provided a choice between an incumbent and a Republican opponent even more unacceptable on policy grounds offered, of course, no chance to achieve the goals the reformers envisioned. When the challenge to the incumbent did not succeed—at least along the lines intended—and as the reformers came to face arbitrary and outmoded nominating rules and a control vested in the party establishment, then their objectives changed. Reform of the party's nominating process became the vehicle through which the eventual policy and leadership changes the reformers held to be so important could be realized.

Finally, the party's nominating process was vulnerable to attack. Its procedures were arcane—unknown to even the most diligent scholar or party professional. They were indefensible. What the reformers found, and what they communicated to the media and the general public, was an unpleasant mix of unresponsive, outdated, and arbitrary practices badly in need of improvement. The system was biased and repressive. Even the regulars found little to specifically defend, and with the uproar at the Chicago convention, even those most comfortable with the system as it was felt a review of possible changes might be warranted. In a sense, the reformers had history on their side—and they seized the moment.

The McGovern-Fraser Commission, then, had chosen the most significant area within the party's domain in which to work. Potentially, its influence could (and as events turned out, would) go to the core of the American political system.

Second, there was a clear line of development between the insurgents, the McGovern-Fraser Commission, and the Reform Movement that followed. Once all hope of capturing the nomination had faded, the insurgents spent the last few weeks prior to the 1968 convention in marshalling their forces to advocate change. The effort had been led by the seven-member Ad Hoc Commission on the Democratic Selection of Presidential Nominees, chaired by then Governor (and later U.S. Senator) Harold Hughes of Iowa. The group was not an official arm of the party (as was the McGovern-Fraser Commission and later reform committees). What it did was to prepare a report on very short notice on the diversity of state nominating practices within the Democratic party and their discriminatory aspects. It then recommended changes. The report, *The Democratic Choice*, was to serve as a model for the later McGovern-Fraser efforts, which were to reflect both its tone and substance.

The Harold Hughes Ad Hoc Commission report was then distributed to the national convention committees and delegates—the first time either had any such analysis available of a previously obscure and little understood process. The report helped reform-minded delegates within the convention's Rules and Credentials Committees argue the need for change, and it provided background for the convention deliberations. The orientation and areas of concern analyzed by the Ad Hoc Commission fed through the national convention to the McGovern-Fraser Commission and heavily influenced its agenda.

The parentage is unmistakable. Harold Hughes was selected as vice-chair of the McGovern-Fraser Commission and Congressman Donald M. Fraser of Minnesota, who had been vice-chair of the Harold Hughes Commission, was made a member of the new reform body and later its chair (succeeding McGovern).

McGovern, Hughes, and the consultants invited to appear before the commission's first meeting stressed themes and objectives that would have made the Ad Hoc Committee and its sponsors, the activist and dissident wing of the Democratic party, comfortable.

There was then a continuity between the movement and groups that demonstrated for reform and the creation, specifically, of the McGovern-Fraser Commission and a delineation of its substantive concerns. There are clear historical lines connecting the beginning of the reform agitation with the McGovern-Fraser deliberations.

A third major characteristic of the McGovern-Fraser Commission was its aggressiveness. Not only had it taken for review a critical aspect of American political institutions, but it chose to pursue its objectives all-out.

Most party committees are rather insignificant assemblages that meet sporadically over a period of time to consider some problem, make some mild recommendations, and then disband. The recommendations are conveniently forgotten and business continues as usual. Government by committees is common in political parties (and, for that matter, any other institution). Usually, it is a safe way to avoid action and defuse tense situations. The appearance of concern and the potential for change are enough to satisfy the offended until emotions subside and the precipitating events are pushed into the background. Non-decision-making of this nature is particularly effective and popular with party leaders because of the high turnover in participants and the changeability of their concerns from one election year to another. There is an absence of any effective organizational memory within party organizations and only the broadest continuity in personnel, factional concerns, and emotional commitments among party bodies over time. The rush of events often makes last year's politics akin to ancient history. It is fair to believe that those among the party regulars who supported a party committee to review delegate selection and those regulars within the national convention who voted for it had something along these lines in mind.

Such was not to be the case. The McGovern-Fraser Commission sought to vigorously ascertain the dimensions of the problems with which it was dealing and then even more aggressively to reform the entire delegate selection process within each of the states. It is unlikely that the party regulars even envisioned such a monumental undertaking by a party committee, one reason they were slow to comprehend what was taking place and even slower to organize any effective resistance to the proposed changes. Even the commission's leadership did not fully appreciate the magnitude of their job until it was at least a year into its work. At that point, it had committed itself.

Nonetheless, it was clear from day one that the commission was an ambitious and determined one, undeterred by the fate of similar bodies in the past. George McGovern, in his opening remarks to the first assemblage of his reform commission, made the point that the group's mandate was both clear, broader, and more audacious than that ever given to such a party committee. McGovern, at least, intended that the commission's work would have a fundamental and lasting impact on party processes.

Clarifying Its Mandate

To add emphasis, McGovern called upon Alexander Bickel, a Yale Law School professor and a former member of the Harold Hughes Commission, and Anne Wexler, who had been a McCarthy anti-war organizer and a forceful proponent of a strong reform resolution within the national convention's Rules Committee hearings, to "explain" the genesis of the McGovern-Fraser Commission and to interpret its power as contained in its mandate.

The move was a significant one in quickly firming up within the commission a no-nonsense approach to its work. Naturally, the two official "consultants," as they were called, took a hard-line approach to the commission's obligations. This was particularly true of Wexler, who devoted her remarks to addressing the meaning of perhaps the most significant phrase within the commission's mandate, that of "all feasible efforts," the test of whether a state party had satisfactorily responded to the commission's directives. Wexler argued, and after a debate, the majority of the commission agreed, that *a state party would have to enact the rules demanded by the commission.*[1] This is an extremely important point and one, more than any other, that set the McGovern-Fraser Commission off from its predecessors (with the possible exception of the Richard Hughes Special Equal Rights Committee).

Committee Operations

The McGovern-Fraser Commission also began very quickly. Fred Harris had appointed the group on February 9, 1969. Within a month, they had appointed a first-rate staff, which more than most such committee staffs, gave the commission deliberations guidance. It was, for example, the staff that proposed and then lobbied for the eighteen guidelines adopted by the commission and it was the staff, basically reduced to two people that oversaw the sensitive implementation stages.

Following its first meeting in March 1969, the commission undertook an exhausting schedule of regional hearings designed to tap the discontent within the party and to solicit recommendations for change. Selected commission members attended the regional airings.

The full commission then met again in September to consider its recommendations. While postponing its final decisions until its meeting of November 19–20, the group actively solicited reactions to its impending recommendations from regulars and reformers; party leaders; members of congress, state legislators, governors, mayors, and other elected officers; the media; academicians; and any interested citizens. With these reactions in hand, it met in the late fall to agree upon its final set of "guidelines." These then were distributed to the state parties in early December 1969, and by the end of its first year the committee's substantive work had been completed.

The Guidelines

The new regulations attempted to fulfill the commission's mandate to ensure "full, meaningful and timely" delegate selection. The guidelines sought to do this by requiring the state parties to adapt their policies for presidential nomination delegate selection to conform with the following provisions. The state parties were directed to:[2]

- Adopt written party rules concerning presidential delegate selection and to make these readily available.
- Establish "quotas" that ensured the representation of blacks, women, and youth in proportion to their numbers in the electorate.
- Adopt "timely" procedures for delegate selection by conducting the entire process within the calendar year of the national convention.
- Select 75 percent of the delegations to the national convention at the congressional district level or lower.
- Select no more than 10 percent of the national convention delegation

through state committees, considered to be the least representative of party procedures.

- Ban the unit rule, a regulation that forced all national convention delegates to vote for the majority's candidate, a vehicle intended to squelch minority representation; proxy voting; delegate selection meetings with a quorum of less than 40 percent; mandatory assessments or fees required of delegates; any fee of over $10 and/or petition requirements of more than 1 percent of the Democratic vote; ex-officio (i.e., unelected or appointed) delegates.
- Require adequate public notice of all party meetings involved in delegate selection; hold delegate selection meetings within a state on the same days and at the same time (except for rural areas); select alternates in the same manner as delegates; have open procedures for forming delegate slates refrain from giving preferential treatment to the slates themselves, and allow them to be subject to challenge; and require all candidates for delegate positions to state on the primary ballot the presidential contender they intended to support at the national convention.

The new rules were intended to give the grassroots party member a direct say in, and influence over, presidential nomination decisions. With the adoption of the guidelines by the commission, the second, or enforcement, phase of its operations began.

Assessing the Commission's Work at the End of Its First Phase

It is worthwhile to pause here to place its first year activities in perspective. If the McGovern-Fraser Commission had stopped at this juncture, its work would have been highly acclaimed and would have been considered basically noncontroversial. Of course, it did not. It repeatedly indulged in the rhetoric of enforcement, reminding listeners that it intended to demand change. Without enforced compliance, it is probable that the regulars, including the state party leaders with authority over delegate selection, would have generally endorsed its contribution and embraced (figuratively) its recommendations as "guidelines" intended to ensure fair, open, and representative processes. Most of the state parties would have encouraged token changes, and by 1972 they would have proclaimed themselves "reformed" and ready to meet the demands of the new election year.

Whether the reformers would have been equally contented with a superficial face-lifting is another matter. Still, the basic power configurations would have been left unchallenged and the appearance of reform would have given the party and its leaders grounds for heralding their responsiveness to the criticism that helped precipitate the troubles of 1968.

The response may appear shallow and, of course, in a more fundamental sense it would have been. But even under these conditions, the McGovern-Fraser Commission could lay claim to being one of the most important groups in its party's history. The Committee would have explored in depth one of the least understood and most confusing aspects of American politics. It would have offered reasonable suggestions for reform that might have led in time to the elimination of some of the grossly discriminatory aspects of the system and, over the even longer run, to a more modernized and efficient nomination process. The change would be incremental, a process with which the party could feel comfortable, and more importantly, it would not have disturbed traditional power relationships (the exact thing, of course, the reformers intended to do). Finally, the extensive regional hearings would have allowed for the largest mass participation exercise in the off-year history of either party. The party could be proud of what it had done, and the McGovern-Fraser Commission would have been honored for what it had accomplished while working within and extending the traditional bounds of what such party groups were expected to do.

That this was not to be the case became quickly apparent. The fact that the McGovern-Fraser Commission had no intention of stopping at this point provides an idea of how inclusive and fundamental its commitment to immediate change was. Further reactions from the party regulars could be expected and the conflicts over reform that surfaced in the delegate challenges in 1972, in particular, should have surprised no one.

The Right to Demand Enforcement

The McGovern-Fraser Commission was aggressive in approaching its job and in completing its work early. The commission was aggressive in a far more important way also: It demanded that the state parties enact its rules. This strategy was novel. It is questionable whether the commission had such authority. The national convention and the party leaders who controlled its deliberations certainly did not consciously award the reform bodies they authorized such power.

Where then did this right to enforce its decision on the state parties come from? First, there was a little bit of flim-flam in the operation. What the commission said was that the state parties that did not enact their rules were subject to judgment by the 1972 national convention and *could* be denied their convention seats. Actually, this constituted a rather weak threat. Judging by the experience of past conventions, with one possible exception (discussed below), national conventions were most reluctant to deprive a state party of its convention seats, whatever the provocation. Strong disciplinary measures of this nature were resisted by national conventions. The reason are not hard to discover.

The prevailing belief among party members was that the national party was a loose alliance of state and local parties. The party was extraordinarily weak at the uppermost levels. The national committee did not represent a national party constituency in any real sense. As noted, it had limited powers, an episodic life, few resources, high turn-over among staff, and recurring financial problems. It made few, if any, demands upon the state parties. Its prime concern was to manage the quadrennial national convention.

At this point, the Democratic party was perceived as the Republican party still is, as a heterogeneous grouping of state and local parties which met periodically in convention to select a presidential nominee. The idea that the national party could mandate rules and could, and more significantly, would require their implementation was a new departure in American party politics. The belief that the state parties meeting in convention would punish their own was also rather new. It was exactly the type of fight party regulars went to extremes to avoid.

There is another element in the thinking here also. The prevailing wisdom among party leaders was that the national party and its candidate needed the goodwill and strong support of the state and local parties to control elections. The dominant purpose in selecting a presidential nominee was to win the office of president. The candidate was chosen in a convention system through a process of negotiation in which the state party leaders attempted to settle on a contender who could best help state and local leaders with their tickets. Once selected, the nominee was dependent on the local party chieftains to fully support his candidacy and to turn out a good following on election day. That the politics of such an arrangement could be sacrificed to the enactment of generalized rules of fair play in state presidential delegate selection did not appear possible: the principal reason that the broad-scale challenges and the resultant convention decisions in 1972 caused such a stir. Punitive actions on such a scale on behalf of abstract standards of justice were a new departure of consequence for either national party.

The McGovern-Fraser Commission then had to make it appear that it had the power to actually require change. This it quietly and effectively did. It avoided drifting into public debates over what the upcoming national convention might, or might not, do. The strong emphasis the commission placed on compliance, the professional way in which the staff isolated and then proceeded to work on each state individually, and the confidence they displayed concerning the commission's authority and the inevitability of enacting what it demanded all worked to their advantage.

The national convention's mandate, of course, did confer on the McGovern-Fraser Commission the responsibility "to aid the State Democratic parties in fully meeting the responsibilities and assurances required for inclusion in the Call for the 1972 Democratic National Convention."[3] This was a long way from giving the reform commission the power to force change. The "Call" would be put out by the national committee and would specify the way in which delegates would be selected to the upcoming national convention. This was traditional. By inference, possibly, the national committee, composed principally of party regulars from the states, had some discretion as to what rules in what form they might incorporate in the "Call." If so, this could have superimposed another review body between the McGovern-Fraser Commission and the state parties and one that could be expected to be far more sympathetic to the regulars at a state level than to the reformers.

The McGovern-Fraser Commission chose to follow another tack. From the very beginning, its leaders emphasized that their body would expect, even demand, compliance with their somewhat misnamed "guidelines." They chose to place their emphasis on how difficult the standards applied to certify acceptable compliance with the guidelines would be and how the state parties would need to begin early to adapt their processes to meet the reform specifications. And they made relatively little reference to the national convention and what it might do to back their demands. The presumption they made then was in the form of their committee having a forceful and activist role in seeing actual the reform through to completion in each of the states.

This approach was clear in the very first meeting of the commission, as indicated, when the commission leadership selectively emphasized one, decisively important, phase in its mandate. This was the "all feasible efforts" charge as interpreted by pro-enforcement hard-liners.

The full commission membership held only one other meeting of consequence after its first year. This was in July 1971 when it met to assess its progress. It was torn between conflicting claims of laxness in enforcement (from the reform element) and the beginnings of serious resistance by several states awaking to what they felt was a hard-nosed enforcement policy. The commission gathered to clarify again its meaning as to what was required in the quotas and by "all feasible effort." Essentially, the meeting one year before the national convention was a test of will. The commission was being forced to reassess its willingness to follow through on the implementation of its guidelines. After much confused debate, the answer seemed to be yes. The commission went on from there to the national convention without a serious reconsideration of what it was demanding of the state parties: effective, total compliance with its model of fair representation and open procedures for delegate selection.

One Precedent: The Special Equal Rights Committee

Clearly, the McGovern-Fraser Commission had not proven to be the retiring, obscure party committee most regulars anticipated. Actually, however, it had one little-noticed precedent operation that served it well. Another group, the Special Equal Rights Committee, chaired by Governor Richard Hughes of New Jersey, during the period 1964–1968 had pioneered the implementation process the McGovern-Fraser Commission had adopted. The Special Equal Rights Committee had been set up by the 1964 national convention to resolve the problems posed by southern delegations that refused to admit blacks to their proceedings. First under Governor David Lawrence of Pennsylvania and, on his death, and during its most active phase, under Richard Hughes, the Special Equal Rights Committee attempted to ascertain the seriousness of the discrimination and the extent to which it involved party-related processes. After holding several little-publicized meetings and consulting with the U.S. Commission on Civil Rights, the special committee drafted six resolutions that it hoped would put an end to racial discrimination within the party. As adopted, the rules were as follows:

1. All public meetings at all levels of the Democratic Party in each State should be open to all members of the Democratic Party regardless of race, color, creed, or national origin.
2. No test for membership in, nor any oaths of loyalty to, the Democratic Party in any State should be required or used which has the effect of requiring prospective or current members of the Democratic Party to acquiesce in, condone or support discrimination on the grounds of race, color, creed, or nation origin.
3. The time and place for all public meetings of the Democratic Party on all levels should be publicized fully and in such a manner as to assure timely notice to all interested persons. Such meetings must be held in places accessible to all Party members and large enough to accommodate all interested parties.

4. The Democratic Party, on all levels, should support the broadest possible registration without discrimination on grounds of race, color, creed or national origin.
5. The Democratic Party in each State should publicize fully and in such manner as to assure notice to all interested parties a full description of the legal and practical procedures for selection of Democratic Party officers and representatives on all levels. Publication of these procedures should be done in such fashion that all prospective and current members of each State Democratic Party will be fully and adequately informed of the pertinent procedures in time to participate in each selection procedure at all levels of the Democratic Party organization.
6. The Democratic Party in each State should publicize fully and in such manner as to assure notice to all interested parties a complete description of the legal and practical qualifications for all officers and representatives of the State Democratic Party. Such publication should be done in timely fashion so that all prospective candidates or applicants for any elected or appointed position within each State Democratic Party will have full and adequate opportunity to compete for office.[4]

These rules are the forerunners of those the McGovern-Fraser Commission were to adopt. They represented a significant departure for either party in the 1960s. While, in retrospect, the regulations do not seem overly bold, they did signify the end of the Democratic party's willingness to tolerate racially discriminatory practices. This was important.

The proposals were the first explicit standards the Democrats had adopted on the racial question. They were acceptable to national and northern state party leaders who had been severely embarrassed by the 1964 convention exposition of the racial practices employed by the southern states parties. The new rules were meant to end once and for all the provocations of the southern all-white delegations that had plagued the Democrats for generations. The non-southern party leaders had little sympathy for the problems and racist politics of the state parties in Mississippi, Alabama, Georgia, Florida, and other deep southern states that had flared up in one form or another at each national convention since 1936 and that had led to a walkout of some of the southern states in 1948. While the old-time southern whites were indifferent in their support of the national party, blacks were emerging as the single, most loyal voting bloc within the Democratic coalition. The civil rights legislation of the 1960s ensured that blacks would be voting in increasing numbers in the south. Their problems with the state parties could no longer be ignored. Intelligent self-interest in line with changing social values led the Democratic party leaders to support, with no apparent difficulty, the special committee's initiatives. The party regulars favored the proposals and consequently, since they had no practical significance in the northern states, did not concern themselves with how they were implemented.

Here, the special committee again broke new ground. Its "six basic elements" (later also adopted by the McGovern-Fraser Commission) were promulgated to the state parties in July 1967. The special committee assumed that under its mandate it had the right to *require* the changes it outlined. The threat was that the national party would use these standards to judge compliance with its rules and state parties found in violation would be denied seating at the 1968 national convention. This is exactly what happened. The Democratic National Committee later endorsed the rules, and Richard Hughes was made chairman of the national convention's Credentials Committee. This committee then employed these rules to determine the suitability of southern delegations and in fact refused to seat any state delegations not conforming to the new requirements. In due course, the regular Mississippi delegation was barred from participating in the national convention proceedings and the Georgia delegation's convention vote was divided equally between the regulars and the challengers.

The important point for the McGovern-Fraser Commission was the assertion by the special committee that it had the power to enforce its own standards. The special committee was hardly flamboyant and its actions occasioned little notice, mostly because the party leadership was in sympathy with what it was trying to accomplish. When a new reform group, not in accord with the party regulars, would employ the same device to require a far broader set of reforms, the reaction would not be so accommodating.

A fourth distinctive feature of the McGovern-Fraser Commission was that it was destined to serve as a model for all later reform bodies. The McGovern-Fraser Commission took a number of bold initiatives that broke new ground and came to symbolize the *sine qua non* of what would, henceforth, constitute acceptable reform enterprises. All commission meetings were open to the public. Each commission member was given an equal voice in deliberations. Decision-making was open. All proposals were subject to discussion and were adopted by majority vote. An effort was made to bring all elements of the commission along on issues and to achieve near-consensus on the major rules to be required of the state parties. The commission files were open to the media, state party leaders, and the public. Volunteer help in commission work was encouraged, and in the aftermath of the Nixon election, it became somewhat fashionable among students, liberals, and anti-war activists to work for the group during the hectic days it researched procedures and attempted to settle on its recommendations.

The regional hearings were highly publicized, and everyone with a grievance against the party (the vast majority who appeared) or who wanted to speak in favor of the existing arrangements or on behalf of something new was invited. These hearings proved to be a public relations bonanza. They were heavily covered by the media, and the transcripts of the field hearings provide the most thorough documentation of party procedures ever assembled. Other committees were to attempt to duplicate such hearings, but with little success. Once the initial wave of emotion following the 1968 election had passed, the party's grassroots membership and the press were to show little interest in succeeding reform bodies. Nonetheless, party reform committees were to schedule such sessions dutifully and then employ them as a justification and legitimation for whatever proposals they put forth.

The Media

The media played an important role in the work of the McGovern-Fraser Commission. The commission set out to make its case through the media. All sessions were open to the press and the commission leaders and staff made every effort to cultivate the media, to keep them abreast of what was happening, and to educate them to its significance. The field hearings provided occasional dramatic outbursts, for example, when party regulars such as Mayor Daley appeared or when the issues they discussed involved such things as the role of television in allegedly inciting or overplaying the events in the streets of Chicago. In many respects, the deliberations of the McGovern-Fraser Commission provided a natural extension of the disruptions of the 1968 election year and therefore were ready-made for media attention.

The commission wanted as much media exposure as possible. It wanted to educate the public and the party to the issues involved in reform and it wanted to develop as large a constituency as possible for change. It hoped to pressure party leaders on the state and national level toward a more receptive stance on reform questions by nurturing as pro-reform a media orientation as it could.

The journalists tended to be skeptical. They had seen party committees operate before and they expected few results. The pro-reformers on the commission and the staff, nonetheless, worked hard to ensure that media representatives had a rudimentary understanding at least of what was happening and, more importantly, that they reported it extensively. In large part, the strategy worked.

Wide media exposure was used by the commission also to ensure that it, or its proposals, would not fade from public consciousness. By alerting the media to upcoming events—for example, the national committee meeting intended to issue the Call to the 1972 convention—the commission could define the issues to come before the group as they saw them and the outcome they would consider acceptable. Anything less than the goals the commission wanted could be considered something less than pure reform. Again the approach worked. The national party agencies involved with questions relating to the McGovern-Fraser guidelines proved remarkably conciliatory and supportive of proposals which, on the face of them, they could have been expected to oppose.

The media helped the commission establish itself in a favorable light. The reformers became the "good guys" and those who opposed them the "bad guys." The burden was placed on those against reform to explain themselves to a public and a press generally favorable to what the McGovern-Fraser Commission was trying to do. The anti-reformers never effectively dealt with this handicap.

The Commission and the National Party

Finally in this regard, the commission used the media and the public goodwill that reform seemed to generate to quietly coopt the national party leadership. The McGovern-Fraser group attempted to avoid confrontations on policy issues and to work as independently as possible from the national committee (which housed it and helped support it financially) and national party leaders. It presented its proposals as a *fait accompli* and asked neither approval nor support for what it had done.

Nonetheless, its independence—much like its power of enforcement—were somewhat illusionary. It needed the backing of the party leaders at critical periods in its enforcement drive.

The commission's relationship with the national chairman that had named its membership, Fred R. Harris, was generally good. Harris supported reform and believed widespread change along the lines anticipated by the McGovern-Fraser rules to be necessary. Harris, however, fell into disfavor with national party leaders, including Hubert Humphrey, because of his liberal views and, in part, his reform stance. He was replaced in the spring of 1970 by Lawrence O'Brien, a party regular who had come into prominence with the John Kennedy campaign of 1960. The new national chair was an unknown quantity on reform issues.

O'Brien did not encourage confidence among reformers when he reopened the sensitive question of the commission's powers to enforce its rules. O'Brien called in the Democratic party's legal counsel, Joseph Califano, to decide precisely what the national convention had mandated. Califano made his judgment just prior to the May meeting of the national committee: Yes, the McGovern-Fraser Commission did have the authority to require compliance with their guidelines. The reformers breathed easier.

Yet, reformers never were completely comfortable with O'Brien. They expected the worst, and they continually prepared themselves to do battle with him and the national party at each juncture in the long road to implementation. The national committee did, at one point, modify the reform guidelines to allow themselves ex-officio (non-elected) delegate status at the national convention. Under pressure from the reformers, and O'Brien, they modified their stand to extend automatic delegate rights at national convention to only those national committee members elected during the nominating years. A small break with the McGovern-Fraser rules, but not a serious one.

At another point (the fall of 1971) the more ardent reformers wanted Harold Hughes to be chosen temporary chairman of the upcoming national convention's credential committee, thus ensuring that the credentials committee would enforce the McGovern-Fraser rules. They felt also that such a choice well before the national convention would alert the state parties that no backsliding would be permitted.

The reformers were incensed when O'Brien, responding to pressure from the regulars and relying on his own instincts, refused to appoint Hughes. In fact, O'Brien went on to mobilize support behind another candidate, Patricia Roberts Harris, a black not associated with reform. Not unexpectedly, O'Brien's choice carried in the national committee (which makes preliminary decisions on such matters) overwhelmingly (72–31).

Harris went on to be a forceful chairperson at the 1972 Credentials Committee hearings. She applied the new rules fairly and the reformers found little to complain about. Still, the incident emphasized the lack of trust between the reformers and O'Brien. They continued to be wary of each other, but at each important test, O'Brien demonstrated his support of reform.

Ironically, O'Brien's rulings at the 1972 national convention that some observers felt were partial to the reformers and to the reform candidate, McGovern, infuriated many party regulars and the leaders of such important interest groups as the AFL-CIO. They were not to forget O'Brien's "disloyalty" and their enmity may have been a contributing factor in O'Brien's decision to leave politics. He co-managed

McGovern's losing 1972 presidential campaign and then retired, later to become commissioner of the National Basketball Association.

The model of how to do what was needed to achieve its goals would be followed in varying degrees by the other reform commissions. None, however, would ever achieve the success in communicating its objectives, publicizing its activities, and successfully pressuring for what it wanted than the model's originator, the McGovern-Fraser Commission.

A final distinctive feature of the McGovern-Fraser Commission was its impact. Its work fundamentally changed the way in which the Democratic Party (and in somewhat modified form, the Republican Party) would nominate its presidential candidates. More than likely, the changes are permanent.

The magnitude of what the McGovern-Fraser Commission attempted can be indicated. It required fifteen proposals (three additional ones were only "recommended" to the state parties and these were ignored), designed, it believed, to open nominating practices to all concerned Democrats and to increase the representation of blacks, youth, and women in the process. When the McGovern-Fraser Commission began its drive for the implementation of its rules in early 1970, not one of the state parties met all its requirements. To the shock of some, reform was to touch each and every state. Ninety-eight percent of the state parties did not meet the highly publicized "quota" requirements. The nominating practices in two-thirds to 95 percent of the states did not have specific rules governing their operations, delegate apportionment formulas, slate-making procedures, or timeliness provisions (nomination processes beginning in the year of the presidential election) that satisfied commission standards. On the average a state party was out of compliance with two out of three of the McGovern-Fraser Commission's rules. At the end of the implementation period, the commission reported to the 1972 national convention:

> Four years ago, the Democratic National Convention directed the Party to open its procedures at every level so that all Democrats who wished to participate in the choosing of delegates to the 1972 Convention would have the opportunity to do so. . . .
>
> Uprooting old, entrenched customs of the past and replacing them with new and different procedures is not easy.
>
> Shifting the historic concept of a system from one of tight central control to open participation by party rank-and-file members constitutes a national political revolution. Including large numbers of women, young people, and minorities in National Convention delegations means turning years of tradition around.[5]

Nonetheless, the commission could claim:

- 40 state parties, the territories, and the District of Columbia, have complied with the Guidelines in their written rules, procedures, and local law; and the remaining 10 are in substantial compliance.
- 99 percent of the Guidelines have been met overall by state parties in new, written rules and statutory revisions.
- 98.3 percent of the delegations to the 1972 convention will have been elected by either primary or open caucus or convention procedures, with only 1.1 percent being elected by state party committees.
- The percentages of blacks and women delegates have nearly tripled over 1968 and the percentage of young delegates has increased fourfold.
- all fifty states, the District of Columbia, and the territories have adopted new official written party rules.[6]

Ten states did not fully implement all the guidelines. According to the commission, most of these did not comply with one, or part of one, guideline and most would have required state legislative action to accommodate themselves to the commission's standards. Ironically, the commission reported it had "made no judgement" as to whether the state parties had met its criterion of "all feasible efforts" in their attempts to comply. The threat of the criteria and the stringency of its provisions apparently had been enough.

Conclusion

The record is impressive. It does amount, as the commission had claimed, to something of a "political revolution."[7] Such success would not be seen again. In fact, the future reform commissions to deal with delegate selection would act in response to what the McGovern-Fraser Commission did. Most also would attempt to mute some features of the new system or even (as with the Winograd and Hunt commissions) to reverse its direction.

The McGovern-Fraser Commission would stand alone. Its achievements could not be duplicated. In some respects, the reform movement both began and substantially ended with the commission's work.

SEVEN

Presidential Selection II: The Mikulski Commission

The period following the introduction of McGovern-Fraser rules and the election of 1972 was one of consolidation and of reconsideration. The emphasis of reform during this phase was on reassessing, and constantly modifying, the reform guidelines. This was particularly true in presidential selection; each election begat a new "reform" committee which in turn begat a new set of rules for the succeeding election.

The continual redefinition of the rules was tiresome and confusing. Some committees attempted to amend the rules slightly, smoothing their rough edges and making them more palatable to the regulars; others claimed simply to apply the values enunciated—engaging in no interpretive function; and others did their best to reverse the entire direction of the reform movement. The result was constant uncertainty and a presidential selection system in continual flux.

The first of the groups to so concern itself was the Mikulski Commission (1972–1974). The commission met in the aftermath of the bitterly decisive 1972 presidential election. McGovern, the man most identified with reform, had run a disastrous and embarrassing race against incumbent President Richard M. Nixon. The general election followed a tumultuous convention in which a large number of delegations had been challenged and many party regulars, including the most powerful local leader within the party, Mayor Richard J. Daley of Chicago, had been unseated for not abiding by one or more of the reform guidelines in their delegate selections.

The party regulars were furious. They were out for blood and their intention was to scuttle the McGovern-Fraser Commission's guidelines. The vehicle to accomplish this was the Mikulski Commission. In effect, this commission was to prove a battleground, once again, between reformers and party regulars over the future direction of party change. The issues then were fundamental. If the regulars had succeeded, the McGovern-Fraser reforms would have represented a brief interlude in the party's long history.

The regulars failed. Mikulski's Commission endorsed the reformers. It refused to open their assumptions to broad public or party debate. Modifications were introduced to make the mechanisms of reform more acceptable to their critics, and a number of concessions were made to party regulars that increased their role and influence in both delegate selection and national conventions. The reforms themselves, however, remained basically intact. Thus, with modest changes, the reforms were endorsed and their permanent place in the presidential selection process virtually assured.

The Mikulski Commission gave way to the Compliance Review Commission (1974–1976), a curious group that grew out of the battles within the Mikulski Commission and between this group and the national party leadership. Through this body the party regulars, in control of the national party's operations, attempted once again to reverse the direction of the reform emphasis. These efforts were not similar to the broad public debate and factional fights evident in the commission decision-making. The strategy had changed and the emphasis was on control of the nominating system and the major party agencies. The belief was that by controlling implementation, an effort could be made to dull the reform drive. Later and once the tide had turned, attention could be turned into a more direct attempt to scuttle the entire fabric of the reforms. Control of implementation would be the key.

In both Compliance Review Commissions (1972–1976 and 1978–1980), the party regulars attempted, through unpublicized rule-making and a quiet accommodation to the needs of the state party leaders, to blunt any controversy and to constantly push reform—through the reinterpretation of rulings or their application—back toward the dominance of party regulars of the pre-1972 era. Through the control of the staff and the day-to-day monitoring of state-level delegate selection, the faction of party regulars represented by National Chairman Robert Strauss (1973–1976), and later those pushing the interests of President Jimmy Carter (through National Chair John White, 1977–1980) did enjoy some successes.

There is a limit to how much can be accomplished in this manner. Hence the creation of the Winograd Commission. This group was established by the national chair (Strauss) allegedly to deal with some of the pressing, and unintended, consequences of reform. A specific concern was the profusion of presidential nominating primaries and the problems these caused state parties. An unarticulated assumption underlying the creation of the new body was that it would help reverse the direction of reform and restore control over party deliberations and presidential selection to the old-line party professionals.

Because of the specificity of its original focus (presidential primaries) and confusion over its actual role, the fact that it was authorized by a national chair and not mandated by the national convention, the first such reform body to be so created, its first months were marked by an uncertainty and aimlessness that resulted in no work of substantive value. Unable to clarify its intentions or legitimize its operations, the commission effectively suspended work until the 1976 nomination and election outcomes had been decided.

The national convention of that year sanctioned the efforts of the Winograd Commission and mandated its continued operation with a much broader official charge. The national convention authorized it to conduct a complete reassessment of the entire nominating process. Its membership was considerably enlarged and recast to allow the incoming Carter administration to appoint, and control, the balance of its members. The Carter representatives, along with those party professionals who opposed reform on principle, dominated commission deliberations. The Carter appointees and the party regulars had one thing in common: Both wished to close presidential nominating practices—and specifically the 1980 contest—to the extent feasible.

The work of the Winograd Commission, the oddest of all the "reform" groups, was a serious effort at revisionism. It worked quietly, with little media or public notice, but (in its reborn phase) with clear objectives. It was only partially successful; primarily, because it went too far, invoking a reaction from liberals and reformers of sufficient magnitude to force a modification of some of its more controversial proposals.

In line with each national convention since 1968, the 1980 national convention created its own reform body to rewrite (in the post-1980 election period) the rules for the 1984 presidential election. The new group (the Hunt Commission) was to extend the work of the Winograd Commission, further closing many of the participatory avenues that traced back to the McGovern-Fraser Commission. It effectively created an enlarged "quota" of delegate seats to be reserved for nonelected (through presidential primaries or caucuses) party officials.

A continuing effort to change the nominating practices, in order to close the system and return control as much as possible to those in party or elective office, has been the hallmark of the newer reform era.

First, however, there is the Mikulski Commission.

The Mikulski Commission and the System of '76

The results of the presidential election of 1972 had sent shock waves through the party. The regulars were determined to reverse the reform rules to avoid in the future the damage they believed these had inflicted on the party. The reformers were dispirited and some appeared ready to capitulate. George McGovern, the party's losing presidential nominee, in a post-election address to a reform group, indicated the new direction the party would take: "The reforms were not written in stone," McGovern told the group.[1] This seemed an open invitation to change the rules, and the regulars and their allies in organized labor were more than eager to try. The battle was to be fought in the Mikulski Commission.

The commission was led by Baltimore City Councilwoman, and later Congresswoman, Barbra Mikulski. The choice, in effect, was a mistake. Supposedly, organized labor and ethnics were discriminated against by the McGovern-Fraser reforms. To symbolize its determination to change this condition, the party leadership decided on Leonard Woodcock, the president of the UAW (United Automobile Workers) to chair the new commission and the little-known Mikulski (representing ethnics) to serve as vice-chair. When Woodcock decided he could not spare the time to lead the body, Mikulski was elected to head it. She turned out to be a fiesty and independent chair, not at all what Strauss and the party leadership intended.

Surprisingly, as the commission deliberations evolved, it became clear that the balance of the group felt the intent of the guidelines to be good and the rules themselves relatively equitable and reasonable. They did believe some aspects of the regulations to be unnecessarily harsh and they did move to cushion the impact of the rules on the representation of party regulars at national conventions.

The Mikulski Commission enjoyed a wild and tempestuous life; its struggles—aired through the media—became some of the bitterest in memory among party factions. Clashes among the stronger personalities on the commission, and especially between the unexpectedly forceful Mikulski and the equally outspoken national chair and advocate for the party regulars, Robert Strauss, were common. The AFL-CIO, determined to regain its dominant role in party affairs, also made its contributions to the proceedings. The Mikulski Commission's deliberations became a particular target of its concern. As it lost on several key issues, its anger and, correspondingly, the public and intra-party attacks it directed against the commission and its leaders, and the pressure it placed on Strauss to do its bidding, increased proportionately.

As a consequence, when the commission concluded its deliberations and made its recommendations in 1974, it opted to turn over the enforcement of its rules to a committee specifically created for the task (the Compliance Review Commission). This decision was reached by the various factional leaders on the commission and National Chair Strauss in a meeting that excluded Mikulski. It was intended as a compromise to terminate the squabbling committee—setting a precedent other such groups would follow—and for allowing a considerable amount of discretionary power to gravitate back into the hands of pro-regular faction controlling the national committee. At the time, however, it was accepted with a sigh of relief by both party regulars and reformers.

The 1976 prenomination season and the succeeding national convention were—from the point of view of the continuing fights over presidential selection procedures—unusually tranquil. The party did not turn in upon itself; record numbers of party members participated in its proceedings; and party voters were given a clear set of issue and personality choices among contenders for the presidential nomination. In short, the nominating system worked much as the reformers had hoped in opening the process and allowing participants a meaningful voice in its decision-making. At the same time, the procedures used did not offend party regulars; while still not accepting the assumptions of a reform system, they could at least live with the manner in which it operated in 1976.

In part, at least, this was due to the regulations advocated by the Mikulski Commission. The commission's rules were adopted, with minor alterations, by the Democratic National Committee in March 1974 and included in its Call to the 1976 national convention.

The rules are about as able, clear, and fair a set of regulations, within the reform assumptions, that could be devised. They accommodate the major objectives raised by the party regulars while remaining basically faithful to the values and priorities of the reformers. They also allowed for modest adjustments in response to the existing political conditions of an election year while still retaining their basic integrity.

Not everyone was totally happy with the 1976 system and not every state met all the guidelines (Wisconsin's retention of its historic "open" primary is one example). Nonetheless, the 1976 procedures reflect political realities. They balanced a reform-oriented system, simple and easy to understand and apply, with compromises (revised quorum provisions, an enlarged role for state party committees and leaders) intended to placate the regulars and to modify the features they found to be the most objectionable. The system employed in 1976 adjusted reform assumptions to the practicalities of the political process and the coalitional divisions within the party. The '76 system serves as something of a model in these regards (and offers a pointed contrast to the complex and poorly understood rules used in 1980). For this reason, the rules are reproduced at some length.

The System of '76: Presidential Delegate Selection Rules in the Democratic Party, 1976

1. PARTY RULES: State Parties must adopt and make available clear and comprehensive party rules describing and explaining the delegate selection process by January 1, 1976 or at least 90 days prior to the beginning of the process, whichever is earlier.

2. DEMOCRATIC PARTICIPATION: Steps must be taken to restrict participation in the delegate selection process to Democrats only. Parties must encourage unaffiliated and new voters to register and enroll as Democrats.

3. PUBLIC NOTICE: All steps in the delegate selection process, except the election of state committee members, must take place in 1976. Meetings must be held in convenient public places and begin and end at reasonable hours. Meetings at each level must take place on the same date throughout the state (i.e., all precinct caucuses must be held on the same date in a particular state), unless meeting such a requirement would significantly reduce public participation. The times, dates, places, and rules for these meetings must be effectively publicized and information explaining the purpose of the meeting and how it relates to the delegate selection process must be distributed.

4. COSTS AND FEES: No one may be excluded from any stage in the delegate selection process for failure to pay a cost or fee.

5. PETITION REQUIREMENTS: No petition requirements in excess of 1% of the registered, enrolled or voting Democrats in the applicable district may be imposed.

6. PROXY VOTING: A person attending a meeting who must leave before business is concluded may, if no suitable alternate is present, leave a proxy vote with another participant, provided that the person to whom the proxy is given holds no more than 3 proxies.

7. QUORUM REQUIREMENTS: At least 40% of the members of any party body above the first level of the delegate selection process must be present to constitute a quorum for any business pertaining to the selection of convention delegates.

8. UNIT RULE: The unit rule may not be used at any stage of the delegate selection process.

9. APPORTIONMENT: National Convention delegates must be apportioned within the state on 1 of 4 formulas based on different measures of Democratic strength.

   (1) Equal weight given to total population and to the average of the vote for the Democratic candidates in the two most recent presidential elections; or

   (2) Equal weight to the vote for the Democratic candidates in the most recent presidential and gubernatorial elections; or

   (3) Equal weight to the average of the vote for the Democratic candidates in the two most recent presidential elections and to Democratic Party registration or enrollment as of January 1, 1976; or

   (4) A formula giving ⅓ weight to each of previous three formulas. Other party bodies must be apportioned on the basis of population and/or Democratic strength. At least 75% of the National Convention delegates must be elected from units no larger than a Congressional District.

10. PRESIDENTIAL PREFERENCE: All candidates for delegate must be identified as to presidential preference, uncommitted or no preference status. The presidential candidate has a right to approve delegate-candidates identified with his candidacy. The presidential preferences or delegate-candidates must be effectively publicized. All public nominating meetings must be held simultaneously within each state so that no person may participate in more than one such meeting. Participants in the meetings may be required to sign statements of support for the presidential candidate on whose behalf the meeting is being conducted. No delegate may be required to vote against his or her expressed choice.

11. FAIR REFLECTION: Delegations at all levels must be divided according to the expressed preferences receiving at least 15% support of the voters in binding primaries and of participants in caucuses or conventions. In primary states with no binding presidential preference poll, delegates must be elected from units no larger than a Congressional District.

12. SELECTION OF AT LARGE DELEGATES: In states with no state convention authorized to elect delegates, the publicly elected delegates or the state committee may select not more than 25% of the delegation if the committee is

    (1) apportioned on the basis of population and/or Democratic strength;

    (2) elected in an open process;

    (3) elects the 25% at a public meeting following the public

election of the other 75% of the National Convention delegates;

(4) elected no earlier than January 1, 1974; and

(5) the 25% reflect the preferences of the publicly elected delegates.

13. AUTOMATIC DELEGATES: The Democratic National Committee is urged to give Democratic Governors, Senators, and Congressmen and Democratic National Committee members delegate privileges, except the right to vote. No person may automatically become a delegate because of public or party office.

14. SLATE MAKING: Any person or group may form a slate, but no slate may receive preferential treatment or ballot position, may not be designated as the "official slate," and must meet identical qualifying requirements.

15. ALTERNATES AND VACANCIES: Alternates are to be selected according to the same rules for the selection of at large delegates so far as state law permits. If an elected delegate resigns or is unable to serve, the delegate selects his or her own alternate who shall be of the same presidential preference, residing in the same political unit if possible. If the delegate dies or is disabled, the alternate is selected by the delegation and must be of the same preference of the delegate replaced and resident of the same political unit if possible. Vacant alternate positions are filled by the delegation. The selected alternate must be of the same presidential preference and political subdivision as the alternate being replaced.

16. AN OPEN PARTY: State Parties are required to adopt and implement the Six Basic Elements which require that

(1) all public Party meetings be open to all Democrats;

(2) loyalty oaths be banned if they condone discrimination;

(3) times and places must be effectively publicized for all Party meetings, and meetings must be held in accessible places;

(4) voter registration must be supported;

(5) procedures for being elected as a Democratic Party or public official must be effectively publicized;

(6) complete descriptions of the legal and practical qualifications of all positions of officers and representatives of the Party must be effectively publicized.

17. NON-DISCRIMINATION: Discrimination on the basis of race, sex, age, color, national origin, religion, ethnic identity, or economic status is prohibited.

18. AFFIRMATIVE ACTION: The National and State Democratic Parties must adopt and implement affirmative action programs whose goal shall be to encourage the participation of all Democrats, particularly minorities, native Americans, women, and

youth, in all party affairs as indicated by their presence in the Democratic electorate. Mandatory quotas may not be imposed. A State Party which has adopted and implemented an affirmative action plan may not be challenged solely on the basis of delegation composition or primary results.

19. STATE LEGISLATIVE CHANGES: State Parties must take provable positive steps to change any state law conflicting with these rules.[2]

The major changes these rules introduced were as follows:

- A proportionate division of all national convention votes being contested in a primary or caucus among all contenders receiving a minimum of 10 percent (later amended from 10% to 15% at the discretion of the state party) of the vote case (a rule favored but not required by the McGovern-Fraser Commission).
- The restriction of party processes to participation by Democrats only (another position favored but not required by the McGovern-Fraser Commission).
- A loosening of provisions relating to proxy voting and quorum requirements, rules originally instigated to curb some of the more arbitrary abuses of the party regulars.
- The requirement that all delegates running on behalf of a candidate be sanctioned by the presidential contender.
- The provision that state party committees be allowed to select up to 25 percent of a national convention delegation in order to better represent party and public officeholders *and* minorities.
- The omission of the controversial quotas on blacks, women, and youth, which were replaced by less stringent, vaguer, and clearly nonmandatory "affirmative action" programs.

Restricting party processes to party members only was favored by regulars and most reformers (although serious divisions arose over the stringency of tests to be applied in determining the party members who could participate in party decision-making). The proportionality requirement was a major victory for the reformers and a clear extension of the reform initiatives. To a lesser extent, this also was true of the rule requesting presidential contenders to sanction delegates who sought national convention seats in their name. The changes in proxy vote and quorum limits, the expanded role permitted state committees, the implicit acceptance of the argument that more party and elective officials should be included in national convention proceedings, the discretion allowed party agencies in selecting and appointing such officeholders, and the elimination of the minority quotas all represented substantial victories for party regulars and their allies in the AFL-CIO.

The system of 1976 maintained a mix of primaries and state caucus/

convention systems at 60/40 (in favor of the primaries). The balance was arrived at by chance—i.e., it was not required by party rules—but it appears about right. It combines the public forum of primaries with enough of the supposedly party-building caucuses and state conventions to satisfy most elements within the party.

Implementation

The Mikulski Commission went out of existence in 1974. It left in its wake the twenty-five member Compliance Review Commission to oversee the enactment of its rules and, in particular, the requirements as to affirmative action. The composition of the commission was intended to represent all the warring factions within the party. It was led by former mayor Robert Wagner of New York City, who had little interest or stake in the reform controversy, and its staff was appointed by the party regulars through the office of the Democratic national chair. As a consequence, it went to lengths to avoid controversy and to accommodate the state parties. The commission proved to be an extension of the national chair's office and, by choice, systematically diluted the meaning and impact of the reform guidelines. Control over nominating practices—although within the context of the new rules and a participant-oriented grassroots system—was returned in fact, if not name, to the states.

For the reformers, something was lost in the transition. For the party as a whole, however, most of the acrimony of the preceding eight years was laid aside and the 1976 process proved to be the smoothest that could be expected. In this sense, the Mikulski and Compliance Review commissions were outstanding successes. After hearing seventeen challenges from fifteen delegations in 1968 and eighty-one challenges from thirty-one delegations in 1972, both successive records for national conventions, the 1976 Democratic National Convention entertained *no* credentials challenges. The outcome was a result of the general acceptance of the new rules, the weariness with internal bickering within the party, and an accommodation to the fact that one candidate, Jimmy Carter, had the nomination assured by the time the national convention met. In the latter regard, few cared to initiate challenges that might weaken Carter's candidacy and thus Democratic hopes for capturing the White House in November.

Conclusion

The presidential selection system, as it operated in 1976, gave voters an immediate and decisive voice in the presidential nomination decision; it offered rank and file participants in the process a choice among thirteen candidates representing all shades of party opinion; and the nomination was won through the cultivation and support of the party's grassroots membership. These accomplishments would all be considered desirable by reform advocates.

There were no major objections to the 1976 system; no particular rules were judged to be overly restrictive on voters or candidates or too onerous (excepting the Wisconsin "closed primary" debate) for the state parties to meet. No major faction within the party (regulars, organized labor, who had begun to direct its energies elsewhere, or reformers) took issue with the guidelines or their results.

Nevertheless, change was in the offing. A new commission, the Winograd Commission, had already (prior to 1976) begun its deliberations. The new group had begun to consider means of limiting the proliferation of primaries and of moving the state parties back toward a caucus/convention preference. Before it would complete its deliberations, its work would result in a new set of rules far more encompassing than early efforts promised and far more of a challenge to the operations of a reformed presidential nominating system than any that had been encountered since the reform era had begun.

EIGHT

Presidential Selection III: Turning Back the Tide with the Winograd Commission

Presidential primaries had spread at an alarming rate: from 16 in 1968 to 23 in 1972, to 30 in 1976 and post-Winograd, to 33 in 1980. The proportion of delegates elected *and* bound to a presidential contender in primaries had increased from a handful in the 1960s to 75 to 81 percent of the active national convention membership by the late 1970s (in, respectively, 1976 and 1980).

It was a development that many party members, regulars, and reformers alike, feared. They felt that the proliferation of primaries served to weaken the party and its control over the nominating process. Primaries—with their attendent costs, media hype, and supposedly, party-debilitating effects—threatened to engulf the entire nominating process.

Hence the rationale for creating a new reform commission in 1975. Its job was to find ways to curb the spread, and to lessen the influence of, primaries in presidential selection. Judged by this standard, it was remarkably unsuccessful. Not only did the number of primaries increase from 1976 to 1980, but there was nothing in the commission's report that would help reverse the movement. In fact, a reading of the commission's recommendations provides little to remind one that this was the original justification for the group's existence.

But the commission was to serve another purpose. Many party regulars, still unreconciled to the reform developments, hoped that the new group would review and, if possible, reverse the reform initiatives taken by the McGovern-Fraser and Mikulski commissions. In those regards the group enjoyed some successes.

Since the creation of a new commission was not authorized by the national convention and since it received little media attention, initially or at any point in the deliberations, the national chair (Strauss) was free to appoint the membership (in 1975) and to intervene as he chose in structuring the commission's agenda. He had little fear of an adverse public or grassroots reaction. Nobody inside the party or out knew much about the committee, what it was doing, or what it hoped to accomplish. If anything, this strengthened the commission's hand. It had few external checks to worry about, while its powers—especially after the election year of 1976—were theoretically as great as any of its predecessors. The commission's chairmanship was awarded to Morley Winograd, a little-known political figure who had served as the Michigan state chair and who was close to the AFL-CIO. Winograd had no previous association with the reform movement. He was not known outside his state and he was open to direction, sometimes subtle, sometimes not, from the national chair's office and staff and from organized labor.

The commission did little its first year. At the 1976 Democratic National Convention a proposal was adopted to legitimize its existence and to expand its deliberations. After the national convention, the commission's membership was increased to include a bloc representing the wishes of the new president, Jimmy Carter. As finally constituted, about one-third were people directly appointed by and responsive to the White House; another third were independent (of the President) party regulars, or those sympathetic to their position; and the final third were people with a reform orientation or with no clear commitment (pro- or anti-reform one way or the other).

By 1978, the revised body had made its recommendations. In light of what previous commissions had done, the results had constituted a 180-degree turn in direction. The Winograd Commission attempted to *close* the presidential nominating process. The recommendations were very much at odds with those that had come from the earlier reform bodies. The new direction in reform perhaps should have been predicted, given the commission's makeup, the intent for which it was established, and most significantly, the desire of the White House to effectively reshape the nominating process to discourage competitors.

The representatives of the Carter administration—their chief a product of the reform system—were not sympathetic to a totally open, and potentially competitive, nominating process: In their eyes, and given the serious opposition evident in party ranks to Carter's leadership, this represented too much of a risk. Their intention was to significantly close the process at the top—making it difficult for other candidates to mobilize the support necessary to meet the qualification requirement for running within the state presidential selection systems. The commission did not attempt to close participation at the grassroots level, although it did dilute the direct impact of the rank and file on nominations by adding appointive delegate positions and by returning control over much of the nominating procedures to the state parties. The latter development did not evoke the concern it would have several elections earlier in many if not most states. Nonetheless, there were still a number of state parties with an unreconstructed view of their discretionary powers and a lingering resentment of a broader participation in party decision-making. Allowing such state parties to reassert themselves in presidential selection could prove to create future problems for the party (and the experience of the Michigan party under Winograd's prodding supplied one example of what could happen).

The Commission's Contribution

The reform impulse had been spent by 1974. The work of the Mikulski and Party Charter commissions had effectively ended the creative phase of the reform drive. Most of what occurred after 1974—and the Winograd and Hunt commissions are prime examples of this development—was intended to placate the regulars and accommodate their (and between 1976 and 1980 the White House's) political needs. Only a handful of reformers, led by former Congressman Donald Fraser of the original McGovern-Fraser Commission, remained interested and active in the continual battle over party revitalization. These reformers carried enough weight to force revision of several of the more blatant extremes of the anti-reform drive, including several of the proposals that came out of the Winograd Commission. They did not have enough power, however, to keep modified revisions of the same recommendations from being enacted by the national committee. In effect, also during the years 1976–1980, the reformers were fighting the White House and the battle was hardly an even one.

Also of significance, the media had lost interest in the continuing party bickering over reform and it refused to cover it in any depth. The media could hardly be blamed for its lack of attention. Reform had turned into technical and boring arguments over regulations, debates more suited to the skills of lawyers than to the interests of the public or the party's grassroots element. Reporters often missed the significance of alternative proposals and could not perceive their long-run implications. There was little human interest left in the reform fights. Difficult to personalize, obscure in content and application, impossible to dramatize, the ongoing reform (or, more accurately, anti-reform) movement excited little notice.

With an absence of media attention, the public and the grassroots party membership could not be expected to know what was transpiring. A lack of public information was a factor that played into the hands of those attempting to further close the system. With this in mind, a look at what the Winograd proposed is in order. Among its recommendations were the following:[1]

• A proposal to restrict the nominating primaries and caucuses to a three month period (from the second Tuesday in March to the second Tuesday in June) of the election year. The argument was that this would save wear and tear on the candidates and cut the costs of nominating campaigns. In truth, any shortening of the nominating period favors an incumbent (or any other well-known national party leader) who already has the name identification and potential for fundraising and organizational development necessary for victory. It hurts newcomers and less-known candidates who need all the time they can muster to gain attention, to educate party members to their policy views, to raise funds and to qualify as a media celebrity.

Clearly, a candidate will still begin campaigning two to four years before the presidential election year. What he now had to do was in effect to be organized, funded and relatively well-known before any of the primaries or caucuses began. Of necessity, he had to contend with winning all of his delegates during a short ninety day period. He no longer had the luxury of building a campaign and a coalition as he went along; depending on the victory in one state to supply the momentum, media coverage and support necessary to succeed in other primaries over the once long (January to June) nominating season. A candidate could not do what Jimmy Carter did in 1976; focus on an early state, such as New Hampshire, and hope a win there would lead to the financial and public response sufficient to sustain an all-out run.

The White House representatives on the Winograd Commission did provide for one exception. They introduced a resolution to exempt from the three month restriction any state that in 1976 had begun its delegate selection process before the second Tuesday in March. The exemption was justified on the basis that these states might have to deal with Republican legislatures or governors and, consequently, could not be expected to get the necessary statutory changes approved. Its intent was more political, however, The proviso safeguarded the position of Iowa and New Hampshire. Iowa was the early-bird caucus state that had launched the Carter campaign in 1976 and it was expected to do so again. New Hampshire's first-in-the-nation primary was the contest that established Carter in the media and the public mind as the 1976 front-runner. The president expected to launch a successful renomination drive in 1980 with repeat victories in both the Iowa and highly publicized New Hampshire contests.

The media attention given the New Hampshire results, in particular, is lavish, well out of proportion to the state's electoral vote, the representativeness of its electorate or the practical value of the delegates won. By isolating New Hampshire (and Iowa) even further from the rest of the pack, it assured, if anything, that increased media significance would be given these races. This ploy offended many party regulars who believed that a more closed party better represented the interests of Democrats. It is evidence of the White House muscle on the commission that the exception still passed by a two to one margin.

Other Winograd Commission requirements included:

• A proposal that would require candidate filing deadlines for primaries or caucuses be set by the states at least fifty-five days before the delegate selection. Originally, the White House wanted ninety days, but under pressure reduced the number. The intention was to limit the pool of contenders by forcing them, again, to organize early, well before the primary or caucus, and, in many cases, before public interest had been aroused. Secondly, the hope was to avoid late-comers. Even if the front runner should stumble in later delegate contests, if a candidate had not already filed for the upcoming state primaries or caucuses, he could not then enter the race. As an example, Governor Edmund G. (Jerry) Brown, Jr., of California, and Senator Frank Church of Idaho, in 1976 and Robert Kennedy in 1968 were late entries into the race. Under the new rules, they would not have qualified to run.

• A proposal to require a floor of from 15 percent to 25 percent of the vote in a primary or caucus before a presidential contender could claim a proportionate share of *any* of the state's national convention delegate vote. In 1976, the floor had been 10 to 15 percent and there had been no difficulty with it. The argument for the change was that it would force the party to coalesce behind candidates in each of the states, thus encouraging a cohesiveness not previously encountered. It would be a "party-building" or "coalition-building" mechanism that would create a "party consensus" behind a candidate, to call upon the favored clichés of the day. The arguments against the measure were that it further closed the nominating process, that it discriminated against candidates without the initial name recognition and media attention a primary race brings, that it favored the incumbent (or well-publicized national party leaders), that successful challenges to a front-runner would become exceedingly difficult to engage in as the primary season went on (under the proposal, 15 percent was needed for the first month, 20 percent for the second month, and 25 percent the third month for a contender to be awarded any national convention votes), and that it was a radical departure from previous experience for no apparent reason. There had been no discontent with this aspect of the 1976 system. Originally, the White House representatives desired a flat 25 percent of the vote in *all* primaries or caucuses, regardless of when held, before any delegate votes could be claimed. They compromised by accepting the step-wise increase in succeeding stages of the selection process, but they would go no further. The proposal was contentious, but passed narrowly, 30–25.

• A proposal to ban cross-over primaries. A party member could vote only in the Democratic or Republican primary for which he or she registered. Regulars and reformers alike supported this resolution (although it was bitterly opposed in Wisconsin and a handful of other states).

• The rejection of a proposal to require equal female representation of state delegations to the national convention. The balance of the commission felt it too closely resembled the McGovern-Fraser quota concept. (This was later overturned by the Democratic National Convention, which did mandate that state parties "promote" an equal division between men and women on national convention delegations.)

• Allowed "winner-take-all" elections, banned in statewide races or at the congressional district races, in single-member districts. The White House felt they could win the majority of the votes in most of these districts and thus would profit from the regulation. Calculations of this nature can be risky ventures. Things do not always work as intended. Nonetheless, supporters of presidential candidates will vote for whatever they believe will provide an advantage to their candidate. The reformers, of course, objected. They argued that it was one step further away from the proportional representation of candidate strength, a *sine qua non* of the reform movement.

• A proposal (the "add-on" delegates) to allow state party committees to appoint an additional 10 percent of each state's national convention delegation. These seats were reserved for state party officials and public officeholders who supposedly would provide an element of independence and wisdom and a practical perspective allegedly not found in an all-grassroots assemblage.

• The institution of the "bound delegate" rule. A national convention delegate elected on behalf of a presidential candidate was required to vote for that candidate at the national convention. If a delegate chose not to, he or she could be replaced at the discretion of the presidential candidate.

This rule ranked with the least publicized adopted by the Winograd Commission. It came to public attention only at the national convention when the (Edward) Kennedy partisans chose it as an issue over which to force a floor fight in hopes of derailing Carter's nomination. The ploy failed. The controversy over the rule at the national convention was a power move with no reference to the reform movement, and it was seen as such by the media and all concerned in the contest.

Nonetheless, the issue is a thorny one, and at the very least, it deserves further consideration. It may appear to be a logical extension of the grassroots participatory effort, further linking delegates for convention seats to the candidate they support. However, the rule is a first for the Democratic party and it reverses a traditional commitment to a "freedom of conscience" choice. The assumption has been—even by reformers—that events may intervene between a primary or caucus vote and that issues and personal commitments may change. This would normally not be the case, but it could happen. The delegate— at his own political risk—could switch from his public commitment if he chose to face the consequences. Any disciplinary action was left to the state parties or to the constituents who elected the delegate originally. This was a comfortable arrangement and neither regulars or reformers publicly advocated any change.

There is one other consequence of the rule. The national convention has been declining as a vehicle for exercising an independent influence on the selection of a presidential nominee. Power has gravitated to the rank and file who participate in the primaries and caucuses. The new provision pretty much eliminates whatever discretion—at least on the early ballots—the national convention might exercise on nominations. It makes a further contribution to the weakened role of the national convention.

These, then, were the major contributions of the Winograd Commission. They were controversial, but their full implications were not appreciated in 1978. They were passed with some minor modifications by the Democratic National Committee in June 1978 and later included in the *Call* to the 1980 national convention.

In comparison with 1976, the major rules changes employed in 1980 included the following:

- The abolition of the "open" primary in presidential selection.
- The equal representation of men and women on each state's delegation (and among alternates). The failure to include an equal representation of women was not, however, in itself a *prima facie* grounds for a challenge before the national convention's credentials committee (thus making the rule harder to enforce).
- The development of a model for "affirmative action" programs that required the state parties to institute "outreach" and "remedial action" programs for women, blacks, Hispanics, and Native Americans

containing specific goals and timetables. In the context of the 1980s (as against the 1940s), such provisions verge on the meaningless.

- The legalization of the election of delegates from single-member districts.
- The required selection of 25 percent of the national convention delegation at-large by the state convention, the state committee, or the publicly selected delegates.
- The reservation of 10 percent of the delegation for public and party officeholders. The commission mandated that "priority must be given" in such appointments to (in order) Democratic governors, state party chairs and vice chairs, Democratic National Committee members, U.S. senators and U.S. representatives.
- The awarding of more control to the presidential contenders over delegate candidates who ran in their name (although the rule required the potential nominee to authorize at least three times the number to be elected, thus giving final choice of who actually went to the national convention to the party's voters).
- The confinement of presidential delegate selection to the period between March 11 and June 10, 1980 (with the exceptions indicated) and specified that all delegates and alternatives must have been selected by June 23.
- The tightening of the rule requiring that only avowed party members could participate in delegate selection.
- The binding of all delegates to vote on at least one ballot at the national convention for the presidential candidate for whom they pledged.
- The specification of filing deadlines for presidential candidates at no less than thirty and no more than ninety days before the primaries.
- The modification of the "floor" provision from a 10 to 15 percent base to a step-wise method. This was later complicated further by the national committee by amendment that was contingent on the number of delegates to be elected. The proposal was unusually cumbersome and confusing. It read as follows:

Rule 12. FAIR REFLECTION OF PRESIDENTIAL PREFERENCES

A. The Call for the 1980 Democratic National Convention shall include provisions that assure that the delegates to the 1980 Democratic National Convention be chosen in a manner which fairly reflects the division of preferences by those who participate in the presidential nominating process in each state, territory and the District of Columbia.

B. At all stages of the delegate selection process, delegates shall be allocated in a fashion that fairly reflects the expressed presidential preference or uncommitted status of the primary voters or if

there is no binding primary, the convention and caucus participants, except that preferences securing less than the applicable
percentage of votes cast for the delegates to the National Convention shall not be awarded any delegates. The applicable percentage in presidential primary states shall be calculated by dividing
the number of National Convention delegates to be elected in
that Congressional District or other smaller delegate selection
unit into 100, provided however, that the applicable percentage
shall be no higher than 25%. In caucus states, at the level at
which National Convention Delegates are selected, the applicable
percentage shall be no lower than 15% and no higher than 20%.
Each state using a caucus procedure shall, at least 90 days prior
to the first step in the delegate selection process, select a percentage within these limits. In At-Large and in Party Leader and
Elected Official delegations, the applicable percentage shall be
no lower than 15% and no higher than 20%, and each state shall,
at least 90 days prior to the first step in the delegate selection
process, select a percentage within these limits. The CRC [Com-
pliance Review Commission] shall adopt regulations to prevent
winner-take-all outcomes at the Congressional District or other
smaller delegate selection unit. The CRC [Compliance Review
Commission] shall adopt regulations to govern the allocation of
delegates in instances where no candidate reaches the applicable
percentage.[2]

Not surprisingly, more than one district party leader asked the
Compliance Review Commission to interpret for them exactly what
this meant and how it applied to their situations.

The proposals adopted on the shortened nominating season, the
candidate filing deadlines, the introduction of a complicated higher
base vote to gain convention representation, the reservation of 10
percent of a delegation for selected party officials, and the single-member concept for district-level elections were all significant rejections
of the assumptions underlying the reforms proposed by the McGovern-
Fraser Commission and modified by the Mikulski Commission.

The Implementation Process

As with the Mikulski Commission, a 25-member Compliance Review
Commission (CRC) staffed from and by the national convention's headquarters was appointed in 1978 to monitor enforcement. Originally,
it was intended that the Compliance Review Commission only, or principally, concern itself with implementing "affirmative action" guide-

lines, an emphasis meant to alleviate the fears of blacks, women, and liberals that the gains made by the quotas would slip away. The charge to the CRC was clear in this regard:

> A Compliance Review Commission . . . shall be appointed . . . to administer and enforce affirmative action requirements for the National and State Democratic Parties; review Affirmative Action and Delegate Selection Plans submitted by State Parties and ap-prove or recommend changes in such plans; conduct periodic eval-uations and provide technical assistance to State Parties on affirma-tive action and delegate selection implementation, and hear and recommend solutions to affirmative action complaints unresolved by appropriate State Party Bodies.[3]

Several factors insured that the main body's power would range well beyond anything a strict reading of its mandate would suggest. First, of course, there is an escape clause in the charge depicting the commission's responsibilities. This is the phrase giving the CRC power to "conduct periodic evaluations and provide technical assistance to State Parties on affirmative action *and delegate selection implementa-tion"* (italics added).[4] It was a loophole that any good lawyer, or politi-cian, could be expected to exploit.

Second, the commission's membership was named by the national chair, John C. White, a Carter appointee who saw his job as advancing the fortunes of the Carter renomination effort. In addition, it was staffed and funded by the national committee, which in turn was, for all practi-cal purposes, an extension of the Carter reelection committee. The staff would play the major role in implementation decisions and its work would be closely supervised by the national chair and by the White House's political operatives.

The CRC, as a result, came to exercise enormous discretionary power. Not surprisingly, the Kennedy people felt that it blatantly dis-criminated in favor of the Carter forces. In one of the more publicized incidents, while the CRC permitted the pro-Carter states of Iowa and New Hampshire exceptions to the "window" concept (the three-month period specified for presidential delegation selection) on the basis that those states had made a "good faith effort" to change their delegate selection dates—a highly questionable evaluation—but could not be-cause of a Republican-controlled legislature and/or governorship, it put strong pressure on the Massachusetts Democratic party to move its primary back from early March (7th) to a later date (preferably the third week or so in April). Ostensibly, this move would place the state party in compliance with the guidelines. Politically, it would also have denied Kennedy an early, and as it turned out, badly needed boost to his campaign. The CRC and the Carter people aligned themselves with anti-Kennedy forces in the state (including the Democratic governor and Carter supporters in the state legislature) and the controversy simmered for some time. Eventually, Massachusetts held its primary in March, but the CRC withheld its sanction of it (and the delegation chosen), warning that its representatives might not be seated at the national convention. This did not happen. The incident was a heavy-handed example of the CRC at its worst and a reminder of the problems partisan committees of this nature can create.

The directors of Kennedy's delegate selection drive later claimed that the rulings in favor of the Carter candidacy cost them between three and five delegate votes per state. If true, this—and the role of a group such as the Compliance Review Commission—could be decisive in a close prenomination race.

A third factor of consequence in the accretion of power by the Compliance Review Commission was the complexity of the rules governing presidential delegate selection in the Democratic party. The end result of the tinkering, political infighting, and constant efforts to change, or render impotent, the reform rules illustrated the confusion, complexity, and overall absurdity that had crept into the process by 1980. Take but one example. Following is the Compliance Review Commission's clarification of Rule 12 above (on the proportional representation of candidates):

Reg. 6.14 Rule 12A.   The method for allocating publicly-elected delegates in primary states pursuant to Rule 12B shall be as follows:
1. Divide the number of delegates in the delegate selection district into 100% to find the threshold.
2. Calculate the percentage of the vote received in that district by each presidential candidate.
3. Divide the threshold into the percentage of the vote received by each presidential candidate whose percentage is equal to or greater than the threshold. This results in the allocation of whole delegates.
4. Compare the remainders of the division in step #3 and allocate any extra delegates starting with the candidates with the largest remainders until all delegates have been allocated.

Example

1. CD #1 has 4 delegates. $100 \div 4 = 25$.
The threshold is 25%.

2. Distribution of the vote.

Candidate A—46%

B—29%

C—21%

D— 4%

3. Division

A $46 \div 25 = 1$ r 21

B $29 \div 25 = 1$ r 4

4. There are two remaining delegates, each candidate receives one.

The final allocation is:

Candidate A—2

B—2.

Example

1. CD #2 has 5 delegates. $100 \div 5 = 20$. The threshold is 20%.

2. Distribution of vote.

Candidate A—46%

B—29%

C—21%

D— 4%

3. Division

A $46 \div 20 = 2$ r 6

B $29 \div 20 = 1$ r 9

C $21 \div 20 = 1$ r 1

4. There is one remaining delegate. Since Candidate B has the largest remainder, that delegate will go to him.

The final allocation is:

Candidate A—2

B—2

C—1

Example

1. CD #3 has 6 delegates. $100 \div 6 = 16.6$. The threshold is 16.6%.

2. Distribution of vote.

Candidate A—46%

B—29%

C—21%

D— 4%

3. Division
   A $46 \div 16.6 = 2$ r 12.8
   B $29 \div 16.6 = 1$ r 12.4
   C $21 \div 16.6 = 1$ r 4.4

4. There are 2 remaining delegates. Since Candidates A & B have the largest remainders, they each receive the remaining delegates.

> The final allocation is:
>> Candidate A—3
>> B—2
>> C—1

Reg. 6.15 Rule 12B.   If only one candidate reaches the applicable threshold, a delegate shall be awarded to the next highest vote getter.

Example

1. CD #4 has 4 delegates. $100 \div 4 = 25$.
   The threshold is 25%.

2. The distribution of the vote is:
>> Candidate A—61%
>> B—18%
>> C—13%
>> D— 8%

3. Since only one candidate has crossed the threshold, Candidate A receives 3 delegates and Candidate B receives 1 delegate.

4. The allocation is:
>> Candidate A—3
>> B—1[5]

A process that should be fair, simple, and easily comprehended had degenerated into one that was virtually incomprehensible, open to arbitrary interpretation by officially sanctioned bodies, and amenable to partisan manipulation. The local party leaders who attempted to explain the rules to potential delegates and then to enforce them could not understand them. Power gravitated upward to a small body of staff members—beholden to one contender—whose real job, in practical terms, was to promote the fortunes, as best they could, of one candidate.

Conclusion

This type of enterprise is a far cry from the original reform intentions. It could happen again; in fact, there is no reason why it should not be repeated in varying guises in election after election. One faction—liberal, conservative, centrist, or whatever—or the supporters of one candidate could capture control of the national party's implementation mechanism and use it to promote their own ends. Such a process hardly lends legitimacy to a system badly in need of it. Its major contribution may be to reemphasize the feelings of uncertainty in application (evident in 1980) and of a process in constant change, one stripped of its integrity and without a real core or discernible substance. If so, we are all the losers.

NINE

Presidential Selection IV: The Hunt Commission and Post-1980 Nomination Changes

The Hunt Commission was created by the 1980 Democratic National Convention to assess presidential nomination practices and to recommend rules for 1984. Its objectives, according to its leader, Governor James B. Hunt, Jr., of North Carolina, were to:

1. Strengthen the party.
2. Help the party win elections.
3. Ensure that the party could govern once elected.[1]

Any rules that could achieve these objectives should be emblazoned in granite. No one set of procedures is likely to begin to achieve such ambitious results.

The charge to the Hunt Commission by the 1980 national convention was comprehensive enough. The new group was mandated to undertake "a complete review of the presidential nomination process."[2] Areas of particular concern would include:

- The length of the primary season (a continuing source of debate).
- Primaries in which non-Democrats were permitted to vote (the Wisconsin "open primary" controversy).
- The binding of delegates to presidential candidates (the controversial innovation in the rules introduced for the 1980 national convention); resisted by party regulars and reformers alike, it was quickly repealed.

- The effort to increase participation by "previously underrepresented groups," a euphemism for the struggle to implement some type of generally acceptable affirmative action program.
- The role and influence of elected and party officials in the nomination process, by all odds the single most important issue to come before the commission and the main reason for its existence.

The list constitutes an honor roll of sorts of the issues still dividing the party. Most of the other problems could be resolved by simply reaffirming decisions made by previous reform bodies or by allowing the states greater leeway in meeting national party standards (while maintaining the essential objectives of the original reforms). The extension of the role of party officials in national convention, and presidential nomination, decisions represented the Hunt Commission's most singular contribution to the evolution of presidential selection practices.

Commission Operations

The Hunt Commission was composed of seventy members from all wings of the party who shared but one thing (beyond party affiliation): All were screened (by the national chair, Charles T. Manatt, who appointed them) to ensure that they held no strong reservations against expanding the role of party professionals in the nominating process.

The group held its first meeting in August 1981. Within six months, it had completed its four regional hearings, held three other substantive meetings, made its recommendations, and gone out of existence. The month after it presented its report, the Democratic National Committee met (in March 1982) and adopted the nominating rules for 1984. The commission was succeeded by a seventeen-member Compliance Review Commission in April 1982, appointed by the national chair, and as in 1974 and 1978, charged with monitoring state party conformance to the newly adopted rules.

If nothing else, the post-1980 performance has to represent some kind of record for speed and efficiency in this type of operation. Perhaps it is an indication of how cut and dried these operations had become and how professionalized the party was in dealing with them. Again, as with its predecessor the Winograd Commission, the media, the public, and the grassroots party membership showed little interest in the proceedings.

Major Issues

Much (although not all) of the substance of the Hunt Commission's deliberations dealt with extensions (with minor modifications) of previous reform group recommendations. In relation to the major items on its agenda, it acted as follows.[3]

Concerning demographic (minority groups) representation in national conventions

By 1980, the traditional debate over minority group representation was no longer volatile. The "affirmative action" and "outreach" plans the state parties had implemented under the national party's direction and the clear acceptance of nondiscrimination standards in party processes had succeeded reasonably well. Black representation in the 1980 national convention was up to 15 percent (and averaged just under 14% for the three post-reform conventions). This figure was higher than that for the black population in the nation as a whole but well below the group's relative contribution to the Democratic vote. Women, more assertive and politically better organized than the blacks in the 70s and 80s, had been guaranteed 50 percent of the national convention's delegate positions (and in 1980, held 49%). Youth were no longer of direct concern to the party. With the adoption of the 18-year-old vote and the end of the war in Vietnam, youth as a political bloc of consequence had faded. The party targeted a 10 percent share of seats for those under 30 (its definition of youth), but no one seemed to know (or care) whether the informal objective had been—or in the future would be—reached.

In terms of demographic representation, the main question in the 1980s appeared to concern the adequate representation of lower income groups. The problem was not new. National conventions are stratified toward those at the higher level of the income scale. In 1980, for example, the median income of the delegates was $37,000 (as against a national median of $13,000), and 65 percent held college or graduate degrees (compared to 10 percent and 4 percent for the U.S. population as a whole).[4]

The 1972 national convention recognized the imbalance and provided that 8 percent of the national party's revenues should be reserved to subsidize the expenses of low income delegates who otherwise would be unable to attend the convention. The provision was never implemented. The party was in continual debt from the obligations it had assumed after the 1968 presidential campaign (a debt not retired until 1982), and the Federal Election Commission had ruled that the funds it made available to the state parties for national conventions could not be used to pay the expenses of individual delegates.

These concerns operated on the fringes of the Hunt Commission's deliberations. The 1980 national convention had established another group (the Commission on Low and Moderate Income Participation, under Congressman Mickey Leland of Texas) to explore the problem and the same national committee meeting (March 1982) that had endorsed the Hunt Commission's recommendations stipulated that each state party in its "affirmative action" programs "include outreach provisions to encourage the participation and representation of persons of low and moderate income and a specific plan to help defray the expenses of those delegates otherwise unable to participate in the national convention."[5] This was one of the Leland Commission's recommendations. It is unlikely to do much to improve the situation.

Concerning the length of the prenomination season and the scheduling of primaries and caucuses

The commission believed that this area contained the potential for the greatest conflict between state and national parties. The reason was that most significant changes (as, for example, relating to the scheduling of state primaries) would require state legislative action, a long and arduous process and one, that in one way or another, would involve both parties in the outcome.

Previous reform commissions had required that "all steps" in the presidential delegate selection process take place "in the calendar year of the national convention" (the "timeliness" standard of the McGovern-Fraser Commission), with the exception (made by the Mikulski Commission and continued by the Winograd and, eventually, Hunt commissions) that at-large delegates could be selected by state committees which had been elected as early as the January of the year preceding the national election. This modification represented a compromise attractive to the regulars and to the state parties and was not in dispute.

The Winograd Commission had attempted to introduce a limit to the prenomination season, defining its beginning (the second Tuesday in March) and ending (the second Tuesday in June of the election year), restrictions that constituted a new departure in party rule-making. The commission, and more accurately, the national party headquarters and its Compliance Review Commission, then granted exemptions to two primary states (New Hampshire and Massachusetts) and three caucus states (Iowa, Maine, and Minnesota) that fell in varying degrees outside the designated period (or "window" as it was called for some curious reason). One area of the Hunt Commission's decisions involved whether to continue to support a well-defined delegate selection season and whether or not to allow deviations from it.

The problem was intertwined with several others: First, the spread of primaries and the efforts to contain these, or reduce their number and influence. Primaries had better than doubled since 1968 and the proportion of delegates selected through, and committed by, primary elections had increased from 49 percent in 1972 to an all-time high of 81 percent by 1980.

Second, there was the phenomenon of "front loading," or the tendency of candidates to focus their resources on the earliest of the primary/caucus tests in hopes of emerging as the early front-runner and quickly capturing the nomination. The trend has several related aspects. As the presidential contenders concentrated more and more on the Iowas and New Hampshires, other states began to move their delegate selection dates up, making the election year seem longer and ensuring that most of the delegates would be chosen, and the presidential nominee decided relatively early in the nomination season (38% of the delegates were selected by the second week of May in 1972; by 1980, this figure had jumped to 55%).

A point of bitter contention within the party, the earliest states— Iowa and, especially, New Hampshire—received disproportionate media attention and political influence within the system, often at the direct expense of states far more politically and electorally significant. Many of the states that came late in the primary season (California, New Jersey, Ohio) provided a better test of a candidate's abilities and his electoral appeal. These states were also far more significant contributors to a party's general election victory. Yet they were underrepresented and often ignored within a process that emphasized early success. The development was a direct contradiction of the balance of power within the old party system in which the late states—and California in particular—had enormous influence in deciding both parties' nominees.

A number of options faced the commission. Among the more interesting were proposals to strictly regulate the earlier primary/caucuses, with hopes that state parties might opt to hold their delegate selection late in the period when they would have more control over their proceedings; to place a freeze on primary/caucus dates, thus preventing more states from moving theirs up (California and New York were considering just such a move) and further overloading the early part of the nomination schedule; to relax proportional representation requirements for all, or later entry, states, thus allowing "winner-take-all" elections (outlawed by earlier reform commissions as diluting the strength of the lesser-known candidates) for some of the larger states, making them more attractive to candidates and more directly influential in the nomination outcome; and a plan advanced by Congressman Morris K. Udall (Arizona) to specify four dates only on which states could hold their primaries or caucuses (a proposal that while controlling for the length of the primary season does not address the question of "front loading").

The general discussion focused on the limits that should be applied to the length of the primary/caucus selection processes, a continuation of the initiatives begun in the Winograd Commission and a type of restriction that appeared to be popular with the public and the media (although such evidence tends to be superficial). The idea of a carefully prescribed delegate selection season had its supporters. Basically, the arguments for continuing such a time limitation should be familiar to even the most casual followers of presidential politics.

The presidential selection process, it is alleged, is too long. It:

- Exhausts the candidate.
- Is expensive.
- Gives the media an undue influence over the outcome (and, some would contend, becomes primarily a media event).
- Adds to the devisiveness within the party and further weakens it going into the November election.
- Magnifies the power of the early states, some of whom are among the most unrepresentative in the nation (New Hampshire is the primary example).
- Favors candidates with the time necessary to devote to full-time campaigning.
- Bores the public (possibly the argument heard most about the very long nominating season).

Those who prefer an unrestricted delegate selection period would argue that a long prenomination season:

- Acquaints the party members with the candidates and their views.
- Provides extensive free publicity and media exposure for the party and its candidates.
- Gives everyone a fairer chance (including the underdogs) to eventually win the nomination.
- Provides an extensive, and realistic test, of a candidate's political savvy and abilities, one that allows new candidates to enter late in the season if the front-runner falters (virtually an impossibility in an abbreviated nomination period).

Further, limiting the actual delegate selection to the three-month period does not cut down on the length of presidential prenomination campaigns. This last argument seems irrefutable. Presidential campaigns now begin two to four years before the election. Such a lead-time is necessary to build public support, acquire the name identification necessary to score well in the polls, cultivate the media, establish an independent political identity and party following, raise the necessary funds, build an organization nationally and in the key states to be contested, and establish the cordial relations with the major interest group and party leaders deemed essential to a candidate's campaign.

The Hunt (or Winograd) Commission's accommodations do not (and cannot) deal with these realities of political life. Cutting the time of actual delegate selection in half (from six months to three) as the Winograd Commission did, would appear to favor those with the name recognition, funds, and organization to do well in the early tests. Such time restrictions minimize the possibility of a serious challenge in the later primaries. It would not seem too much to ask that each candidate undergo a prolonged testing period under a variety of conditions before aspiring to his/her party's presidential nomination.

Nonetheless, this was not the position taken by the commission. There is an intrinsic—although, it is argued here, false—sense of security and economy in placing limits on the delegate selection period. The Hunt Commission chose to reaffirm the stand taken by the Winograd Commission, endorsing the same restrictions while allowing specified exceptions (Iowa and New Hampshire, in particular), but under a more tightly controlled format (New Hampshire could hold its primary no earlier than one week and Iowa its caucuses 15 days before the rest of the states).

Concerning the issue of "Democrats-only" party processes and the "open primary"

The McGovern-Fraser Commission favored restricting participation in presidential selection primaries and caucuses to party members only. This prohibition was endorsed by the Mikulski Commission, which, along with the party charter (endorsed in 1974), specifically applied the restrictions to "open primaries" (the latter allowed anyone who wished—Democrats, Republicans, or Independents—to vote on the party's nominees). Both party regulars and reformers agreed with the assumption underlying the rule and it was not a matter of debate between the camps.

The Winograd Commission further endorsed the principle and tightened the screws on the state parties (only four of which were out of compliance with the provision) by specifically stating that no state would be allowed an exemption on this point, even though they may have taken "probable positive steps to achieve legislative changes to bring state laws into compliance" with national party directives. The exemption phrase went back to the early reform days and was meant to add flexibility to the standards, provide both state and national parties an escape clause when needed, and not unduly penalize Democratic state parties that had to deal with unsympathetic Republican legislatures or governors in attempting to bring about the required statutory changes in primary laws. The Winograd Commission specifically denied this recourse to the Wisconsin party, the last one with an "open primary," in part because the state party had gone through a sham process of initiating legislative change.

Wisconsin was adamant. It had no intention of dropping its "open primary," a practice that went back to the days of "Fighting Bob" LaFollette in the early years of the century. The primary reflected the state's commitment to Progressive and Populist values. The factor that makes the confrontation significant is the pains the state went to in efforts to void the national party directives.

Wisconsin brought suit in state court (*LaFollette v. Democratic Party of the United States*, 1980), which ruled in favor of the state party and ordered the national party to officially recognize the results of the state's "open primary." The national party then took the case to federal court, where the Supreme Court handed down its decision on February 25, 1981 (*Democratic Party v. LaFollette*).

The Supreme Court revised the state court's action and reaffirmed its path-breaking ruling in *Cousins v. Wigoda* (1975). In *LaFollette*, as in *Cousins*, the Court declared that a political party can decide the qualifications, selection procedures, and eligibility standards for its party's presidential selection process, and that those are binding on the state parties. If state law is in conflict with national party rules in this area, then the national party prevails.

> A State, or court, may not constitutionally substitute its own judgment [in presidential selection] for that of [a] Party. A political party's choice among the various ways of determining the makeup of a State's delegation to the party's national convention is protected by the Constitution. And as is true of all expressions of the First Amendment freedoms, the courts may not interfere on the ground that they view a particular expression as unwise or irrational.[6]

The outcome of all of this, and a by-product of the entire reform movement, is the virtually absolute legal power national parties now enjoy in establishing and implementing their own regulations for presidential delegate selection. It represents a highly significant addition to, and centralization of, party authority. One, in fact, can wonder if it has not gone too far. The states and the state parties have no viable legal recourse in opposing what could be arbitrary and pernicious national party directives relating to presidential selection.

The Wisconsin party had been given a bye in the 1976 national convention while the case was being argued in the courts and because

there was insufficient time to institute some form of alternative delegate selecting procedures. This is unlikely to happen again. The Hunt
Commission followed the only course it could and reaffirmed the ban
on non-Democrats participating in party decision-making (and thus
went on record as opposing the last of the "open primaries").

Concerning the issue of the proportional representation of a presidential contender's strength at all levels of the nominating process

Proportional representation (or "fair reflection" as the reform commissions termed it) of a candidate's vote from local caucus or primary
to national convention was one of the *sine qua nons* of the reform
bible. The reformers believed that this was the fairest way to accurately
gauge the actual grassroots party support for each of the presidential
contenders.

The McGovern-Fraser Commission urged (but did not require) that
such a rule be adopted (feeling it "too momentous" a step to take so
early, according to McGovern). The Mikulski Commission embraced
the idea, setting a floor of 10 percent of the vote—later amended to
15 percent—in caucuses and primaries as the figure above which a
candidate must receive his proportionate share of the vote. The idea
of the base figure—intentionally set low—was to allow all candidates
with any significant party backing their fair allocation of the votes
while eliminating those with little support whose candidacies could
lead to a hopeless profusion of choices and serious overload on the
system. The idea was to be practical while still remaining fair and
open to all reasonable candidacies.

The Mikulski Commission and the party rules did permit "loophole
primaries," a term used to cover some ambiguous wording in the party
regulations that appeared to allow "winner-take-all" primaries at the
congressional district level or below. In a "winner-take-all" election
the candidate who received a plurality of the popular vote won all
of an electoral unit's delegate votes. No provision was made for representing the electoral strengths of the losing candidates.

In 1976, twenty-one caucus/convention and sixteen primary states
used proportional representation in allocating national convention delegate votes. Thirteen states employed the "loophole primary" in some
form and the matter came before the 1976 national convention. The
national convention, in response, outlawed the practice.

With this as precedent, the Winograd Commission engaged in a
series of controversial maneuvers intended to introduce floors of up
to 25 percent for some stages of delegate selection and to permit plural-

ity, "winner-take-all" elections in single-member districts, seemingly
a direct repudiation of the national convention's position. After much
interplay between the commission, the Compliance Review Commission of 1978–80, national party leaders, and the White House, and a
series of resolutions, modifications, and reversals, the national party
settled on a virtually unintelligible set of rules that, in practice, allowed
some use of "winner-take-all" primaries (as in Illinois and West Virginia,
for example) and the imposition of a complex formula that did permit
a graduated base of between 15 and 25 percent (depending on electoral
conditions and the number of candidates running for delegate positions
in an area). It is difficult to believe that these compromises satisfied
anyone.

The Hunt Commission recommendations are not likely to please
many either. The group came closer to the Winograd Commission's
position than to, for example, that espoused by the Mikulski Commission. It attempted to add flexibility to the system by "open[ing] up a
range of possibilities, all falling within the standards of fair reflection,
from which the states may choose in light of their own perferences
and traditions." It is proposed to do this by setting a base of 20 percent
in the caucus states and 25 percent in the primary states; by allowing
states to award "bonus votes" to candidates if thought needed to better
reflect their strength within the state, a practice that led to enormous
confusion under the old party system; and the introduction of some
types of plurality election, "winner-take-all" delegate races under certain conditions.

As with 1980, the rules are again complex and needlessly confusing.
They may allow for the flexibility and experimentation the commission
wished for. Proportional representation of a candidate's strength was
a basic tenet of the reform movement, although the efforts to dilute
it have resulted in few objections. The early reformers and successive
reform commissions and national committees came to believe that
"winner-take-all" systems are basically unfair to both candidates and
party voters, failing to represent the strength of losing candidates (regardless of how well—short of winning—they might run in a state)
and effectively disenfranchising any bloc of voters who happen to support a candidate who did not finish first. The work of the Winograd
Commission was regressive in this regard, and the Hunt Commission,
with somewhat less certainty, is continuing in the same direction. It
might be appropriate to ask in this context if it is too much to require
clear, simple standards that make a permanent—and easily understood—commitment to one type of political representation? Judged
by developments since the mid-1970s, the answer would seem to be
yes.

Concerning the representation of elected and party officials in national conventions

By any criteria, this was the single most important issue to come before the Hunt Commission. The question is a simple one: Who should be represented at national conventions? The reformers would argue that only those elected by primary or caucus participants and committed to a candidate (or who ran as uncommitted on the ballot) should be. They believed that this allowed the grassroots party member a decisive say in the nomination decision and made for more representative and accountable party decision-making. The reformers would not permit anyone who had not presented himself to the rank and file, with a declared candidate affiliation (or uncommitted status), to participate in the choice of a nominee.

The party regulars took quite a different position. Many did not like to commit themselves to a contender or to place themselves before the party's electorate in support of a candidate, thus encountering the very real possibility that they could be rejected by party voters. They liked to believe that they deserved a place in the national convention by virtue of their elective or party office and previous work on behalf of the party and its candidates. This had been the practice prior to 1972. Party regulars felt that they brought expertise and insight to national convention deliberations that could not be duplicated. Proponents argued that the presence of a large bloc of uncommitted party professionals would add a flexibility to the convention proceedings and a reality-orientation that they believed was missing from the post-reform conventions. Finally, such proponents, they argued—and this was incontrovertible—that the representation of upper-level party and elective officeholders in national conventions was down by as much as 80 percent from pre-reform days.

As presented to the Hunt Commission, then, the gains from increased participation in nomination decision-making by party professionals would be substantial:

- These leaders and officials, as experienced politicians, would bring seasoned and sensitive judgment to the selection of a nominee and to the conduct of other party business.
- Convention participation would create stronger ties between the party and its officeholders, promoting a unified campaign strategy and teamwork in government.
- The inclusion of more elected officials would strengthen the party's ties to their constituencies and its broad mainstream appeal.[7]

The Winograd Commission had proven receptive to such appeals. As a consequence, it had provided for a 10 percent "add-on" to each state's national convention delegation (literally, an additional 10% to be added to the delegation's elected membership) to be reserved for state and party officials (and, in a vague way, to help meet "affirmative action" guidelines). Those favored were to be governors, state party chairs, Democratic National Committee members, U.S. senators and U.S. House members.

The "add-on" was in stark contrast to early reform regulations. It did not appear to contribute much to national convention deliberations, although the Hunt Commission was to report that all of the twenty-three governors who were delegates to the national convention came as "add-ons," as did six of the eight U.S. senators and seventeen of the U.S. House members. The major fault the commission found with the provision was that it had been too limited to incorporate significant numbers of U.S. representatives, state legislators, and city and county officials.

There is a problem here that proves somewhat of a contradiction to the main arguments concerning the antipathy of the post-reform conventions to party officeholders. While the number of *high-ranking* party officials was down, CBS News estimated that 57 percent of the delegates in 1976 and 64 percent in 1980 held some kind of party or public office.[8] Party professionals and officeholders would appear to be well represented in national convention deliberations.

Nonetheless, and whatever the figures, the Hunt Commission decided that the most needed change in national convention operations was the inclusion of far greater numbers of party and elective officeholders in convention decision-making. Given the purpose for which the commission was created, this conclusion was not unexpected.

What the commission proposed to do was increase the nonelected "add-on" contingent to approximately 25 percent, the minimum figure the group believed would be needed to accommodate all the party and elected officials it felt should be represented at the national convention. As with the proportional representation amendments, the provision for the increased delegation is anything but simple. According to the commission's (and national party's) rules, the states would retain the 10 percent "add-on" seats reserved for elected or party officials pledged to a candidate or officially uncommitted as in 1980. "In addition, each state will have a larger add-on to be composed of unpledged delegates. The size of this add-on will be determined as follows: (a) each state will receive two slots for its Democratic Chair and Vice-chair; (b) 400 slots will be allocated to the states in proportion to the size of their base delegations; and (c) states for whom those allocations are insufficient to include their key Democratic elected officials (Governors, U.S. Senators, U.S. Representatives, Mayors of cities over 250,000 in population) will be granted additional slots sufficient to make the add-on equal to the number of such officials."[9]

The commission figured that the new quota would ensure that most of the major party officials would be represented at the national convention and that approximately two-thirds of the total, unlike 1980, would be unpledged and thus able to give the convention the flexibility and direction that many saw as lacking in the post-reform era. The Hunt Commission believed that this change would constitute its most lasting contribution to decision-making in presidential selection.

Conclusion

The most distinctive contributions of the Hunt Commission then were:

- The repeal of the controversial "bound delegate" rule of 1980 and the return to the "good conscience" standard that guided previous conventions.
- The relaxation of the proportional representation requirements.
- The significant increase in the number of party and elected officials to be included in the national convention membership.

This last point is the most controversial. By providing for significant additions of nonelected officials, the Hunt Commission accomplished one other thing: It ensured the largest national convention in either party's history (with a membership of 3,850, up from the previous high of 3,300 in 1980).

TEN

Reform and the National Conventions

The O'Hara Commission

If one made a list of the major problems facing national conventions today, it would probably include the following needs:

- To modernize convention machinery and the methods of conflict resolution required to provide a basis for quick but practical decision-making, relatively equitable to all concerned (party factions, candidates for the party's nomination, individual delegates).
- To reduce the discretionary power of the national party chair and the national committee over the critical preconvention preparations (the designation of the "temporary" convention chair and other convention officers, the selection of the membership and leaders of the key convention committees, the designation of the convention site, the awarding of accommodations), all potentially significant decisions in an election year.
- To limit the arbitrary power of the national convention's presiding officers, in effect making them creatures of the convention membership, accountable and dependent on the body of the convention for their support and their authority.
- To clarify and increase the powers and role of the average delegate.
- To "return" the national convention to a position of prominence (preeminence actually) in party decision-making.

The reform of national convention procedures within the Democratic party succeeded on the first point and failed on each of the others. More than likely, the commission established to consider these problems did not see their role in this context. It set a limited objective (convention modernization) and never really addressed some of the more pressing problems confronting national conventions in the late twentieth century.

The perspective was unfortunate. With the exception of the last area (which may have more to do with delegate selection methods relating to how and when a president is selected, a more proper concern of the committees or presidential nominations), all were within the realm of the commission established to assess convention performance.

Such an evaluation was certainly needed. The 1968 national convention which mandated the convention reform commission hoped to avoid future repetitions of its own unhappy experience. It was a tumultuous and trying ordeal for all who attended—the most violent and disorderly national convention in the modern era. While not going to the same extremes as the bloody confrontations that took place outside, the proceedings inside the convention hall had proven to be unmanageable. They helped inflame, rather than soothe, hostilities, and they presented to the country a picture of a political party in total disarray, unable to govern itself much less the nation.

The Democratic party needed to avoid such disruptive gatherings in the future. It believed the answer lay in institutionalizing a set of rules that would provide for the orderly consideration of party business while still allowing for the free expression of opinion and an equal opportunity for all candidates and factions to work their will.

Reformers could endorse these objectives, while at the same time wishing to carry them somewhat further. In line with their grassroots emphasis, they hoped to provide a meaningful role for the individual delegate in convention proceedings. Their objective was to do this by writing fair and impartial rules for the transaction of business, and rules that they hoped would effect a shift in power from the highly centralized, and even autocratic, management of national conventions experienced by both parties in the past to more democratically run gatherings with power centered in the delegates. They failed to realize these latter objectives. Nonetheless, the work of the O'Hara Commission, the group charged with improving convention operations, did receive praise for its contributions to convention modernization. Anything would have been an improvement over previous practices.

Commission operations

The 1968 national convention mandated that the new commission "be charged with the duty of studying and evaluating and codifying the rules of past Democratic National Conventions."[1] The national convention directed the group (although it did not confine it to these topics) to consider permanent rules for the national convention and its committees. It also specified that the new commission be composed of "members knowledgeable in matters of parliamentary procedure and familiar with [the] Convention procedure of the Democratic party."[2]

The O'Hara Commission was appointed the same day as the McGovern-Fraser Commission. It got off to a slow start—and it maintained an unhurried pace through the four years of its existence. During its first year, it contented itself with identifying the areas it would investigate and some of the proposed alternative solutions it would consider. It did not begin its substantive sessions until the fall of 1970. Its delay in attacking its work was to cost the group support and influence that it could later have used to mobilize behind its more controversial proposals.

The substance of its deliberations and the leisurely manner in which it went about its duties ensured that it would pass its days in the shadow of the more flamboyant McGovern-Fraser Commission. Few were aware of its existence when it was in operation and fewer yet could later recall its accomplishments.

In contrast with the McGovern-Fraser Commission, the O'Hara group did not cultivate the press. As a consequence, it developed no national constituency that was continually aware of, and identified with, its work. When the commission's proposals encountered unexpected difficulties—as, for example, when the national committee and the national chair (then Lawrence O'Brien) decided to change the O'Hara Commission's formula for allocating national convention delegates to the states, a politically sensitive issue—the group could not turn to any politically significant group in the national party's coalition for immediate support for its position. Yet the issues involved in the controversies were important. The difference among the allocation strategies were technical but the outcome would determine which states would assume the greatest influence within national conventions and, correspondingly, which would cast the greatest number of votes on presidential nominations. Unexpectedly, under O'Brien's direction, the national committee reversed the O'Hara Commission's lead in devising formulas closer to the "one man, one vote" or "one Democrat, one vote" standards the reformers sought. The national committee, a malapportioned body sensitive to the interests of the smaller states (each state enjoyed equal representation on the committee, a practice that worked against the more populous states), chose to favor the small states by protecting their interests as best it could.

The episode points up additional differences between the O'Hara and McGovern-Fraser commissions. The O'Hara Commission did not prepare well for the tests it would encounter. The chair, O'Hara, a Democratic congressman from Michigan, was considered a parliamentary expert within the House of Representatives. He had aspirations to become Speaker one day (and actually made, and lost a bid, for the majority leader's position during the commission's life). He was a close ally of organized labor, and like many House chairs, he tended to run a tight ship. He allowed the commission only one permanent staff aide during most of its life: a lawyer who was a personal friend. As a consequence, alternative solutions and their ramifications—who gained influence, who lost—to the problems facing the commission were seldom adequately or fully researched. The commission members were expected to make ad hoc decisions on the issues brought forth before them based on their own instincts and personal judgments. This is a difficult position to be in and one fraught with dangers. On many—if not most—of the questions to come before the commission, its members had no previous knowledge of the issues involved, the alternatives available or the consequences of their decisions.

Such procedures may be useful in operating congressional committees—and the O'Hara Commission operated somewhat like these—when each congressperson has an expert's knowledge of the legislation being considered and represents clearly defined interests. Even then, most committees supply their members with voluminous background reports. The O'Hara Commission did not. Such an approach weakened the legitimacy of the commission's position when it became involved in tugs-of-war with other party groups.

When the national party committee chose to substitute its judgment and political instincts for those of the reform commission, the members of O'Hara's group were stunned and offended by the national party's actions. They had not expected it—along with ineffective preparation and failing to lay adequate groundwork for their proposals, they somewhat naively trusted the goodwill of the national committee and its leaders. Unlike the McGovern-Fraser Commission, they were vulnerable and the national party was to take repeated advantage of their weak position. Throughout the remaining years leading up to the 1972 national convention, it appeared that the criticism and frustration that logically should have been directed at the adventuresome McGovern-Fraser Commission was targeted at the relatively unprotected and less politically astute O'Hara Commission. This effectively limited its freedom of operations and, consequently, what it could be expected to accomplish.

The substance of the national convention changes

The Democratic party had *no permanent rules governing its convention deliberations.* This fact is extraordinary and it was to dawn on the commission slowly. The commission spent considerable effort in its early phases reviewing old convention records attempting to locate and then hopefully codify the relevant bylaws. It could not locate any single body of convention laws of consequence. The practice of the Democratic party had been to pass "by reference" in each national convention a resolution specifying that the rules governing the deliberations would be those of the last national convention. The practice had been going on for generations and the number of potentially relevant rules had proliferated (until, by one estimate, about 5,000 precedents existed for convention rule-making).

The party supplemented its nonexisting bylaws with the rules of the House of Representatives, in themselves extraordinarily complex, and on occasion, *Robert's Rules of Order*. It was expected that the national convention's presiding officer would somehow manage to keep the proceedings moving along through political judgments and adept and selective reference to the rules he felt relevant. The approach invited disaster; and, of course, it came with the 1968 convention.

The commission did improve procedures, although the rules it adopted were not radical departures from previous approaches. The power of the national convention chair was not diluted and an effort to permit a wider range of groups to influence the management of conventions failed. The rights of the delegates were never clarified and their situation is as nebulous and ineffective now as it was in pre-reform days.

The commission did accomplish the following:[3]

- It specified the powers and duties of the National Chair and the national committee in arranging for national conventions (a series of provisions that have had little significant impact).
- It increased the size of the three national convention committees from 100 to 150 and provided for representation on the committees by states in rough relation to the size of their delegations (previously all states had two representatives regardless of size).
- It provided fairly elaborate procedures for bringing credentials challenges. These procedures were intended to resemble something like a court action and they were supposed to introduce due process guarantees to all individuals involved in the process.
- It authorized the random seating of state delegations on the convention floor (to avoid, as in the past, those in control of the national committee being given the choice spots close to the center of decision-making).
- It attempted to ensure all delegations would have adequate communication facilities (in order to keep abreast of developments) and an equal chance for the most desirable off-floor and hotel accommodations (intended to resolve complaints in each of the national con-

ventions over the years directed against the party faction that controlled the convention's management).

- It provided for adequate media facilities.
- It mandated that the financial and business arrangements for the national convention be made public (prior to this, they were considered private matters not open in either party to public or press scrutiny).
- It rewarded states with national delegate votes in relation to their population and record of party support in past elections (a decided improvement over the previous system that inflated the strength of southern and smaller states in the convention deliberations by awarding delegate votes on the basis of the state's electoral college vote combined with a complicated "bonus vote" arrangement), a recommendation that was substantially changed by the actions of the national committee.
- It restricted the hoopla, candidate demonstrations, bands, and frivolity that it felt wasted much of the convention's time and did set effective limits on the length and number of speeches to be given.
- It limited the nomination process to only those serious presidential contenders who could (through rigorous petition requirements) demonstrate support in a number of states (a minimum of ten), a provision that both reduced the number of nominations to be presented to the national convention and effectively eliminated "favorite son" and nuisance candidacies from coming before the convention membership.

The language of the O'Hara Commission's report is dry and legalistic, one reason (although not the only one) its recommendations excited little public attention. Many of the procedures outlined are cumbersome. Yet they represent a major step forward for a political party whose reliance in previous conventions on ad hominum combinations of little-known and largely unconfided precedents had led to a continuing bitterness that threatened to erode the legitimacy of the national convention decision-making process. The elaboration of a fair, clear, and accessible set of national convention rules constituted a significant contribution to orderly convention deliberations. It ranks as the O'Hara Commission's most successful legacy.

Conclusion

The failings of the O'Hara Commission were two-fold. First, it did not detail the responsibilities of the national convention's presiding officer and the limits on his power. And second, it never made clear what the rights of the delegates were. Both political parties face the same problems in these regards.

O'Hara's relationship with the party's leaders had improved by the eve of the 1972 national convention and O'Brien appointed him to chair the 1972 national convention's Rules Committee. The choice indicated the party's acceptance of his group's proposals. The rules were to prove noncontroversial. They did not seriously challenge the convention leadership's positions while adding order and predictability to a process that needed it. They were basically apolitical. They offended few. With minor changes, they should be around for years to come.

In sum then, the procedures instituted were a considerable improvement over the chaotic and highly personalized approach that characterized previous national conventions. They *did not, however, affect any redistribution of power within the national convention.* The measure of their impact would be simply that they were adopted by the national convention and have proven serviceable to the party and its leadership.

The Platform Accountability Commission

If the party system is coming into an age of an increasingly issue-oriented vote, as appears to be the case, then the party's mechanisms for deciding on its policy commitments—and then enacting these once in office—should acquire new relevance. At least, this was the thinking of the Democratic party when in 1980 its national convention authorized the creation of another reform committee to find ways to establish an "effective and disciplined effort to implement the Platform of the National Democratic Party."[4]

The national convention outlined the objectives that a party's platform ought to strive for[5]:

- The platform "ought to be the party's contract with the people," a view first popularized by Harry Truman.
- Voters "should rightfully expect that candidates . . . when elected to office will be guided by the Platform."
- "The election of the Party's nominees to office ought to be a legitimate and effective means for implementing the Platform."
- The platform "ought to be an authentic expression of the assembled delegates as to [the] policies which are desirable and possible in [the] contemporary environment if . . . the nominees of the party are elected to office."
- "The formulation, proclamation, and implementation of the Platform [ought to be] among the highest responsibilities of any political party."

Simply outlining these views suggests that the party's policy-making procedures and commitments (as symbolized by the platform) fell somewhat short of the ideal. Certainly, this has been the case. If the platform is some type of "contract" between the party, its leaders and its officeholders, and those who support it, the contract is more akin to one in contemporary sports; subject to constant renegotiation and redefinition and, when convenient, capable of being ignored. Outside of attempting to win votes in an election year through a "wish list" of promises to major interest groups that also, hopefully, are attractive to voters, no one is quite sure what the purpose of a platform is.

It could be argued that the party platform represents a consensus-building device within the party. This much does seem clear. The platform also has an electoral function, advertising party positions to prospective voters and it can serve as a convenience for the media in contrasting major party stands. Interest group leaders use it as a benchmark against which to measure the party's commitment to their cause and then its performance in making good on its obligations. The platform is taken seriously by the political parties and it does appear to influence party members' actions once in office. Potentially, a party's platform is an important document.

Yet the manner in which a party arrives at its policy obligations, who it attempts to represent, and how effective it can be in encouraging its elected officials to implement platform commitments are all subjects of concern. The development of a more meaningful party coherence on policy matters and an accountability once in public office to the voters and policy views that helped put them there have long been objectives of reformers and party critics. In a time of a more policy-based electoral decision-making, they appear to have become of increasing concern to the political parties also. The problem far exceeds any assessment of the uses of the platform. Introducing policy coherence into a system known for its diversity and independence would appear to strike at the very roots of the contemporary party structure.

This begins to suggest the magnitude of the task facing the 52-member Platform Accountability Commission named in late 1981. The extent of the problem awaiting the new body was clear in the charge given the group. It was asked to find:

Methods of using the Platform as a tool to improve the relationship between the National Party, state parties and the electorate.

Methods of party-building by involving Democratic office holders and constituencies in the Platform process.

Methods of using Platform as a means of informing the electorate of the Party's ideological and programmatic commitments.

Methods of encouraging elected officials to actively share in the platform process and participate in the Democratic National Convention.

Methods by which the Platform can be implemented as a clear expression of Party policy.

Methods of developing a platform that defines Democratic ideals.

Methods of using the platform and its processes to implement the Democratic legislative agenda.

Methods of evaluating accountability at all levels of the Party.[6]

It is a tall order. It is unlikely that the commission can move beyond nibbling at the edges of an area that speaks to the most fundamental of weaknesses ingrained within the current party operations.

ELEVEN

Reform and the National Party

The last major target of the reform movement was to be the national party. An effort was made to extend to the national party operations the same guarantees of openness, fair procedures, and responsiveness to a grassroots constituency that had been used as the base for restructuring presidential selection. In addition, there was a problem not faced with presidential nomination practices: how to make the national party processes relevant to broader party, and social concerns, and attractive to large numbers of party members. In short, beyond instituting the reform assumption, there was a need to revitalize an antiquated national party structure.

If this aspect of reform had succeeded, the national parties, for the first time in their history, would have had one party relatively independent of any faction's control and even, if need be, domination by an incumbent president of the same party. The party would begin to constitute the expression of a rank and file national constituency's interest. Such, of course, was not to be. The national parties remain awkwardly structured vehicles, utilized for their own interest by whatever party faction, candidate group, or cluster of individuals that happen to be in control at a given point in time; politically ineffectual (in the case of the Democrats, at least), unrepresentative of the rank and file, and generally irrelevant to the conduct of modern politics.

The reformers did try. They set a number of ambitious goals that could have transformed the national party in both spirit and operations, and they did make a serious attempt to realize their objectives. The avenue for this was the Party Charter Commission.

The Party Charter (Sanford) Commission

Reformers and party regulars alike were well aware of the national party's impotence. It remained, of course, in the interests of many of the most powerful elements within the party's ranks to keep it as such. A critically weak national agency infringed on no one. The congressional party, the AFL–CIO and other organized interests, the principal funders of political campaigns, presidential contenders, governors and mayors, the state and local party leaders, all could lose from the institution of a more assertive party at the national level. These groups, the balance of those influential in the "old party" system, used the Party Charter Commission as a forum to air their objections and to resist fundamental change.

Background

National party reform had been included in the original mandates given the reform groups in 1968, and in actuality, both the McGovern-Fraser and O'Hara commissions claimed jurisdictions in the area. Both could cite support for their claims. In fact, both commissions had been authorized by the 1968 national convention (in an overlap of jurisdictions) to investigate reform of the party's structure, and both were jealous to maintain what they believed to be their principal responsibility for the area. The McGovern-Fraser Commission did establish a subcommittee to analyze and recommend change in national party operations, but its work was largely overlooked in the rush to reform presidential selection. The O'Hara Commission, in turn, focused its energies on convention modernization. Outside of recurring skirmishes over who enjoyed principal responsibility for the area, little was done. Belatedly, however, the commissions swallowed their antagonisms, and in an uncharacteristically cooperative mood, they jointly (or at least their leadership did—Fraser, on behalf of his group and O'Hara on behalf of his)—produced a "draft" party charter. This they presented in the late spring (May) of 1972 to the party, the media, and ultimately the national convention.

In reality, it was much too late to assess the ramifications of such an all-encompassing project. The party and the national convention were tied up with more pressing matters: the belated challenge of Hubert Humphrey for the presidential nomination; a series of controversial credential challenges including the Chicago fight; the drafting of a new, McGovern-type party platform; and the search for an acceptable vice-presidential candidate, a task that would, unexpectedly, take months. National party reform was far down on the list of priorities.

The national convention did not debate the party charter. Instead, it felt it advisable to create a new body to investigate the possibility of reforming all levels of the party organization. The new commission (1972–1974) was led by Duke University President and former North Carolina Governor Terry Sanford. A moderate, Sanford was acceptable to all party factions.

The substance of the recommendations

The Party Charter Commission was the last of the creative reform exercises. With its death, there ended, for all practical purposes, the real reform era. The years from 1975 on witnessed a second phase of the reform period, one which accentuated retrenchment. During this second reform stage every effort was made to make the new rules as unobjectionable to party regulars as possible without totally violating the spirit of the reform enterprise. From the mid-1970s on then, although reform bodies continued to be established, "reform" took on a quite different character.

The Sanford Commission, like the Mikulski Commission, led a volatile life. Nonetheless, it completed its work on time and its report attempted to spell out new directions for the party. Its proposals were intended to institutionalize the party structure (it had evolved as ad hoc responses to immediate necessities), open the organization to influence from Democrats at all levels, and provided party members with the basic procedural safeguards implicit in presidential selection (as a result of the McGovern-Fraser Commission's work). To accomplish these goals, it proposed an amended "party charter." The new charter was a document intended to correspond to a constitution that would govern all party affairs. Not incidentally, it was hoped that it would provide a mechanism for resolving intra-party squabbles without resort to external agencies such as the courts.

Some aspects of the party charter were clearly visionary: a judicial council, resembling the Supreme Court, to resolve intra-party disputes; and a "National Education and Training Council," vaguely modeled on European party developments and intended to expand the party's influence to new areas of social concern. As adopted in December 1974, the party charter[1]:

- Requested the national party to take stands on policy issues that represented the views of its rank and file.
- Recognized the national convention as the party's supreme governing body (as, in party law, it always had been) and asked the state parties "to take provable positive steps" to adjust their forms and policies to the national party and, as adopted, the party charter and its requirements.
- Reaffirmed the new delegate selection rules for national conventions.
- Enlarged the national committee to 350 members in an effort to make it more functionally representative of groups within the party (the congressional party, Young Democrats, Democratic mayors and governors, state chairs, etc.) and in order to give the larger states more (although still disproportionately low) representation.

- Attempted to make the national committee's executive committee more responsive to and dependent on the national committee's membership (an effort that basically failed).
- Allowed for midterm policy conferences to be held (but in deference to organized labor and the party regulars who feared them, did not mandate such conventions).
- Established a judicial council composed of people knowledgeable in law and party rules to arbitrate party disputes.
- Created a national finance council to fund national party operations (the council was to be modeled after the highly successful Republican party's funding device and was intended to help the virtually bankrupt national party pay off its substantial debts and begin to mount a professional and aggressive national party staff operation, a development which has yet to occur).
- Banned discrimination and supported affirmative action programs in party affairs.
- Encouraged "full participation by all Democrats, with particular concern for minority groups, native Americans, women and youth" in all party activities.
- Required that all meetings of the national committee, its executive committee and those of all party commissions be open to the public and that all votes be made public (a new departure for either party).
- Required an annual report of the national party, to include an accounting of its finances. (Again, a new departure for the parties. Prior to this, such information was considered private and the parties themselves were generally treated by their leaders as private organizations, publicly accountable to no one. This state of affairs remains basically true for the Republican party, and the Democratic party has been slow to make its financial reports available for public or media scrutiny).
- Required written rules of all state parties for the conduct of all party business. (A provision that has not been actively enforced, and unlike the situation with presidential selection, has made little difference in the operations of the state parties or in their openness. In general, neither the party charter nor the commission dealt with state or local party concerns in any depth.)
- Provided that the party charter could be amended by a majority vote of the national convention or by a two-thirds vote of a national conference called for that specific purpose, or under certain conditions, by a two-thirds vote of the national committee.

Given the lax organizational structure that characterized the Democratic party, the party charter did signify a potentially evolving interest in developing a cohesive organizational style. A restructured and more democratically representative party could result in an organization more responsive to contemporary political and social concerns.

This did not happen. Most of the changes introduced proved marginal in any important respects in transforming the national party. The restructured national committee, for example, remained as moribund as it had been prior to reform. No new direction emerged at the top, and the state and local parties continued to operate much as they had in the past. When President Jimmy Carter decided in the post-election period of 1976, under the tutelage of advisor Hamilton Jordan and pollster Patrick Caddell, to "Carterize" (their term) the national committee,[2] it proved as susceptible as it had in its previous incarnations under Franklin Roosevelt or in the Kennedy-Johnson years (or in relation to any other Democratic administration one might name). In this regard, little had changed.

The national party and its national committee still had no sense of responsibility to a national constituency or of standing for any issues or party concerns distinguishable from those of the immediate occupant of the White House. In effect, and despite the reforms and all that had transpired, the national party structure remained a shell, representing nothing of consequence, and easily manipulated by the faction controlling the presidency. As far as party regulars are concerned, of course, this is exactly what its role should be. No sense of "national" party purpose or rank and file commitment or representativeness of consequence to the national party organization emerged from the reform period or from the changes instituted by the Party Charter Commission.

The commission did do one thing that had never been attempted before. The party charter did—explicitly and implicitly—indicate the goals (openness, representativeness, stability, professionalism, intramural impartiality in party affairs, fair procedures, and a policy-oriented voter appeal) toward which the national party should direct itself. This, at least, sets a standard against which to measure future party achievements.

The Midterm Policy Convention

The single most significant step taken by the Party Charter Commission was the introduction of off-year policy conferences, representing the party's rank and file, to debate issues and update the party's platform in the intervals between presidential elections. The idea was to give the national party a policy-based appeal and to make it flexible and responsive to public concerns. If it worked as it should, the platform and the party's issue commitments would prove adaptable to changing social pressures, and at the same time, more internally consistent in their fundamental assumptions. Party members, in turn, would be likely to demand more accountability from elective officeholders. The party could strengthen its linkages to its supporters through its policy network.

A look at the policy conferences: fears and prospects

From the beginning, the entire concept of a midterm convention made party regulars uneasy. They attempted, with some success, to control delegate selection procedures to such conventions so that they would not be as open, lively, or unpredictable as delegate selection in presidential years. The national chair at the time of the first midterm convention, Robert Strauss, scheduled the midterm meeting for December 1974 (they were originally intended to be held prior to the off-year elections, in the late spring or during the summer, to develop a policy base for all candidates to run on). Strauss hoped that it would not attract much attention and he was determined to see that it did not embarrass the party. Strauss then established a committee, with himself as chair, to review any potential credentials disputes and to set the agenda for the gathering.

To appease the regulars, the first midterm convention was to be limited to the debate over the ratification of the party charter. Policy concerns were not to be discussed. With a few modifications, party regulars found the charter acceptable, and they and the reformers combined to pass it. The only party group adamantly opposed to the charter was the AFL-CIO. Organized labor had the votes in both the Sanford Commission and the midterm convention to force changes in significant sections of the document (for example, it opposed anything resembling the quota concern and it pushed, with success, for much milder "affirmative action" guarantees). The AFL-CIO, however, did not have the strength to scuttle the entire project.

The national chair feared discussions of policy issues would prove divisive to party unity. He did not allocate any time during the first midterm convention for consideration of public issues. Curiously, as the midterm convention approached, the party regulars became upset with the restrictions. At that time, they had just won major victories in the off-year 1974 Watergate election, and they wanted to capitalize on the momentum provided by the election to further attack a Republican administration on the defensive. They were never given the chance.

As the 1978 midterm convention approached, the same type of restrictions were once again enforced. The situation was different—a

Democrat now sat in the White House—but the basic approach to the convention was not. The White House controlled party affairs, and it was sensitive to any criticisms of its policies. Its conception of the 1978 midterm convention was a gigantic pep rally. It was intended to showcase the administration's accomplishments, gain valuable media exposure, and launch Jimmy Carter's drive for renomination. As a consequence, again delegate selection was tightly controlled. The midterm conference's agenda and membership selection procedures were determined by the national chair (now John White of Texas) in consultation with the White House. In addition, the national chair and a select group from the national committee served as gatekeepers for the convention. Virtually all proposals for discussion had to be cleared in advance with them.

Given those objectives, the rules created for the midterm convention were ingenious. First, delegate selection was left in the hands of the regular party organizations at the state level. Second, the agenda for the three-day conference provided for speeches by party notables the opening night, twenty or so workshops to continue all during the next day, and a plenary session on the final day. The business meeting on the last day would participate in an ecumenical service, debate and adopt the permanent rules for the convention, hear the workshop reports, debate and vote on the resolutions, and adjourn.

To further ensure no unforeseen developments occurred, a torturous process for the certification of proposed resolutions was instituted. To be presented to the membership during the plenary session, a resolution had to be submitted to and endorsed by the party committee established by and responsive to the national chair. The resolutions had to be submitted to the special committee two weeks before the midterm convention met.

Failing this, a resolution had to have the signatures of 406 delegates (25% of the membership) and be submitted to the party headquarters several days before the gathering convened. Anyone desiring to have a resolution considered after the delegates met would need the 406 signatures. Such proposals would be heard only after all the resolutions endorsed by the designated party committee had been debated and voted on (and there was no limit on the number of these that could be considered). Those submitted prior to the convention with the necessary signatures also had precedence over any introduced at the convention.

The restrictions were not well received by party members. Several state parties petitioned the national committee and its chair to revise the procedures, and several reform groups, led by Congressman Donald Fraser, once more geared for battle. They were modestly successful at best. The Carter administration had never been particularly sensitive to the reform issues (as the work of the Winograd Commission indicated), and their ties to any of the party factions—regulars, organized labor, blacks, liberals—were fragile. The administration had no intention of allowing any semblance of open debate, and its will prevailed. Still, there were costs involved that illustrates why officeholders are wary of such policy gatherings. Carter had intended to make ceremonial appearances at several of the meetings to endorse the administration's policy directions. Despite the careful supervision of delegate recruitment and the control exercised over the agenda, problems arose. In fact, in face-to-face confrontations with the president, Carter and his policies were severely attacked by both delegates and members of Congress. The president's address to the full convention was coolly received. In contrast, a speech by his prospective opponent for the presidential nomination, Senator Edward Kennedy, was enthusiastically applauded. This is not the type of situation incumbents positioning themselves for reelection seek out. The midterm convention proved to be an embarrassment to the administration.

The 1982 policy conference was held in June of the midterm election year, more in line with the original intention of providing a cohesive statement on national issues for congressional candidates to present to the electorate. The national party chair, however, announced that the conference would be held as essentially an expanded version of the semi-annual national committee meeting. Roughly, this is what happened. The state parties had primary responsibilities for chosing the delegates. In addition, selected officeholders were invited to attend. Policy alternatives were discussed and issue stands taken, a less controversial process when the Democrats could direct their fire at a Republican president. The distinguishing characteristic of the policy conference appeared to be the opportunity it provided potential candidates for the presidential nomination to appear and test their popularity.

Conclusion

The midterm conferences as they operated in 1974, 1978, and 1982 represented a considerable departure from what the reformers had envisioned. Nonetheless, the midterm conference has considerable potential for debating policy issues, and for voicing the concerns of the party's grassroots constituency. It could force the party's leadership to address these directly. Many party regulars appear to be increasingly comfortable with the idea, although future Democratic administrations are likely to react much the same as the Carter administration did. The midterm convention, if handled properly, could provide an effective instrument for evolving a policy-oriented party, in touch with contemporary concerns, much as the reformers had intended. Its potential is such that it continues to remain the most valuable contribution to the Party Charter Commission.

TWELVE

Issues in the Reform Debate: Who Gets Represented?

Two basic concerns dominated the reform debate: who should be represented in the party, and what kind of party should it be. The two came together in the controversy over the nature of the party system that could best serve a changing political order and help ensure survival and relevance for political institutions of great value to a democratic system. Many other issues—addressed and fought over by the successive reform groups—came to dominate the debate at various points in time (cross-over primaries, national party powers, definitions of party membership, procedures for reviewing credentials disputes, the flexibility allowed state parties in meeting criteria, the fairness or practicality of individual requirements, and so on) that reflected conflicting perspectives between reformers and regulars, or within each of the groups, over the substance, implementation, and impact of the changes. All though, in some way, traced back to the broader questions of representation within the party and the purpose and future evolution of the Democratic party. It is these basic concerns, beginning with the question of representation, that we will explore in depth.

Who Should Be Represented?

Langston Hughes wrote in one of his poems:

> I swear to the Lord
> I still can't see
> Why democracy means
> Everybody but me.[1]

This nicely reflects the views of the groups excluded from party influence. The blacks, of course, were the most severely discriminated against. The issue came to a head in the 1964 national convention and resulted in the creation of a special committee to find ways to end racially discriminatory practices within the party. The regulations of the committee, endorsed by the national party leadership and the party leaders of the major industrial states, became party policy and were forced on the southern states, the focus of the problem. These regulations, plus the enactment of the 1965 Voting Rights Act, were expected to effectively bring an end to racial bias in party and political affairs. The impetus of these events did much to fuel the subsequent reform move within the Democratic party.

A centuries-old problem was not to be so quickly resolved. A representative of the U.S. Commission on Civil Rights reporting to Congress in 1969 on the progress in implementing the 1965 Voting Rights Act, testified that:

> Instead of accepting the 1965 Act, many [state and elected officials] have violated or attempted to circumvent it whenever possible. Officials charged with managing elections in some areas of the South have withheld information from black party members about party precinct meetings and conventions, or have prevented them from participating fully. They have omitted the names of registered Negroes from official voter lists. They have failed to provide adequate voting facilities in areas with greatly increased Negro voter registration. They have refused to provide or permit adequate assistance to illiterate Negro voters. They have given inadequate or erroneous instructions to black voters. They have disqualified ballots cast by Negroes on technical grounds. They have failed to afford black voters the same opportunity as white voters to cast absentee ballots. They have established polling places in locations, such as plantation stores, likely to discourage voting by Negroes. And they have maintained racially segregated voting facilities and voter lists.[2]

Racially discriminatory practices continued also in explicitly party affairs. As documented by the McGovern-Fraser Commission, for example:

- The county executive committees in one southern state (Alabama) switched from district elections to at-large elections to dilute the impact of the black vote and prevent the election of blacks to these party committees (an action that was later overturned by the courts).
- Members of lower-level party committees in the same state (Ala-

bama) decided to personally "extend" their own terms to prevent the election of blacks. The state legislature then officially "extended" by law the terms of state party officials and county party leaders, thus ensuring that they would not have to face election and the possibility of blacks elected in the party primaries from gaining their ranks.

• In Alabama and Louisiana, the party's state executive committee and national committee delegates were elected (or selected—Louisiana and Georgia governors simply chose the national convention delegations) from gerrymandered districts that once served as the basis for congressional elections but were declared unconstitutional (under the "one man, one vote" formula) in 1962. The result was a state-level party executive committee that was all-white and which continued to be elected from districts not reapportioned since 1931.[3]

Such practices were found to be common in many southern states, all intended to minimize black influence in party deliberations. The underrepresentation of blacks (and other minorities) was not confined to the South alone. As events were to show, blacks did poorly nationwide. In 1964, prior to reform of any kind, two-thirds of the state party delegations to the national convention contained no blacks whatsoever; only one southern state had any black representation, and of the total 671 chosen in the South, one-half of one percent were black (see Table 12.1). By 1968, and *after* the implementation of the new bans on socially discriminatory practices by the Democrats' Special Committee and the 1968 national convention, the southern states had advanced to the stage of token black representation: All southern states now had some black delegates, but blacks could claim only 10 percent of the region's total (as opposed to 25% of its population).

The problem was most acute in the South but it was not limited to the region. Only 2 percent of the delegates to the 1964 Democratic national convention were black and 7 percent (in a national population estimated to be 12%) in 1968 (up from the 5.7% originally presented by the states to the national convention for certification). It was figures such as these, and the need to do something decisive to eliminate discrimination in party operations, that prompted the McGovern-Fraser Commission to act.

The debate within the commission was long and heated over the question of black representation—explained in the exchanges among the members to include other "underrepresented" groups, women, and youth (see Table 12.1 for the proportion of women represented in the national conventions of 1964 and 1968).

The idea was formally introduced by then Indiana Senator Birch Bayh. The commission members broke into a number of factions on the issue. These included a centrist group that advocated defining a "moral standard" the party should endorse, a position that failed to resolve the problems of enforcement, the national party's precise expectations of the state parties and the penalties, if any, to be enacted should a state ignore (or, what was more likely, not meet to the satisfaction of the national party) what would obviously be a vague directive. The weaknesses of this middle ground—endorse an ideal but neither require compliance nor allow for enforcement—is illustrated by an excerpt from the commission debates:

> I'm willing to concede that in the structuring of a delegation to meet this requirement that whoever's doing it, our leaders who are doing it in each state, are going to crank that [whatever stand the party adopts] into the thought process. Let me suggest, what do we mean when we say a *moral standard?* Does that mean that we have 25% of the black citizens in this state and we're going to be satisfied with 3%? That's going to be our moral standard? I don't think that's what anybody wants.[4]

The opposition to any such requirement on race argued two points: one related to the impracticality of implementing such a concept, and the other to its (as they saw it) inherently undemocratic aspects:

> In every state of course, obviously, the selection process is different. For a moment think about in your mind all of the different ways of selecting the delegations and then say that in any of those states you have candidates opposing each other to be a delegate to the National Convention. And let's say that a white would want to seek an office, to seek to be a delegate. Who's going to tell him, no, you can't seek that office because if you are by chance elected that would throw our quota system out of balance and we won't be seated at the National Convention. Therefore, don't run because you're going to beat this fellow who might count for our quota system.

———————————

> All right, I understand . . .

———————————

> So you delete his chance to participate.

———————————

> I understand what your feeling is.

———————————

O.K. you can't run. We're going to have to get a black to run against that black or a Mexican to run against a Mexican so regardless of who wins we still maintain our little quota system.

The second basic argument was over the definition of "minority" or "underrepresented" groups. Whom do you include?

The Democratic Party and the Republican Party are both grossly underrepresented as to women and to blacks, as to ethnic groups, as to young people.

You've got a very large minority group that's no longer a minority group that's going to right on you, too. You've got women in this country that have long been called a minority and are no longer a minority . . . and you can look at that and have yourself a big hassle.[5]

In addition to women and youth (ultimately brought under the quota concept as a separate guideline), other groups proposed for recognition were: ethnics, farmers, members of a "red minority, a yellow minority, and a brown minority."[6] Spanish-Americans, Orientals, the poor, Mexican-Americans, the rich, labor union members, and as the discussion wove in and out of what one participant characterized as "total confusion," the proportional representation of minority political views and candidates. These themes—the impracticality of the approach, its anti-democratic bias (when weighed against a standard of electoral strength), and the definition of targeted groups—were to remain points of attack throughout the long controversy over the issue.

A third position in the commission, and the one that ultimately prevailed, wanted a clear and enforceable party commitment:

I think we would strengthen our party, I think we would move ahead if we would have some reasonable relationship for racial minorities, for ethnic groups, for women, and for young people. There's no reason why our National Convention shouldn't have 50% women, it shouldn't have 10 or 15% young people. Well, you just have to face up to it and decide that we are going to change it, we are going to change the male domination of the national convention and turn what people are afraid of in this word quota as it is applied to the racial groups, turn it around and make it an advantage, build in an appeal to women and to young people and the ethnic groups, where let's say much of the racial friction exists, assure them adequate representation, they're underrepresented in the National Convention. I'm not for a specific quota but why shouldn't they have some reasonable relationship between their share of the population and their participation in our party at our National Convention?[7]

This is exactly how the commission came out. It did not officially institute "quotas"—although this is how the state parties saw the matter and it was enforced as if they had—but it did call on the state parties to "overcome the effects of past discrimination by affirmative steps to encourage minority group [defined as blacks, women, and youth] participation, including representation of minority groups on the national convention delegation *in reasonable relationship to the group's presence in the population of the State*" (italics added).[8] This stipulation actually underrepresented the blacks' proportionate contribution to the Democratic vote, but it was the strongest the commission members would endorse (initially passing only by a 10 to 9 vote). The commission members then explicitly stated (and had included with the rules) a provision to the effect that "it is the understanding of the Commission that this is not to be accomplished by the mandatory imposition of quotas."[9]

The outcome appeared to satisfy few. Ironically, the strongest objections were raised by those most in favor of an explicit pro-quota commitment. Senator Harold Hughes (Iowa), for example, voted against both proposals to come before the group—the first a general statement encouraging nondiscriminatory practices in the party and the second, somewhat more explicit, proposal adopted as commission policy. Hughes voted against the individual proposals "because I didn't think they were strong enough."[10] Hughes, and the others who supported his position, did vote for the final compromise on the grounds that it was the best that could be achieved and on the assumption that it clearly stated the party's position of unalterable opposition to discrimination.

This then provides an indication of the tortured deliberations that led to the most controversial of the McGovern-Fraser guidelines. Many more years of controversy and redefinition would lie ahead for the party. In the short run, the quota rules as interpreted by the McGovern-Fraser Commission staff and the 1972 national convention did lead to significant increase in the representation of the groups affected: Blacks were up from 7 to 15 percent over 1968, women from 13 to 40 percent, and youth from 4 to 21 percent (Table 12.1). The Democratic party was to become more sensitive to providing a role within its deliberations in the years to come to minority groups with the organizational power to demand attention and the political know-how to build on these early commitments. Over the longer run, blacks, women (especially), and to a far lesser extent, youth (those under 30)

TABLE 12.1 DELEGATES TO THE 1964 AND 1968 DEMOCRATIC NATIONAL CONVENTIONS, BY RACE AND SEX

State	1964			1968		
	Total	Women	Blacks	Total	Women	Blacks
Alabama	37	2	0	50	2	2
Alaska	18	1	0	22	1	0
Arizona	34	4	0	34	4	1
Arkansas	53	9	0	54	12	1
California	154	21	4	174	25	13
Canal Zone	7	2	*	8	5	0
Colorado	42	8	1	42	5	3
Connecticut	43	7	1	44	7	3
Delaware	22	2	0	22	2	1
D.C.	18	6	6	23	7	14
Florida	59	26	0	63	30	4
Georgia	59	7	4	64	4	17
Guam	7	0	*	8	1	0
Hawaii	23	4	0	26	1	0
Idaho	26	4	0	26	3	0
Illinois	110	8	6	118	8	8
Indiana	67	4	1	68	4	4
Iowa	52	10	0	52	10	1
Kansas	42	8	0	42	10	1
Kentucky	62	10	0	62	11	5
Louisiana	50	11	0	52	4	9
Maine	28	2	0	30	3	0
Maryland	48	7	2	49	3	4
Massachusetts	82	6	1	82	10	1
Michigan	102	26	14	102	19	20
Minnesota	62	8	0	62	10	3
Mississippi	44	2	0	45	4	9
Missouri	78	15	5	78	10	3
Montana	32	8	0	32	8	0
Nebraska	21	3	0	30	5	0
Nevada	24	4	0	30	5	2
New Hampshire	22	2	0	26	3	0
New Jersey	82	4	3	82	9	7
New Mexico	34	3	0	34	4	0
New York	228	20	8	227	18	20
North Carolina	74	11	0	74	6	4
North Dakota	22	8	0	25	7	0
Ohio	128	16	3	128	7	5
Oklahoma	58	8	0	58	12	5
Oregon	24	5	0	35	8	0
Pennsylvania	161	22	4	162	15	8

TABLE 12.1 (continued)

	1964			1968		
State	Total	Women	Blacks	Total	Women	Blacks
Puerto Rico	13	1	*	14	3	0
Rhode Island	34	5	1	34	4	1
South Carolina	42	1	0	42	3	6
South Dakota	22	4	0	26	4	0
Tennessee	66	7	0	66	6	7
Texas	121	8	0	120	13	6
Utah	24	8	0	26	6	1
Vermont	18	2	0	22	4	0
Virginia	66	7	0	64	6	6
Virgin Islands	8	2	*	8	1	4
Washington	54	18	0	54	13	0
West Virginia	37	2	0	38	2	1
Wisconsin	62	12	0	62	12	1
Wyoming	28	5	0	28	6	0
TOTAL	2934	416	69	3049	405	211
Percent	100%	14%	2%	100%	13%	7%

* Unknown.
SOURCE: Democratic National Committee.

improved their representation significantly (and in both parties) in the national conventions (Table 12.2).

The Counterattack

The response to what the Democratic party had done was immediate and strong. The opposition built on objections first raised within the commission itself. Ethnics, a core part of the New Deal constituency, felt rejected and demanded recognition. From the limited data available (Tables 12.3 and 12.4) it appeared that they had a case. Whether the post-reform conventions were significantly worse in these regards than their pre-reform counterparts is moot (Table 12.3). In neither type of convention system did ethnics do particularly well. The Mikulski Commission was supposed to remedy the imbalance, but could find no acceptable resolution to the problem (short of additional quotas, a concept it was moving away from).

An editorial in a Kansas newspaper exemplifies the usual kind of attack and the one that received the most continuous attention. After

TABLE 12.2 THE REPRESENTATION OF BLACKS, WOMEN, YOUTH, AND OTHER MINORITIES AT THE 1972 DEMOCRATIC NATIONAL CONVENTION

State	Elected Delegates	Women	Percent	Youth	Percent	Blacks	Percent	Other
Alabama	37	7	32.0	4	10.8	10	27.0	
Alaska	21	7	33.3	6	28.6	2	9.5	2 Indian (9.5%); 2 Eskimo (9.5%)
Arizona	25	8	32.0	11	44.0	3	12.0	6 Latino (24%)
Arkansas	27	12	44.4	5	18.5	5	18.5	
California	271	129	47.6	94	34.7	50	18.5	48 Latino (17.7%); 1 Indian (0.36%)
Colorado	36	18	50.0	12	33.3	5	13.9	11 Latino (30.6%)
Connecticut	51	15	29.4	2	4.0	4	7.9	
Delaware	20	9	45.0	2	10.0	3	15.0	
Dist. of Col.	20	9	45.0	4	20.0	14	70.0	
Florida	81	34	41.7	14	17.3	11	13.6	2 Latino (2.5%)
Georgia	53	16	30.2	11	20.8	18	34.0	
Hawaii	20	4	20.0	4	20.0	0	0	12 Oriental (60%); 1 Latino (5%)
Idaho	20	7	35.0	3	15.0	2	10.0	2 Latino (10%)
Illinois	194	68	35.1	36	18.6	29	15.0	6 Latino (3.1%)
Indiana	76	27	35.5	13	17.1	12	15.7	
Iowa	46	19	41.3	7	15.2	3	9.0	2 Latino (43%); 1 Indian (2.2%)
Kansas	35	14	40.0	8	22.8	4	11.4	
Kentucky	47	20	42.6	10	21.3	5	10.6	1 Latino (2.1%)
Louisiana	46	15	32.6	10	21.7	19	41.3	
Maine	20	5	25.0	5	25.0	0	0	
Maryland	56	15	26.8	9	16.1	9	16.1	
Massachusetts	102	49	48.0	19	19.4	11	10.8	1 Indian (0.98%); 1 Latino (0.98%)
Michigan	142	62	43.7	29	20.4	30	21.1	2 Latino (1.4%)

State							Notes
Minnesota	64	30	46.9	12	18.6	6	9.4	4 Indian (6.3%); 1 Latino (1.6%)
Mississippi	25	11	44.0	8	32.0	14	56.0	
Missouri	85	33	38.8	8	9.4	9	10.6	3 Indian (15%)
Montana	20	9	45.0	7	35.0	1	5.0	
Nebraska	24	11	45.8	7	29.2	1	4.2	
Nevada	20	8	40.0	6	30.0	2	10.0	1 Latino (5%)
New Hampshire	20	8	40.0	3	15.0	0	0	
New Jersey	116	50	43.1	30	25.9	22	19.0	2 Latino (1.7%)
New Mexico	20	8	40.0	5	25.0	1	5.0	7 Latino (35%); 1 Indian (5%)
New York	278	136	48.9	70	25.2	35	12.6	17 Latino (6.1%); 1 Indian (o.35%)
North Carolina	64	30	46.9	5	7.8	13	20.3	1 Indian (1.6%)
North Dakota	20	8	40.0	5	25.0	1	5.0	2 Indian (10%)
Ohio	153	56	36.6	18	11.8	27	17.6	
Oklahoma	41	18	43.9	4	9.8	4	9.8	2 Indian (4.9%)
Oregon	34	17	50.0	13	38.2	2	5.9	
Pennsylvania	200	69	34.5	27	13.5	22	11.0	1 Latino (0.5%)
Rhode Island	29	9	31.0	11	37.9	2	6.9	
South Carolina	32	8	25.0	5	15.6	11	34.4	
South Dakota	17	7	41.2	6	35.3	0	0	2 Indian (11.8%)
Tennessee	49	24	49.0	15	30.6	16	32.7	1 Latino (2.0%)
Texas	130	39	30.0	29	22.3	12	9.2	18 Latino (13.9%), 1 Indian (0.76%)
Utah	19	7	36.8	3	15.8	0	0	
Vermont	20	8	40.0	8	40.0	1	5.0	
Virginia	56	21	37.5	20	35.7	16	28.6	3 Indian (5.7%); 1 Latino (1.9%)
Washington	52	20	38.5	7	13.5	4	7.7	
West Virginia	35	2	5.7	2	5.7	0	0	
Wisconsin	67	31	46.3	21	31.3	5	7.5	1 Indian (1.5%); 2 Latino (3.0%)
Wyoming	20	7	35.0	1	5.0	1	5.0	1 Indian (5%)

TABLE 12.2 (Continued)

State	Elected Delegates	Women	Percent	Youth	Percent	Blacks	Percent	Other
Canal Zone	6	3	50.0	4	66.7	2	33.3	
Guam	6	3	50.0	1	16.7	0	0	5 Native (83.3%)
Puerto Rico	14	8	57.1	4	28.6	0	0	14 Latino (100.0%)
Virgin Islands	6	3	50.0	0	0	4	66.7	1 Latino (16.7%)
TOTALS	3,188	1,271	39.9%	683	21.4%	483	15.2%	

SOURCE: Democratic National Committee.

**TABLE 12.3 REPRESENTATION OF SELECTED GROUPS
AT NATIONAL CONVENTIONS, 1968–1980**

National Convention	Blacks, %	Women, %	Youth (under 30), %
		Democrats	
1968	7	13	4
1972	15	40	22
1976	11	33	15
1980	14	49	11
		Republicans	
1968	2	17	1
1972	3	35	7
1976	3	31	7
1980	3	29	5

SOURCE: Democratic and Republican National Committees.

**TABLE 12.4 REPRESENTATION OF ETHNICS AT THE
1968 AND 1972 DEMOCRATIC
NATIONAL CONVENTIONS**

1968		*1972**	
Italians	137	Italians	113
Germans	94	Germans	66
Poles	42	French	32
French	37	Poles	27
Czechoslovaks	37	Czechoslovaks	23
Scandinavians	28	Scandinavians	21
Orientals	23	Greeks	17
Greeks	13	Orientals	14
Yugoslavs	9	Arabs	11
Arabs	6	Russians	6
Finns	5	Yugoslavs	4
Russians	3	Finns	3
		Lithuanians	2
		Hungarians	2
TOTAL	434		381
Percent of Total National Convention Membership	15%		12%

* At the 1972 Convention there were 131 Latino delegates.
SOURCE: Democratic National Committee.

musing that the state would need 1.64 black delegates to satisfy the national party requirements, the newspaper went on to say:

> The [McGovern-Fraser] commission didn't say anything about it, but fair is fair. The over-75 [age] group makes up 4 percent of the population. That should entitle them to a couple of delegates. We haven't worked out the percentages, but in 1960 Kansas numbered 5,069 Indians, 1,362 Japanese, and 537 Chinese. Surely they're entitled to some representation.[11]

The editorial concluded by wondering if the Democratic party could conclude all its arithmetic calculations in time to hold a national convention.

The attack was typical. It was easy to understand and it caught the public's fancy. The state parties opposing reform—often more strongly on other grounds that more directly threatened their control over their state nominating procedures and national convention delegations (the timeliness provisions; requirements for applicable, written rules in delegate selection; and the methods specified for choosing delegates and alternates)—found it expedient to center their attacks against the reforms on the quota concept. The media was attentive to this type of argument, and the issue was easily understood by both party members and the general public.

Years after the initial quota debate had subsided and the party had reverted to "affirmative action" standards that the states had no trouble complying with, strains of the first wave of attacks continued to be heard. Two incidents in the late 1970s illustrate the continuing interest in the topic and its ability to stimulate controversy. One involved the Illinois Democratic party and the other the Democratic National Committee. In Illinois, the state party had been under persistent pressure from the national party to admit a woman into one of its leadership positions and, specifically, to comply with the national party rule to designate as a co-chair of the state party the highest ranking Democratic female official in the state. The leadership of the Illinois Democratic party was all male and had been for as long as anyone could remember. Worse, there were no ranking women in state party positions.

No problem. In a brief meeting of the ruling body of the party, the leadership designated an honorary women's auxiliary group as a proper recruiting grounds and then selected one of its members to serve as co-chair, fulfilling the national party's requirement. Women's groups were furious. "They didn't even let the women [in the auxiliary] make their own choice," said one.[12] When the state chair was asked why the party had not made more provisions for women, he responded that "all the women have to do is run for office." When told how angry the women's groups were, he replied: "Women are angry everywhere."[13] So ended the controversy as far as the Illinois party was concerned.

At the national level, the Democrats decided to add two positions to their national executive committee, reserving one for a black woman. That began the maneuvering. One woman on the national committee argued that if there were going to be two new positions, both should go to women. A black on the committee made the same point concerning blacks. Another member from a farm state said she could support the additions if both posts were reserved for farmers. Another committee member went over the list of thirty-four executive committee appointees and found that none were Italian-American, Polish-American, or Jewish. At this point, the party leadership felt it best to drop the proposal.

Organized Labor Responds to Reform

Only 4 percent of the delegates attending the 1968 national convention were union members. Yet organized labor chose to look at 1968, and the old party system in general, as something of a golden age in terms of its power within the Democratic party and, in particular, its influence over the choice of a presidential nominee. Seemingly, the reform movement would be tailor-made for a strong showing by the unions in helping to shape rules best calculated to increase the representation of its membership. This did not happen. What did occur was that despite organized labor's opposition to the reforms, union representation at Democratic national conventions was to increase from five to eight fold between 1972 and 1980. It would come to approximate the proportion of union households in the nation. Ironically, this was achieved without organized labor's support. More often than not, labor (as represented by the AFL-CIO leadership) was to position itself in diametric opposition to the reform movement, a stance that may have cost it heavily in national politics.

The AFL-CIO leaders did not misperceive their role within the old party system. While the labor delegations to national conventions may have been negligible, federated labor's influence over presidential nominations could be decisive. At a minimum, organized labor exercised a veto over the choice of a nominee. More often though, no one could be nominated that did not have the full backing of George Meany, the president of the AFL-CIO. Reform threatened organized labor's preeminent status within national conventions and the AFL-CIO fought it tenaciously.

Representatives of the AFL-CIO were appointed to the early reform commissions. They boycotted the sessions. "Mr. Meany wanted
no part of it,"reported one of the union political directors who moni-
tored reform developments.[14] From here, the union leadership went
on to strongly criticize the reform proposals, and particularly the quotas on blacks, women, and youth, which incensed them: "They [the
reformers] worried about kids being underrepresented at the convention and about women and blacks," said one representative of organized labor. "But we supply the muscle in November and nobody
thought about our problems."[15] While objecting that the "kids and
the kooks" ran the party, the AFL-CIO failed to organize early enough
or well enough for the 1972 presidential selection contests in the states.
As a result, although the number of union members at the national
convention actually increased to over 20 percent, labor felt left out
of the proceedings, its role and influence on nominations undermined.
Its response was to remain officially "neutral" in the 1972 presidential
election, a decision that helped elect Richard Nixon.

After the election, the AFL-CIO led furious counterattacks within
the party (usually through the national chair) to shape the Mikulski
and Party Charter commissions' recommendations to better suit its
own interests. The controversy ensured lively sessions for both reform
groups. The AFL-CIO was able to mute the effects of the quota rules,
its major target in the ongoing debate. On a more significant level,
it was not able to scrap the reforms or to appreciably reverse their
direction, a failure that led to an increasingly strained relationship
between the national party and its normal ally.

By the late 1970s, the costs involved in this estrangement had
become clear to both the party and the unions. Leaders of the progressive faction of labor, which had remained close to the reform developments, attempted to bring about a rapprochement. Both groups
(the national party in elections and the unions in cultivating receptive
lawmakers) had lost heavily. "Organized labor's mistakes are catching
up with it, and it is becoming a victim of new perceptions of its
strengths and weaknesses," reported the late Jerry Wurf in 1977.[16]
Wurf was president of one of the biggest unions and one of the few
still growing (the American Federation of State, County and Municipal
Employees). According to Wurf:

> What happened is very simple. Organized labor displayed cynicism
> in staying neutral on George McGovern, in its relationships with
> Mayor Daley in Chicago and Rockefeller in New York. It displayed
> blindness on America's role in Vietnam.
>   Suddenly labor made the discovery that it did not have the

real clout it thought it had in Congress. Its ability to be effective electorally had lessened and, so, therefore, did its influence on political leaders. The AFL-CIO treats the situs defeat [a congressional vote to permit one construction union to shut down a construction site with a picket line, an issue the unions took to be a litmus test of their legislative strength] as a tactical error, but it was more—it was the voice of the United States government it helped elect.[17]

By the 1980s, with the retirement of Meany and the long-time director (Al Barkan) of COPE, the AFL-CIO's lobbying and political arm, the situation had begun to change. Organized labor made its peace with the remnants of the reform movement and it attempted to develop a more forceful voice in party affairs and, more importantly, reassert its presence in elections and in the Congress. In the interim, much emotion, time and energy, as well as a considerable amount of resources, had been invested in a fight that profited few.

The Party Professionals

One group that did appear to lose significant influence over the choice of a presidential nominee in the change from the pre-reform to the post-reform presidential selection system was party professionals. At first it was believed that—and most of the controversy centered on this issue—party professionals had been effectively excluded from national conventions. The villain in this debate for the regulars was the quotas; to borrow organized labor's term, the "kids and the kooks" had replaced the party pros. The argument raged from the late sixties to the 1980s. The Hunt Commission found, to its surprise, that party and elective officeholders had not really been excluded (for whatever reason) from national convention deliberations. In fact, CBS News reported that between one-half (57% in 1976) and two-thirds (64% in 1980) of the delegates to the national convention held some type of party or elective position.[18]

This finding should have defused the argument somewhat. It did not. The original charges continued to be made with the same intensity. What was true was that the participation of upper-level party figures (and especially of members of Congress) in national conventions had fallen off dramatically (Table 12.5). The participation of Democratic governors was down from 83 percent in pre-reform days to 67 percent in the post-reform period (although three out of four of the Democratic governors took part in the 1980 national convention). The representation of U.S. Senators decreased from 75 percent to 23 percent and of House members (never high) from 41 percent to 15 percent.

TABLE 12.5   REPRESENTATION OF TOP-LEVEL PARTY AND
ELECTIVE OFFICEHOLDERS IN PRE-REFORM AND POST-
REFORM DEMOCRATIC NATIONAL CONVENTIONS, 1956–1980

	Old Party System (1956–1968)	New Party System (1972–1976)	1980 National Convention
% of Democratic Senators	75	27	14
% of U.S. Representatives	41	15	14
% of Governors	82	67	76

SOURCE: Democratic National Committee.

There is some question as to just how anxious elective officeholders actually are to participate in national conventions. The Mikulski Commission had polled the Democratic membership of the U.S. House of Representatives and found that 45 percent of the total did not want to be included in national convention delegations. This surprised advocates of a stronger party professional presence, but it failed to change the nature of the debate.

The effort to protect the position of the party professionals had begun early. As noted, the only change of consequence in the original McGovern-Fraser guidelines was the national committee's amendment to award themselves ex-officio delegate status (later modified slightly). The Mikulski Commission dealt with the issue by relaxing the national party's procedural requirements in order to return more control over the process to state party leaders, with the expectation that one consequence would be more party officials attending national conventions. The Winograd Commission provided for a 10 percent "add-on," or quota, for party and elected officials and the Hunt Commission expanded this to roughly 25 percent (it is difficult to determine the exact number of such delegates given the formula adopted).

Regulars remained convinced that such changes could only benefit the party. The Hunt Commission can be presumed to speak for those who hold this position:

Why so much stress on increasing party and elected official participation? The [Hunt] Commission regards this as an important way to increase the convention's *representativeness* of mainstream Democratic constituencies. It would help restore *peer review* to the process, subjecting candidates to scrutiny by those who know them best. It would put a premium on *coalition building* within the Party prior to nomination, the forming of alliances that would help us campaign and govern effectively. It would *strengthen party ties* among officials, giving them a greater sense of identification

TABLE 12.6 DEMOGRAPHIC CHARACTERISTICS OF DEMOCRATIC PARTY AND ELECTED OFFI-CIALS

	Total	Men	Women	White	Black	His-panic	Native Amer.	Asian Pac.
Governors	28	28	0	26	0	1	0	1
U.S. Senators	46	46	0	44	0	0	0	2
U.S. Representatives	241	232	9	217	16	5	0	3
Big-City Mayors (over 250,000)	43	39	4	34	5	4	0	0
State Chairs and Vice-Chairs	112	56	56	92	8	7	0	5
DNC Members Not Included Above	249	127	122	191	41	13	0	4
TOTAL	719	528	191	604	170	30	0	15
Percent	100%	73%	27%	84%	10%	4%	0%	2%

SOURCE: Democratic National Committee.

TABLE 12.7 REPRESENTATION IN DEMOCRATIC AND REPUBLICAN NATIONAL CONVENTIONS 1968–1980, BY GROUP

| | National Convention Delegates | | | | | | | | Public | |
| | 1968 | | 1972 | | 1976 | | 1980 | | 1980 | |
	Dem.	Rep.	Dem.	Rep.	Dem.	Rep.	Dem.	Rep.	Dem.	Rep.
Women	13%	16%	40%	29%	33%	31%	49%	29%	56%	53%
Blacks	5	2	15	4	11	3	15	3	19	4
Under thirty	3	4	22	8	15	7	11	5	27	27
Median age (years)	(49)	(49)	(42)		(43)	(48)	(44)	(49)	(43)	(45)
Lawyers	28	22	12		16	15	13	15		
Teachers	8	2	11		12	4	15	4		
Union official	4	0	5		6	0	5	0		
Union member			16		21	3	27	4	29*	18
Attended First Convention	67	66	83	78	80	78	87	84		
College Graduate	19		21		21	27	20	26	11	18
Postgraduate	44	34	36		43	38	45	39		
Protestant			42		47	73	47	72	63	74
Catholic			26		34	18	37	22	29	21
Jewish			9		9	3	8	3	4	1
Ireland			13		19	14	15	9		
Britain			17		15	28	15	31		
Germany			9		9	14	6	12		
Italy			4		6	5	5	6		
Liberal					40	3	46	2	21	13
Moderate					47	45	42	36	44	40
Conservative					8	48	6	58	26	41
Governors (number)	(23)	(24)	(17)	(16)	(16)	(9)	(23)	(13)		
Senators (number)	(39)	(21)	(15)	(22)	(11)	(22)	(8)	(26)		
U.S. Representatives (number)	(78)	(58)	(31)	(33)	(41)	(52)	(37)	(64)		

* Households with a union member.
SOURCE: Warren J. Mitofsky and Martin Plissner, "The Making of the Delegates, 1968–1980," *Public Opinion*, October/November, 1980, p. 43.

with the nominee and the platform. And the presence of unpledged delegates would help return *decision-making discretion and flexibility* to the Convention.[19]

Maybe such a change would accomplish all the objectives indicated. One outcome is more probable: It is likely to dilute the impact of the unofficial quotas/affirmative action guidelines even further. The overwhelming majority of governors, U.S. senators, members of congress, and state and national party officials are white males (Table 12.6). While a quota is unacceptable for many of the minority groups, it has been institutionalized for party officials.

Conclusion

The big winners in the battle over representation appear to be women and party officeholders. Women are guaranteed one-half of the total Democratic seats at national conventions and officeholders between one-fourth and one-fifth (although, of course, their numbers may far exceed this designated share). The big losers are blacks and other minorities and youths (Table 12.7).

Youth is no longer considered a viable political force, which may be unfortunate. With 50 percent or better of those coming into the electorate not affiliating with either party and about the same proportion not taking part in elections, it would seem to be in the party's intelligent self-interest to cultivate this group.

The situation with blacks is more complicated. The civil rights movement was one of the generating forces that led to party reform. The work of the early committee (the Richard Hughes Special Equal Rights Committee) created to deal with problems of discrimination set procedural and substantive precedents that were directly incorporated into the reform movement. Blacks have increased their representation at national conventions to about 14 percent of the post-reform total. This figure corresponds with the black population nationwide, although it underrepresents the black contribution to the Democratic vote. Blacks are more of an electoral force in the South in particular, and blatant discrimination on the basis of race is punishable under both national statutes and party bylaws. Still, it could be expected that blacks would have done better within the party. They did not because as the later stages of the reform movement unfolded, blacks did not field the political organization and aggressive leadership needed to present their case effectively and to defend their early gains. Later developments in the reform movement reflect an accommodation to the realities of political power.

THIRTEEN

What Kind of Political Party?

A National Party

One objective of the reformers was to mold a nationally cohesive party to replace the collection of state and local parties and candidate groups that had little in common beyond the party name. Donald M. Fraser, of the McGovern-Fraser Commission, answered the question "What kind of national party do we want?" this way:

> The major new thrust . . . should be in the direction of creating a more genuinely *national* Democratic Party. By this I mean that we should firmly set our course away from the tradition of 50 state parties, each autonomous within a poorly-defined, national confederation, meeting every 4 years to nominate a presidential candidate. We should set as our goal the creation of a truly national party in which decision-making at the national level is strengthened and the 50 state parties become integral parts of that party.[1]

Obviously, there would be opposition toward a move in any such direction from party regulars and factional leaders holding positions of power within the prevailing party system. They stood to lose influence and freedom within any system that emphasized a greater degree of cohesion and common enterprise. There was then a very real fear of change existing within party ranks.

There was a second point of resistance also. Many attack the effort to change—what reformers saw as adapting institutions to the realities of political development—as a type of "social engineering that attempted to place a rationalist's value perspective on organisms that ranked among the least rational of those found in society. Jeane Kirkpatrick, a neoconservative critic of reform and later the Reagan administration's ambassador to the United Nations, has made the argument that "rationalism" of this nature constitutes a utopianism that can have unwanted, and even disastrous, consequences, potentially leading to tryanny and totalitarianism (in some circumstances).[2] This is strong stuff. Kirkpatrick tended to see in political institutions, rather than a resistance to change or an outdatedness that had severe political consequences, qualities she felt reflected the lifeblood of a civilization. Her emphasis was on "the intractability of human behavior, the complexity of human institutions, and the probability of unanticipated consequences."[3]

Among the "unanticipated consequences" of reform, Kirkpatrick argued, were the lessened ability of the parties to represent voter concerns, a decrease in the influence of ethnic minorities, the use of a "new political class" (see below), a lower voter turnout, decreasing party identifications, the rising influence of the media and candidate organizations, and weaker state and local parties.[4] A reformer would reverse the causal flow. Such conditions within the political environment illustrated the need for a new form of national party.

Many party regulars (although not all), not only favored a decentralized, fragmented, and relatively autonomous national collection of party units, but for them, somewhat ironically, the ideal party system at the local level was the machine: efficient in delivering the vote; bartering with constituents for services, a job, or patronage; benevolent; paternalistic; and an electoral force of consequence in national and state (as well as local) politics. Everyone, they believed, profited from such an arrangement. Few models could be further from the reform conception of what a party should be.

A number of people have argued that a "nationalizing" trend within the party system has begun. They point to the sympathetic position taken by the Supreme Court toward the powers of the national party in presidential selection (*Cousins v. Wigoda,* 1975; *Democratic Party v. LaFollette,* 1981); the restructuring of delegate selection rules with power lodged in the national party; the midterm policy conferences; the party charter; the increased funding available to the national parties (especially apparent within the Republican party); and the aggressive provision of resources and services (candidate recruitment, campaign management, media guidance, polling, voter identification and consulting programs, funding) by the national Republican party to state and local parties for their candidates for elective office.

Whether all of this will result in the type of "national party" envisioned by Fraser and others is problematical. It has, however, affected a redistribution of power that is moving in the direction of a more powerful national party system.

An Accountable Party

A basic division existed between reformers and regulars over the question of party accountability. Reformers believed that to be accountable a party had to be in direct contact with its grassroots constituency. This meant being directly responsive to its views, including the rank and file within party deliberations, and evolving intra-party democratic decision-making procedures. This strain can be seen in many forms during the reform period: the drive to restructure the national party, the promotion of party conferences, and most notably, in the overhaul of presidential selection procedures.

Party regulars believed accountability of this kind and talk of intra-party democracy totally impractical. The assumption was that it would incapacitate a party from effectively engaging in electoral politics. The type of accountability the regulars espoused was through elections. The political party would make its decisions as to nominees and policy commitments in relative isolation. The results would be presented to the voters. They, in turn, had the option of voting the party and its candidate in or out of office. According to the regulars, this was the only practical and effective type of political responsibility that could be exercised within the American political system.

The regulars could call on different political theorists for support for their views. The democratic theorist, Joseph A. Schumpeter, was a particular favorite. In elaborating the conditions necessary for the success of a democracy, Schumpeter contended that "the effective range of political decisions should not be extended too far."[5] He described a political party as:

> . . . a group whose members propose to act in concert in the competitive struggle for political power. . . . Party and machine politicians are simply the response to the fact that the electoral mass is incapable of action other than a stampede, and they constitute an attempt to regulate political competition exactly similar to corresponding practices of a trade association.[6]

Within such a system, the role of the voter is limited. "Voters confine themselves to accepting . . . [the] bid [of a candidate or party] in preference to others or refusing to accept it." And once elected:

> The voters outside the parliament must accept the division of labor between themselves and the politicians they elect. They must not withdraw confidence too easily between elections and they must understand that, once they have elected an individual, political action is his business and not theirs. This means that they must

refrain from instructing him about what he is to do . . . few people realize that this principle clashes with the classical doctrine of democracy and really spells its abandonment.[7]

The individual's role, quite simply, was to vote a party or candidate up or down in an election. Beyond this, he or she had no real voice in party or public affairs. This would be taken care of for the individual by those with the knowledge and experience necessary to ensure the survival of the democratic enterprise. It was a politics of elitism, knowledge, and power, founded on a basic distrust of democratic procedure. As E. E. Schattschneider said, in a much quoted reference: "Democracy is not to be found *in* the parties but *between* the parties."[8]

There is little room for compromise between such polarized conceptions of party accountability.

An Open Party

A theme that ran through the early reform hearings was the closed nature of the party and its coolness to newcomers. References to "the bossism and corruption of hundreds of state and local organizations," a state party "dominated by old and corrupt machines," and the "many areas in [the] party . . . [that were] under the effective domination of one man or group" were heard often.[9]

The party was closed. The matter was stated well by Donald Peterson, a delegate from Wisconsin to the 1968 Democratic National Convention, in his testimony before the McGovern-Fraser Commission:

> What we learned first-hand in 1968 was that as members of the Democratic Party—whether as voters, party leaders, elected or appointed officials—whatever our position, we had and could have no effect on the policies that our party was pursuing.
>
> As the nation was plunged into war abroad and strife at home, as our young people drifted off into hostile separation, we grew progressively more uneasy, more and more opposed to the course of policy. But we could not be heard. With the exception of a few courageous individuals—like Senators [Eugene] McCarthy and [Robert] Kennedy and [George] McGovern, those who finally carried our banners in 1968—with those exceptions, and others I need not mention, the party as an organization worked not to discuss these great issues but to bury dissent and punish dissenters. As individuals, we could not be heard.[10]

The reformers believed that the party should be open to all those party members who wished to participate. They felt it was absolutely crucial in a time of dwindling party enrollments and declining party authority to include as many people in party decision-making as possible. And they contended that the people drawn into party operations should receive a fair and unbiased hearing. These views motivated much of their concern with reform and are reflected in the participant-oriented and procedural due process guarantees that formed the basis for the early reform recommendations. A stagnant, arbitrary, and out-dated party structure with closed decision-making and little public or party member accountability, they believed, was a contributing factor to much of the social and political unrest they found around them.

Again, the opposing camps could not be further apart. The reformers carried the day in the early proceedings and their emphasis on greater involvement in all party areas was incorporated into the rules governing presidential selection, national conventions, and national (and to a lesser extent state) party organization(s). In presidential nominations at least, they achieved their objective (Table 13.1). At a time when turnout in general elections is both low and continuing to decline,

TABLE 13.1 PARTICIPATION IN THE PRESIDENTIAL
NOMINATION PROCESS.1968–1980

	Democrats			Republicans		
	Primary	*Caucus*	*Total*	*Primary*	*Caucus*	*Total*
1968	(17)* 8,247,000	(34) 219,000	8.4 million	(16) 4,571,000	(35) 105,000	4.7 million
1972	(23) 16,715,000	(28) 771,000	17.5 million	(22) 5,887,000	(29) 256,000	6.1 million
1976	(31) 18,884,000	(20) 639,000	19.5 million	(30) 9,724,000	(21) 546,000	10.3 million
1980	(33) 17,580,000	(18) 539,000	18.1 million	(35) 13,301,000	(16) 307,000	13.7 million

Grand Total Participating
(By Year)

1968	13.1 million
1972	23.6 million
1976	29.8 million
1980	31.8 million

* Number in parenthesis represent the number of primaries or caucuses.
SOURCE: Democratic and Republican National Committees.

participation in presidential selection processes increased between 1968 and 1980 by 19 million people, a jump of almost 150 percent.

The increase has not been welcomed by party regulars. First, as noted, they were committed to a restricted involvement. Within such a system, their job was to judge the sentiments of the electorate and the interests that best represented the party's base, and then to act on these as they deemed necessary. Second, they perceived the new-comers as a threat to both their conception of what a party should be and their own role within the party's power structure. Their concern was not ill-founded.

The people attracted to the party in the post-reform era held views on the nature of party and on policy concerns that were profoundly different from those of the regulars. The 1972 Democratic primaries and national convention can be used to illustrate the opposing points of view. The convention's membership is not a totally accurate micro-cosm of the conflicts within the party, since it took place at the height of the controversy over these issues, but it does serve to indicate how dissimilar the delegates' commitments were.

A comparison can be made between those who supported the McGovern candidacy within the party in 1972, a reasonable substitute for those who were pro-reform, and those backing other contenders (Edmund Muskie, Hubert Humphrey, and Henry Jackson primarily) in the primaries and national convention, a representation of those less sympathetic to reform. The differences are quickly apparent (Ta-ble 13.2). Demographically, the McGovern supporters in the primaries compared to other primary voters were younger, better educated, and more urban, more likely to be Catholic, Jewish, women, residents of the northeast, and (surprisingly) members of a urban household. These differences appear also in contrast to Democrats who defected to Nixon in 1972 and to Democratic party identifiers more generally.

The McGovern supporters' policy views were equally dissimilar from those of other Democratic primary voters, Democrats defecting to Nixon, and Democratic party identifiers. Employing indicators of "life style" positions (as against New Deal economic and social issues on which the groups exhibit a great deal of similarity), the McGovern voters were significantly more liberal on these cultural issues than are other party members (Table 13.3). In opposition to the war in Vietnam and in sympathy for liberal positions on amnesty, the use of marijuana, campus demonstrators, aid to minorities, bussing, and government promotion of a better standard of living, the modal group of McGovern voters differed from the modal group backing the other candidates by an average of over 100 percentage points (on a scale from +100 to −100). Ideologically, in addition to their positions on the specified individual issues, the contrasts remain: the McGovern

TABLE 13.2 A DEMOGRAPHIC COMPARISON OF McGOVERN SUPPORTERS WITH THOSE OF OTHER CANDIDATES, 1972

	McGovern Primary Voters	Other Primary Voters	Democrats Voting for McGovern	Democrats Voting for Nixon	All Democrats	McGovern Voters	Nixon Voters
(N)	(67)	(98)	(279)	262	(807)	(445)	(1000)
Age:							
18–24	19%	5%	19%	7%	13%	19%	10%
25–29	10	8	10	8	9	14	11
30–59	55	62	47	58	51	48	54
60+	16	25	24	27	27	19	25
Total	100%	100%	100%	100%	100%	100%	100%
Education:							
Grade School	13%	18%	21%	21%	25%	16%	14%
High School	45	50	45	55	51	44	49
College	42	31	34	24	24	40	37
Income:							
Less than $4,000	12%	17%	17%	16%	19%	15%	12%
$4,000–$7,999	22	21	24	21	25	21	19
$8,000–$14,999	45	42	37	43	38	39	41
$15,000 or more	21	20	22	20	18	25	28
Sex:							
Male	40%	38%	43%	42%	42%	41%	47%
Female	60	62	57	58	58	59	53
Residence:							
Urban	33%	16%	29%	21%	25%	29%	21%
Suburban	36	41	33	37	35	37	43
Rural	31	43	38	42	40	34	36

Region:							
Northeast	33%	11%	25%	17%	20%	29%	22%
Midwest	30	29	31	23	27	32	32
South	13	41	23	46	37	20	29
West	24	19	21	14	16	19	17
Religion:							
Protestant	50%	73%	53%	61%	61%	57%	74%
Catholic	41	23	41	38	35	37	25
Jew	9	4	6	1	4	6	1
Occupation:							
White Collar	55%	55%	49%	54%	47%	54%	59%
Blue Collar	45	45	51	46	53	46	41
*Social Class:**							
Working Class	51%	59%	49%	58%	58%	46%	48%
Middle Class	49	40	51	42	42	54	52
Union Household:							
Yes	38%	28%	35%	28%	30%	33%	23%
No	62	72	65	72	70	67	77

* Respondent's self-perceived social class.

SOURCE: Center for Political Studies, as reported in Arthur H. Miller, Warren E. Miller, Alden S. Raine, and Thad A. Brown, "A Majority Party in Disarray: Policy Polarization in the 1972 Election," A Paper Delivered at the 1973 Annual Meeting of the American Political Science Association, Washington, D.C.

TABLE 13.3 DIFFERENCES BETWEEN McGOVERN SUPPORTERS AND OTHER VOTERS ON LIFE STYLE ISSUES, 1972

	McGovern Primary Voters	Other Primary Voters	Democrats Voting for McGovern	Democrats Voting for Nixon	All Democrats	McGovern Voters	Nixon Voters
(N)	(78)	(104)	(377)	(271)	(1092)	(566)	(1021)
Vietnam:							
Left	79%	34%	69%	30%	52%	69%	29%
Center	17	26	19	31	24	19	29
Right	5	40	12	39	24	12	42
Amnesty*:							
Left	52%	17%	49%	18%	34%	54%	15%
Right	48	83	51	82	66	46	85
Marijuana:							
Left	41%	19%	30%	10%	20%	37%	17%
Center	19	6	11	7	8	11	11
Right	41	75	59	83	72	52	72
Campus Unrest:							
Left	†	†	40%	12%	31%	43%	11%
Center	†	†	18	24	22	20	23
Right	†	†	42	64	47	37	66
Minorities:							
Left	49%	18%	50%	25%	39%	52%	25%
Center	25	35	24	24	22	23	27
Right	26	47	26	51	39	25	48

Standard of Living:							
Left	53%	28%	53%	21%	39%	50%	18%
Center	16	22	23	24	23	24	25
Right	31	50	24	55	38	26	57
Busing:							
Left	19%	4%	23%	2%	14%	22%	3%
Center	10	2	8	2	5	8	4
Right	70	94	69	96	81	70	93
Five Issues:							
Left	51%	18%	45%	15%	34%	50%	16%
Center	30	42	30	33	31	29	34
Right	18	40	25	52	35	21	50
Liberal Conservative:							
Left	48%	24%	50%	14%	33%	54%	13%
Center	38	33	36	44	41	32	37
Right	14	43	14	42	26	14	50

* The format for the amnesty question was suitable for collapsing into two categories only.

† Data unavailable because primary voting and campus unrest questions were on opposite half-samples in the study design.

SOURCE: Center for Political Studies, as reported in Arthur H. Miller, Warren E. Miller, Alden S. Raine, and Thad A. Brown, "A Majority Party in Disarray: Policy Polarization in the 1972 Election." A Paper Delivered at the 1973 Annual Meeting of the American Political Science Association, Washington, D.C.

voters were significantly more "left," the others more "right." The trends in comparing the McGovern supporters with Democratic party identifiers in the general electorate, while slightly modified, were along the same lines.

Not surprisingly, the pro-reform element within the party had a different conception of what a party should be and what standards it should emphasize in rewarding its members (Table 13.4). There was a split approximating a two to one difference in the qualities found desirable for national convention delegates. The McGovern delegates emphasized policy commitments and the party regulars stressed previous work on behalf of the party and the ability to represent of the party's interest as prime considerations. The same type of difference appears in the factors they reported as influencing their decision-making. The McGovern delegates favored issue-oriented candidates who supported a democratized decision-making process within the party. They placed less value on party service, the need to avoid internal squabbles within the party, and the role of the party organization in determining nominations. The party regulars took opposing positions.

On the functions best served by a national convention, the reformers (when measured in relation to those most strongly supportive of the new reforms) and the anti-reformers (those least supportive) again disagreed. Reformers were less concerned than regulars that the purpose of a national convention was to unify the party or put together a team that could win the election. The reformers were more in favor of national conventions that took relevant issue stands and they were strongly supportive of party reform.

The attitudinal and demographic differences between reformers and regulars alarmed the party professionals. One Humphrey supporter described the new breed of McCarthy delegates to the 1968 national convention as "McWhinnies":

> The McWhinnies [McCarthy supporters] are like little boys with marbles; if you don't play by their rules—they want to break up the game. . . . The party structure is always open to people who are interested in working. . . . It's just that we have a sort of seniority system like Congress; those who make the most contribution get the largest say in what we do. That's only fair. . . . The problem is that while the McCarthy kids want into the party they want in at the top. They aren't interested in the status which the beginner usually gets licking envelopes and things like that, which we did, all of us, when we were coming up.[11]

Based on her analysis of the delegates to the 1972 national convention, Jeane Kirkpatrick argued that the "new elite" was unrepresenta-

TABLE 13.4 ATTITUDES OF REFORM (McGOVERN DELEGATES)
AND REGULAR DELEGATES TOWARD VALUES CONSIDERED
IMPORTANT IN PARTY DECISIONS,
1972 DEMOCRATIC NATIONAL CONVENTION

I. Qualities considered important for a delegate to have, by candidate preference:

Qualities of Delegate	McGovern Delegates	Regular Delegates
Works Hard for the Party	33%	60%
(N)	(296)	(307)
Strong Policy Views	50%	26%
(N)	(440)	(307)
Represents Party Interests	40	75%
(N)	(361)	(390)

II. Factors that will influence a delegate's decisions at the convention, by candidate preference:

Factors	McGovern Delegates	Regular Delegates
Counting Party Service in Nominating Candidates	5%	35%
(N)	(34)	(145)
Minimize Disagreements in Party	26%	51%
(N)	(231)	(254)
Stayed Firm for Issue Position	17%	11%
(N)	(136)	(46)
Minimize Role of Party Organization in Nomination	20%	4%
(N)	(164)	(20)
Compromise on Issues to Improve Chance of Victory	13%	25%
(N)	(13)	(120)
Encourage Broad Participation in Decision-Making	75%	50%
(N)	(649)	(245)
Select Candidate Committed to Issues	74%	28%
(N)	(644)	(122)

SOURCE: 1972 National Convention Delegate Survey.

tive of the party; threatened the older cultural values held by most party members; were younger, well-educated professionals with the skills necessary to effectively contest in a more open, media-oriented and confrontational style; and held philosophic and policy views that were detrimental to the political system. As a consequence, the "new class," according to Kirkpatrick, "has an impact on the capacity of the parties to represent voters, most of whom are attached to traditional views and values."[12] It would profoundly alter the assumption that winning the election is the party's principal objective, a belief that is "the foundation of the theory and practice of two-party politics as we have known it" and constitutes the "basis of the expectation that American parties will continue to be inclusive, aggregative, pragmatic, responsive, and representative."[13]

A provocative argument and one believed in varying degrees by many regulars and neoconservatives. The obvious solution was to void the reforms that had brought about these consequences. Hence the reaction to replace the quotas, force the representation of party regulars in national conventions, and put the professionals back in charge of state delegation selection procedures.

It soon became fashionable to talk of "party-building," "consensus," "cohesion," and "governance," as if these abstract goals, once presumably an integral part of the party process, had been somehow lost in the transfer to a more open system. The regulars were determined to reincorporate these virtues "back" into the party. One way to do it, they believed, was to again close the party. The most notable example of an attempt of this nature took place in Michigan. Acting under pressure from Morley Winograd, the state chair and head of the commission studying presidential selection, the Michigan party substantially restricted participation in its nominating system.

By implication, if not in actuality, the state party appeared to require a financial contribution as a precondition for party membership and some formal, party-inspired acknowledgment of membership as a condition for participation in its caucus-centered presidential nominating system. The caucus system instituted for 1980 replaced the primary system in effect in 1976.

The result: 704,149 Michigan Democrats participated in that state's presidential nominating politics in 1976. In 1980, only 40,635 managed to *qualify* to participate in the presidential nominating caucuses and *only 16,048* actually did participate.

What happened to the "lost" 688,101 Democrats? Does such a change promote party vitality? Or party consensus-building? Or party anything? It is hard to believe that it does.

Further, the Michigan Democratic party then held a "beauty contest" primary in conjunction with the Republican primary about six weeks after its delegate selection caucuses. Sixty-five thousand Democrats participated. Neither of the Democratic party's principal contenders for the presidential nomination, Jimmy Carter or Edward Kennedy, appeared on the ballot and the result had no influence on the state party's national convention delegation. The delegates had already been selected. The procedures were close to those employed in the pre-reform era.

It can be argued that the Michigan experience in 1980 was experimental, which is true. It can also be argued that there were foul-ups and misunderstandings, which is also likely and, in fact, which any changes to a more restricted system are likely to entail. It is difficult to say what is gained from such an approach. It is most unlikely that the party can return to pre-reform days, close its nominating processes (and other party procedures) and still survive.

A Policy-Oriented Party

Clearly, the delegates to the post-reform national conventions prized an issue-relevant party more than did the party regulars comfortable with the politics of the old party system. Reformers thought a contemporary party might begin to appeal to the disaffected and politically unaffiliated, possibly even reversing the decline in party influence, by intelligently addressing the major issue concerns of the day. Anti-reform party regulars believed such appeals destroyed the unity and cohesion of the party and, in more extreme form as the Kirkpatrick quote indicates, the very essence of a "winning is everything" political psychology. Reformers would contend that little benefit was derived from parties that stood for nothing of consequence, offered few solutions or alternatives, and refused to be directly accountable to their membership.

The commitment to an issue-oriented party runs through the entire reform movement. Based on her analysis of the 1972 national conventions, Kirkpatrick has argued that the Democratic convention was unrepresentative of its party's base (unlike the Republican party's national convention) and that this result was a direct consequence of the reforms. She then writes that the degree of association between "elite and mass opinion will not tell us whether the political system is democratic. . . . but the extent of correspondence between mass and elite opinion does tell us whether the system of representation is working in such a way that it offers citizens the opportunity of supporting leaders who share their views and values and opposing those who do not."[14]

It is not a bad criteria for assessing the reforms, although it should not be the only one. With the presidential selection system restructured and the real power over nominations placed in the rank and file participants within the states, it should not be too surprising that a national convention comes to reflect the views of the winning coalition within the party. A more relevant standard of the correspondence between elite and mass positions within party ranks would be the range and adequacy of the choices offered the voters in the primary and caucus states. Under the reform system, the focus has changed and questions of representativeness should be addressed to the broader presidential delegate selection processes. The major concerns should be: *the extent to which the activist seeking delegate seats, the presidential contenders, and those party members voting in primaries (or, to a lesser degree, participating in the caucuses) are generally representative of the party's constituencies; whether the party's voters are offered meaningful alternatives among the candidate and policy views relevant to contemporary political needs and reflective of the broad spectrum of potential party contenders and party concerns; and whether the procedures continue to be open enough that the choice of the majority of the grassroots activists participating in the nominating process determines the party's eventual nominee.* The reformed nominating structure would do well by these measures.

Whatever the standard used, the days of "take-it-or-leave-it" party politics are over. Both parties are being forced to speak to the relevant concerns of the voters and to respond to the needs of an electorate in which policy matters have assumed a greater influence in voting decisions. The move toward issue relevance in voter perceptions is a reality of contemporary politics. However persuasive the case appears for a return to the old party system or an issue-less politics, neither is any longer possible. Both parties will have to meet (and both have begun to do so) the needs of an electorate in transition no longer content to render the traditional subservience and blind homage party regulars have grown to expect.

Conclusion

Fundamental differences exist then between reformers and anti-reformers as to the kind of party system best suited to the present-day political world. A party for the few, or one for the many; elitist or participant-oriented; backward- or forward-looking; policy-relevant or "indirectly" representative; open or closed; flexible or static; authoritarian or democratic; and most significantly, relevant or irrelevant to contemporary life. The choices offered are clearcut enough.

The transition from the old party system to one more suited to the modern age has been slow, and in most aspects, remains unfinished. The present party system is a cross between many elements of the old interbred with some of the new. The indecisiveness of the party's commitment satisfies few. One thing is predictable: The fight will continue with the outcome yet to be decided.

PART THREE

A Case Study of Reform and Its Impact at the Local Level

FOURTEEN

Chicago: An Unlikely Setting for "Reform"[1]

Chicago's former mayor, the legendary Richard J. Daley, has left us with several notable quotations and many indelible political memories, not the least of which constituted the bookends of one of the most remarkable eras of party reform in this nation's history. From his behavior as host and leading symbol of the reactionaries at the 1968 Democratic National Convention in Chicago to the behavior of his delegation and its, and his, eventual expulsion from the 1972 Democratic National Convention, Mayor Daley came to serve as a negative reference for some and as a rallying point for others in the efforts to come to grips with the reforms introduced into delegate selection procedures by the McGovern-Fraser Commission. Daley, although the perspective is oversimplified and personalized (no one is as good or bad as some in this episode might lead one to believe), represents a good vantage point from which to view the ramification of the changes that swept through one national party in an unprecedently short four-year period.

First, a few words on the Mayor's good points: Daley long enjoyed a national reputation as the Mayor who made Chicago "work." During his long tenure as Mayor (he held office from 1955 until his death in 1976) he was credited with reviving the city's economy, rebuilding huge sections of its downtown area, introducing to the city one of the most extensive networks of interstate roads, and creating a series of municipal monuments that ranged from O'Hare Airport (the world's busiest) to the Picasso sculpture in the Daley-built Civic Center. Daley had long been a power in national Democratic politics. Richard Nixon (and perhaps others also) credited the Mayor with winning the 1960 presidential election for John Kennedy. Since one of the new President's first invitations for a personally conducted tour of the White House went to the Daley family, others were willing to concede the Mayor had a major role in the outcome. None of this hurt the perception of Daley's influence on national party affairs. For these reasons, the Chicago Challenge to the national party reforms provided an acid test of the party's commitment to its new rules. The challenge of the Mayor's delegation to the proposed changes was the biggest obstacle the new party reforms had to face before being accepted. The test of wills in due time would unalterably change the face of national politics. The issues raised by the confrontation go to the heart of the reform debate. The facts of the struggle are clear enough and by themselves make for interesting reading.

Daley's Chicago

The Mayor was fond of advising one and all that power was dangerous unless, as he used to say, "you have humility." Daley's humility and that of the political machine he headed was legendary. It is reflected in the words of Alderman Claude W. B. Holman, presiding officer in the Chicago City Council until his death in the years after the 1972 convention, the heir to Congressman William Dawson's black South-side organization, a power in Chicago machine politics, a challenged delegate to the 1972 national convention and, above all, a Daley loyal-ist. Holman, appearing before an assembly of national party leaders convened to ajudicate the dispute over the 1972 credentials challenges, compared the possible unseating of Daley (and his colleagues) to the assassination of Caesar. "You can't take Caesar down!" the good alder-man cried.[2] (Daley might have put it differently. As he once said: "They have vilified me, they have crucified me, yes they have even criticized me."[3]) Such "humility" resulted in a blindness to implications of the changes in party rules, a predeliction toward business as usual and eventually a stunned disbelief—a reaction shared as well by those who had no involvement with or even any sympathy toward the Chicago machine—as to the final outcome. Mayor Daley, the symbol of oppres-sion for many in 1968 but also, and unquestionably, the single, most powerful man in the loose coalition of state and local Democratic parties that nominate the presidential candidate, was ousted from the 1972 national convention. A recounting of what happened does much to highlight the nature of the reform movement and to illustrate its impact as well as its strengths and its potentially critical weaknesses.

Chicago's Attitude toward National Party Reform

It is difficult for anyone outside of Chicago to appreciate its political atmosphere. There is a clubbiness, xenophobia, pervasive corruption, and official insensitivity of staggering proportions. Normal political processes have been so compromised as to render any reliance on these virtually useless. Everything of consequence is done through the machine—and for a price. Few appear to question or to care. And fewer yet challenge. The machine operates on the assumption that every person has his price—measured in economic rewards, power, or community honors—a pretty fair and quite successful operating principle. With such an insularity, abuses are bound to grow. The concerns of the outside appear far off, and more significantly, irrelevant. Such an attitude leads to difficulties, and the problems the machine encountered in getting their people to the 1972 national convention vividly illustrated just how much they had become victimized by their own parochialness and indirectly by their own past political success.

In the post-1968 period, reform came slowly to the Illinois Democratic party, an appendage of the Cook County (Chicago) Democratic organization. It came even more reluctantly to Chicago itself. As criticism arose as to Chicago's performance (especially in applying the new rules) in the months immediately preceding the 1972 convention, Daley (who favored hyperbole) brushed aside any hint of trouble. The reforms, he asserted, "worked better here (in Chicago) than anywhere else in the country,"[4] a refrain to be heard often in the weeks that followed. From the Mayor's vantage point, this boast was undoubtedly true. The reforms certainly had done little to inconvenience the machine or to change its mode of operation. As pressure mounted, Daley was pressed further. Angered, his views became clearer. He told a group of party workers that he "didn't give a damn about the rules of the McGovern Commission."[5] He went on to state: "We'll elect our delegates as we always have. Why the hell should we let those people in Washington tell us how we should elect them?" Once they got to the national convention and took their seats, Daley concluded "no one would dare throw them out."[6] It should be noted that the smart money would have bet Daley to be right.

Daley's miscalculation, as it turned out, bordered on the incredible. In the course of pursuing business as usual, he became embroiled in the most far-reaching challenge to the essence of the reforms ever mounted. In fact, as his indignation later expanded, so did his attack on the national party, eventually questioning the authority of a national party convention to rule on its own membership, a power it had been exercising for the 140 years of its existence without serious judicial controversy. He and his lieutenants attempted to force the courts, right up to and including the Supreme Court (convened in an extraordinary summer session), into a repudiation of its historic posture of noninvolvement in internal party matters. The machine would have had the Supreme Court champion its cause—or alternatively coerce the national party to pay a heavy penalty for their actions.

The machine's demeanor combined a blend of arrogance (and as events moved along) disbelief and eventually vindictiveness (which the successful challengers were to live with for a long time to come). All involved, from national party leaders to the media, were quick to grasp the significance of the drama. A record number of challenges were lodged with the national party. Undoubtedly, the one from California, questioning the allocation of its huge delegate vote, had the most significant immediate impact on the nomination. Yet for long-run consequences to the party, the Chicago Challenge was the most critical. It, as one local commentator wrote, "is the blockbuster, . . . both sides appear to agree that the legitimacy of the party and its convention are at stake."[7] Indisputably, this was the case by the time the challenge reached the national convention's Credentials Committee. As a consequence, many long-time party professionals (more significant than the reformers, newcomers or disgruntled holdovers from the 1968 national convention), who would normally have been expected to sympathize with the Mayor's plight and support his position, felt the integrity of the national party was at issue. As a consequence, they joined forces with the reformers to defeat Daley. The mood was best summed up by Matt Troy, a tough Irish boss from New York. In words the Daley delegates could understand, Troy angrily charged Daley with putting "the older line political hacks into the convention so they would do what he told them to." He continued: "I broke my back trying to conform to those new party rules, and I'll be damned if I'm going to let Mayor Daley get away with ignoring the rules and doing things his way."[8]

Quite obviously, the Chicago Challenge grew to be something other than a fight to repudiate a holdover symbol from an earlier, discredited convention; more than a rejection of the "old politics"; and more than a local political squabble bucked up to the national level. It represented an attack on the entire conception of the reform effort leveled at its most vulnerable point (enforcement) by the most powerful individual within the party. The controversy helps to illustrate the impact the reforms were to have on all levels of party operations—from the national to the local level. If the reforms could leave their imprint on the Chicago machine, their success elsewhere would be virtually assured.

The Facts of the Challenge

The incidents leading to the Chicago Challenge are easily recounted. On March 21, 1972, the Illinois primary was held to elect, among other things, delegates to the national conventions. As expected, the machine candidates dominated the Democratic primary results. But the battle had just begun. Within ten days of the primary, ten individuals acting in concert and including Aldermen William Singer, William Cousins, Anna Langford, and the Reverend Jesse Jackson filed written notice of a challenge on behalf, as they phrased it, "of Democrats in general, and, in particular, all Blacks, Latin Americans, Women, and Young People."[9]

The machine at first ignored the challenge, letting the ten-day interval in which they were required to reply to the challenge elapse without official comment. This show of indifference lasted until April 19th. At that point, Alderman Paul Wigoda, a challenged delegate who was a machine stalwart and the law partner of another challenged delegate (City Council President Thomas E. Keane, second in importance in the organization to Daley), filed a civil action in the State Circuit Court asking the following: that Wigoda be declared a proper representative of the "uncommitted" fifty-nine delegates and thirty-one alternates being challenged; that all challenged delegates be declared duly elected under Illinois law and entitled to take their seats at the National Convention; and that the defendants (Singer et al.) be enjoined from taking any action (i.e., pursuing their challenge before the Credentials Committee of the national party) that would interfere with Wigoda and associates acting as delegates. The local courts were chosen because the machine could expect a favorable ruling from these judges, many of whom had been placed on the bench by the machine and some of whom were former law partners of major figures in the city government. In filing his suit, Wigoda was quoted as saying that "first of all, I never read the laws of the [national] Democratic Party and [second] I am not bound by them."[10] The war had been joined.

Previous Practice

Prior to the reform period, the practice of the machine had been to meet before the primary and select (slate) those it wanted elected. Nominations for the delegate positions in each presidential election year were rotated among the fifty ward and thirty township committeemembers that constituted the eighty-member Cook County Central Committee. Party chieftains who made the slating decisions looked on the nominations as a reward for faithful service and an honor for the recipient (although the party workers who had to pay the expense of attending an out-of-town convention did not always share their leaders' enthusiasm). Those nominated to seek delegate positions put themselves forward as "uncommitted" to any major candidate, thus allowing Mayor Daley to control a large bloc of delegate votes and giving him maximum bargaining leverage at the national convention.

While Mayor Daley doubled as Cook County Democratic chair, the decisions as to slating were made by the county organization in cooperation, formally at least, with an essentially moribund state committee. The remaining nonelective delegate posts were filled by the state convention some time after the primary and went usually to party functionaries, fundraisers and public officeholders.

The organization, at the grass-roots level, consisting of the precinct workers, many of whom were beholden to their ward captains for their livelihoods, went out and worked for the machine's official slate in the primary. The machine published and distributed sample ballots with their candidates' names (only) on them, held pep rallies, conducted house-to-house canvases, mobilized the vote on election day, and absorbed the costs of the campaign. In most states, party endorsements in the intra-party, pre-nomination phase of campaigns (much less active support for a factional slate of candidates) is unheard of. The primary is considered an internal party mechanism for deciding the party's representatives for the general election. In Chicago, such was not the case. All-out primary electioneering by the machine was an accepted fact of life. The basic position of the challengers was that despite the reforms mandated at the national level that, among other things, denied preferential treatment to one slate of candidates, things had changed little.

Reform in the Illinois Party

This is not to say that Illinois had remained outside the orbit of the reform. In 1971 (the first state in the nation to so act according to Daley), three changes had been enacted into law. These permitted a potential delegate to declare his or her support of a presidential contender or to have "uncommitted" appear beside his or her name on the ballot; apportioned delegate seats through a formula based on population and former presidential vote, a refinement that both met national party standards and benefitted the machine by increasing the Chicago-area representation; and limited filings for delegate positions to the year of the national convention. The state party also adopted written rules as required by the McGovern-Fraser Commission but did so *after* the primary had been held, a delay that hurt their position in the later challenge. Further, the machine aligned itself against (and thus killed) a bill drafted by an Illinois Muskie backer to require potential delegates who wished to run committed to a presidential contender to receive the candidate's permission in writing. The purpose of the proposed legislation was two-fold: to prevent overfiling (too many candidates running for too few delegate seats, a move that diluted a presidential contender's vote); and to assure that all those elected as delegates pledged to a contender were bona fide supporters. As it turned out, Illinois was the only state in the nation that failed to give a presidential contender some form of control over delegates filing on his behalf.

Such as they were, these changes represented the sum of the reforms. Given the background of Chicago politics and the machine's role in previous primaries, a challenge to the old ways was not unexpected. In fact, Singer (a young, independent Democratic alderman, Daley's chief adversary, and the man behind the challenge) had let it be known before the primary that anyone wishing to challenge elected delegates on the basis of machine irregularities would receive a sympathetic hearing from him and the groups supporting his position. Chief among the latter was the Committee on Illinois Government, a reform-oriented independent group begun approximately two decades earlier by then Governor Adlai Stevenson. Singer and his associates also collected the evidence of organizational involvement and abuse during the primary campaign that laid the basis for the challenge.

On the other side, the state party chair, a Daley functionary, could claim that the organization's candidates would still go to Miami Beach. "We've always done it before. But it won't be easy as it used to be," he conceded,[11] prophetic given the events that were to transpire. Daley meanwhile was his usual voluble, aggressive self. He attacked, as he was to do often, the "so-called Democrats" (those who did not follow the machine line) and labelled the "committed" (nonmachine) primary candidates a "bunch of fakers." If those favoring presidential contenders, he reasoned, have a right to put together their slates, "then we have a right to put together our slates, too."[12] Excluding the bombast, on the face of it, the argument sounds reasonable enough—that is, until the opposition's contention is examined in depth.

The basis of the challenge

The challenge itself was directed against fifty-nine uncommitted delegates and thirty-one alternates elected to fill all but three delegate and three alternate vacancies (these went to Muskie backers) in eight congressional districts in Chicago or overlapping the city and the suburbs. The challengers claimed violations in two regards: that blacks, Latin Americans, women, and youth were grossly and unfairly underrepresented in the delegations; and that the elected delegates were "slated, endorsed and supported by the Democratic Party organization of Chicago without open slate-making procedures, without public rules relating thereto, and by Party officials who had themselves been chosen prior to 1972."[13] These constitute abuses of six reform guidelines.

The reformers claimed that the two thrusts of the challenge were closely related (unrepresentative procedures leading to unrepresentative results). On examination, the inability of the machine's delegation to meet the "quota" standards was obvious. To satisfy the McGovern-Fraser criteria, twenty-one delegates would have had to be black, six Latin Americans, twenty-nine women, and eighteen youth. In turn, the "Daley 59," as the press called them, included twelve blacks, one Latino, six women, and eight young people.

The machine made no apologies for its choices. They were put forward as the elected representatives of the primary voters. Clearly though, the Mayor's organization had no sympathy for the quota concept. As a former president of the League of Women Voters in Chicago was later to testify, when she asked a precinct worker canvassing for her vote why the organization's slate did not contain more women she was told: "Women don't belong in politics."[14]

The crux of the challengers' case rested on the less glamorous set of charges, the argument that the machine had slated and then done its best in the primary to elect its own delegates. To meet the reform rules, the Daley organization would have had to ensure that the people doing the slating had been chosen for that specific purpose with adequate public notice and not prior to the calendar year of the national convention, that the meetings had been well publicized and open to all party members and that there had in fact been widespread participation, and that procedural safeguards had been extended to all participants including the means for initiating meaningful challenges to those included on the designated slate. Furthermore, the slate once assembled would have to demonstrate a "reasonable relationship" to the social characteristics of the district it purported to represent. And party rules would have to exist explaining how party members could participate in the process.

The challengers claimed that the Daley organization defaulted on each count, resulting in "gross and deliberate" violations of the reforms according to Singer. As for the "Daley 59's" contention, and a powerful one it was, that the will of 900,000 Chicago Democratic voters (the primary turnout) would be voided if their delegates were unseated, the Singer group argued that the electors had not been given a meaningful opportunity to participate in the first, and critical, stage of slate-making. The slates were drawn up in secret well before the presidential election year by party officials elected for other purposes. The organization then went out and employed its considerable resources to elect its designated representatives.

The slates themselves were typical machine creations, including mostly old-line politicians who as one precinct worker informed a prospective primary voter had been selected "on account of the fact that they were in the 'Organization' for many years."[15] This last contention appears incontrovertible. The machine showed a decided preference for its own, slating Mayor Daley and thirty-seven of the fifty Chicago ward committeemembers and such other organizational stalwarts as (according to the Credentials Committee report) "the Cook County Clerk [as well as the President of the Cook County Board and the Clerk of Courts], the Sheriff of Cook County, the President of the Chicago City Council [and twelve other machine aldermen], in-laws or relatives of committeemen, the son [and cousin] of Chairman Daley, other party officials, party candidates for public office and persons described as 'confederates of the Chairman or otherwise affiliated with the Democratic organization.' "[16] In each instance, moreover, the slate corresponded exactly to the number of positions available. In short, the organization had done its work as it normally did, effectively foreclosing any realistic chance that a sizable number of others would be represented at the Miami Beach Convention.

The Contest Begins

National party leaders were aware of what was happening in Chicago, and they were upset. In an effort to head off any misunderstanding as to the reforms or their mandatory status, National Chair Lawrence F. O'Brien, in an apparent reaction to the Wigoda suit, issued an unusually strong statement in late April 1972. "Those states that remain in non-compliance with the delegate selection guidelines," he said,

> "must make the necessary changes, promptly. Any state delegation that comes to Miami Beach having been selected by procedures that violate the delegate selection rules of the 1972 Call are certain to be challenged. *The issue is clear beyond debate.*" (Italics added.)[17]

The Mayor disagreed. An ugly and tumultuous battle had commenced.

The Daleyites' defense, initially, was tactical. It was bold and it almost worked. Their belief was that they could prevent the hearing officer from the Credentials Committee assigned to Chicago from even holding the meetings necessary to establish the facts of the case and thus making the report to the full committee necessary for its deliberations. Once the issue went to the floor of the national convention in Miami Beach, they expected little trouble.

They persevered and they almost carried it off. To them, the challenge was a nuisance, little more. Similar to many such incidents in the past, they firmly believed it would disappear, the challengers

Chicago Challenge

Chronology of Events

February 24, 1972	Meeting of ward committeemen when Daley is quoted as saying he "didn't give a damn about the rules of the McGovern Commission" and "once the delegates were seated no one would dare throw them out."
March 21	Illinois primary.
March 31	"Written Notice of Intent to Challenge" filed with Credentials Committee by Singer et al.
April 19	Challenged delegate, Alderman Paul Wigoda, files suit on behalf of all the elected delegates in State Circuit Court requesting an injunction to stop challenge.
April 20	Challengers (Singer et al.) file suit in U.S. District Court to have case removed to federal court.
May 2	Wigoda countersuit to have federal case remanded to state court denied.
May 3	Challengers file suit in U.S. District Court to enjoin organization from getting an injunction.
May 18	Federal judge (in response to May 3rd suit) rules he does not have jurisdiction in Wigoda case; that forum for settling dispute is Credentials Committee of National Convention; does put off action for ten days, permitting machine from interfering with process and thus allowing Credentials Committee hearing officer to hold meeting.
May 24 (24th & 25th scheduled meeting days)	Louis Oberdorfer, first Credentials Committee hearing officer, arrives in Chicago; holds stormy meeting with principals; asks to be relieved.
May 25	Challengers postpone caucuses intended to select alternate slate.
May 26	Second federal judge issues restraining order against "Daley 59" that permits a new hearing officer to conduct investigation into facts of case. Credentials committee chairperson, Mrs. Pa-

	tricia Roberts Harris, appoints Cecil Poole as new hearing officer.
May 31 (Wednesday)	Credentials Committee's Chicago hearings begin with Cecil Poole as new hearing officer.
June 1 (Thursday)	Credentials Committee's Chicago hearings continue.
June 2 (Friday)	160 Convention delegates meet in Springfield to elect 10 at-large delegates.
June 6	California "winner-take-all" primary won by McGovern (who also captures New Jersey, New Mexico, and South Dakota primaries on same day).
June 8	Credentials Committee's Chicago hearings resume and after long day are completed.
June 9	State Democratic Convention meets in Springfield to ratify the election of at-large delegates and alternates; doubles number of at-large delegates from 10 to 20 and alternates from 9 to 18; additional delegates appointed.
June 12	Challenge to expanded at-large delegation initiated.
June 16	Full convention delegation meets in Springfield to elect delegate chairman and other officers and delegates to serve on 3 convention committees (6 per committee); does not select proper proportion of women, leading to rejection of state representatives by convention committee and another Illinois-instituted court suit.
June 17	Watergate break-in.
June 19	Federal District judge in Washington, D.C., upholds Keane, Wigoda, et al. challenge and voids guidelines A-1, A-2, C-4, and part of C-6.
June 20	Federal Appeals Court overturns lower court decision but indicates suit could be renewed pending outcome of credentials Committee hearings.
June 21	Daley returns to Chicago (from mayors' conference in New Orleans) and convenes meeting of party leaders.

June 22	Chairman refuses to seat Illinois representatives (and 9 other state delegations) to Rules Committee of convention (and other convention committees because male/female ratio violates national party rules).
	Challengers hold congressional district caucuses as first step in selecting their delegations; meetings disrupted by Daley forces.
June 23	Daley capitulates and restructures convention committee delegations, giving equal weight to men and women; new delegation permitted full voice in Rules Committee deliberations.
June 24	Challengers convene their county convention to make final selection for alternative delegation; meeting disrupted briefly at opening by Daley forces.
June 26	Credentials Committee's full hearings open in Washington, D.C.
June 27	Credentials Committee meeting continues; Cecil Poole report on Chicago Challenge released.
June 28	Frank Mankiewicz attempts to mediate Chicago dispute.
	Democratic caucus in House of Representatives initiated by, among others, Congressman Frank Annuzio of Chicago, a machine figure, denounces new reforms.
June 29	Humphrey California challenge to McGovern California victory sustained by 72–66 vote in Credentials Committee.
June 30	Chicago Challenge of Singer et al. upheld in Credentials Committee by 71–61 vote; Daley and 58 other machine representatives unseated.
July 1	John Mitchell quits as head of Committee to Re-Elect the President; Clark MacGregor chosen to replace him.
July 3	U.S. Federal District judge upholds Credentials Committee decisions in Illinois and California controversies.

July 4	Credentials Committee ends Washington deliberations.
July 5	U.S. Court of Appeals upholds Credentials Committee decision on Chicago but reverses its ruling on California and returns to McGovern 151 votes he lost.
July 7	U.S. Supreme Court rejects suits (thus upholding Credentials Committee's original decisions) stating that only the Democratic National Convention can determine a delegate's right to sit in on its deliberations.
July 10	Democratic National Convention convenes in Miami Beach.
	First session reverses Credentials Committee ruling on California (returning original 151 delegates to McGovern) and upholds committee's decision on Illinois unseating Mayor Daley and his delegation in session lasting well into the night. (adjournment comes at 4:52 a.m.).
July 12	McGovern wins presidential nomination.
July 13	Democratic National Convention recessed.
July 20	Jerome Torshen speaking for the Daley group seeks contempt ruling against Singer delegation for disobeying Cook County Circuit order not to take their seats in the convention.
September 14	Judge Daniel A. Covelli, on motion of Wigoda argued by Torshen, orders Singer group to show why they should not be held in contempt of Circuit Court; case to continue for years, up through Illinois court system to, eventually, U.S. Supreme Court.
January 22, 1975	The Supreme Court rules on the issues in the Chicago Challenge and in the process codifies in law significant new powers for the national parties in presidential selection. The Supreme Court rejected the contentions of the Daley group and found for the national party. In doing so, it ruled that not only did the national party have authority over the state party in matters relating to presidential delegate selection, but its authority in this area

even extended to state statutes that might be in opposition to its requirements. Contending that "the [National] Convention serves the pervasive national interest in [the] selection of candidates for national office, and [that] this national interest is greater than any interest of an individual State," the Court concluded that party rules relating to presidential delegate selection take precedence over state laws.

---

routed in disarray. In essence, this is what helps to make the fight so arresting: Daley was determined that no national party would apply *its* rules within *his* party. Conversely, if the national party backed down, its reforms—and whatever limited authority it yielded—were meaningless, a point O'Brien fully appreciated.

The Hearing Officers

Oberdorfer leaves

The first hearing officer, Louis Oberdorfer, appointed by the acting chair of the Credentials Committee, Patricia Roberts Harris, became the contest's first sacrifice. The hearing officers were to be persons "known by reputation to be fair and impartial in the context of the challenge and . . . experienced in the law."[18] Thirty-six, all distinguished lawyers, had been assembled (primarily by Burke Marshall, former assistant attorney-general under John Kennedy and a Yale Law School professor). They included men of legal reputation and good party credentials. And they donated their time, serving without pay.

Oberdorfer, an assistant attorney-general under both Kennedy and Johnson, soon found that Chicago politics could be tough. He came to the city and held an exploratory meeting which included all the principals to set procedures and establish the ground rules for the hearing into the facts that would serve as the basis for his report to the Credentials Committee. Under persistent questioning from challenged delegates Keane and Troy, it was established that the law firm with which Oberdorfer was associated represented the American Automobile Manufacturer's Association, whose member firms included General Motors, Ford, and Chrysler, all of whom were defendants in anti-pollution suits filed by the city of Chicago. In the eyes of the challenged members of the city's power structure, this would cause the lawyer to be biased against them. Second, the Daley group's lawyers brought out the fact that Oberdorfer's firm and that of the two chief counsels (Wayne Whalen and John Schmitt) for the challengers were co-counsels in a law case before the courts. An angry and flustered Oberdorfer put in a call to Washington to Harris asking to be relieved. He was, and the first round went to Daley's men.

The organization could not leave well enough alone. Practitioners of the overkill, they went on to demonstrate a flamboyance characteristic of Chicago politics. Troy, a challenged delegate from the 7th Congressional District as well as an attorney for the delegation, concurrent with the Oberdorfer episode (late May) was waging a guerilla war with the national party headquarters. The lawyer wired National Chair O'Brien demanding that Harris be fired because she failed to answer satisfactorily a number of questions he had forwarded relating to the challenge. The effort generated some local publicity but little else.

Poole arrives

Harris, apparently little bothered by the Troy episode, moved quickly to appoint Cecil Poole, 57, a black attorney from San Francisco and a Harvard Law School graduate, as the new hearing officer. An unknown quantity in Chicago, Poole had served at one time (1961–1970) as U.S. Attorney for the Northern District of California and at another had had an appointment to a high court vacancy blocked by Republican opponents. With the arrival of Poole, the game began anew (despite as it turned out, the effort by Keane to postpone the meeting until the local courts had ruled on the Alderman's suit—a decision expected to be favorable—prohibiting the challengers from doing anything to obstruct the elected delegates from taking their seats).

Poole was a shrewd lawyer, and despite a soft-spoken style and calm demeanor, a tough adversary. Perhaps the smartest lawyer in the room—the point was debated in an unintentionally comic scene at one stage by a red-faced, shouting young alderman who insisted that *he* was the smartest man at the hearing—he soon established himself as an unfailingly courteous but no-nonsense arbiter who had every intention of proceeding with and *finishing* the hearing. The organization got more than they bargained for; but as usual, they were determined to find out the hard way.

The initial encounter turned into quite a show. Liking a good thing when they saw it, the "Daley 59" lawyers began by demanding Poole disqualify himself. Their main argument was simplicity itself: Since Oberdorfer had, Poole should. Alternately shouting, pleading, and reasoning, they argued that Poole would undoubtedly be prejudiced against them because of what had happened the first time around.

Furthermore, he had probably read—or would read—the record of the initial meeting. Since it was not particularly pleasant, this review would prejudice his thinking. And by the way, did he perhaps know any of the challengers, serve as co-counsel with their lawyers on any case, or represent any group that was being sued by the city of Chicago?

When such attacks produced little, they changed the arguments: Poole was holding the hearings in violation of state law; the Credentials Committee had no jurisdiction; Poole was chosen as hearing officer in violation of Credentials Committee procedures (i.e., the machine claimed they had never been given a chance to submit their nominees); Poole favored the Black Panthers (a convoluted argument even the machine did not appear to place great faith in); Poole was probably a friend of Oberdorfer's since both had served in the Justice Department at the same time; Poole was a big city lawyer prejudiced against small midwestern (Chicago!) lawyers; Poole would probably favor the challengers on rules of procedure; and so on. But Poole persisted. He answered the objections, some many times over. He remained calm and he unmistakably indicated that the hearing would be held.

But the organization's lawyers—17 in all—were at least as stubborn. They next innundated Poole with over 50 motions, ranging from demands that the challenge be dismissed to requests for information and the clarification of procedural points (the latter were general standards for the most part, and since they had never been applied before, they provided ample opportunity for digression). The motions and verbal attacks were interspersed with veiled threats, often in the form of jokes, to Poole's well-being. The indomitable Troy, among others, asked publicly at what hotel Poole was staying and wondered aloud if he would be safe. Perhaps he should watch his home mail ("if it's ticking, throw it in the trash"[19]), a crude form of humor that the organization representatives thoroughly enjoyed. For others, anger replaced the heavy-handed bantering. Keane, the autocratic and detached leader of the City Council, in particular, seemed incensed with Poole's conduct of the meeting, calling it a "kangeroo court." "All my motions are over-ruled by you without argument," the agitated leader of the City Council complained,[20] not used to sitting while others made decisions. An unruffled Poole responded ("That sometimes happened") and went on with the meeting, a move that did not help Keane's temperament.

The pattern of the hearings

The wrangling continued throughout the four and one-half hour morning session and into midafternoon. Then with a few motions carried over for later decision, the challengers were given the opportunity to make a brief opening statement and to call their first witnesses. Their victory was short-lived. They decided to put the Reverend Jesse Jackson on first, primarily because he was leaving that day to join the McGovern campaign in California and they felt that since he was nationally known, there was a strategic advantage in having him testify. The choice was a mistake. Jackson knew little concerning the facts of the challenge or the contents of the reform guidelines. His testimony took slightly over a half-hour. The cross-examination took over three hours. Aldermen (and delegates) Holman and Vrydrolyak (then a relative newcomer to Chicago politics) painfully demonstrated Jackson's ignorance of the specifics of the issues involved. Jubilant at what they heard, the lawyers from each congressional district's delegation insisted on and received their crack at the witness, taking him over all aspects of Chicago and Cook County government. Flushed with victory, they shouted across the room to Singer that he was next. When bored with their questioning, they took random shots at Poole (as they were to each day) attempting to rattle or provoke him. As the session continued into the night, delay, harassment, and ridicule remained the basic response of the "Daley 59." The only humor of note came at the end of the lengthy first session when Troy pleaded with Poole (who had upcoming court appearances in San Francisco) to postpone in "fairness and good conscience" a scheduled future meeting that conflicted with a convocation of delegates in Springfield.[21] No one in recent memory could recall a machine representative making such an appeal.

The pattern continued into the second day. The first witness took 15 minutes to give her statement. The cross-examination took five times as long, focusing as much on intimidation as anything. Adjournments were sought to allow members to attend City Council meetings. The battle of wits continued to rage. Keane threatened to go into the home of every person who filed an affidavit on behalf of the challengers and take sworn depositions. Other machine supporters felt such bullying tactics went too far. The organization objected to every witness before they spoke (usually on the curious grounds that their testimony would be prejudicial to the machine) and they tried to have their comments stricken from the record when they were finished.

The hearing officer continued to sit it out. He refused to allow the ceaseless, repetitive questioning of witnesses. He asked the lawyers to consolidate their arguments and he attempted to ration the time available to each. The restrictions were difficult to enforce, leading halfway through the day's session to Poole's "Order of June 1st" setting strict limits on the proceedings: establishing the remaining schedule of hearings, requiring written statements of testimony, limiting the time available for cross-examination, and, worst of all, setting aside the bulk of a two-day period for the "Daley 59" to give their side (testimony they had no intention of delivering).

As the day wore on, Poole made it clear that if a pattern existed (i.e., the machine slated candidates at closed meetings and then campaigned for them) this would be sufficient evidence of abuse; witnesses did not have to establish specific guideline abuses *by each and every delegate* personally. In part, it was hoped that this ruling (much disputed by the organization members who would prefer to hang separately) would end the practice of each witness being asked to go down the list of the "Daley 59" by name to testify to violations by each of the delegates. The move met limited success. Still, and despite the delays, the hearings did move on in the late afternoon and in the evening session to some serious and eventually damaging witnesses. Persons began to appear who could testify to personal knowledge of hearing some of Daley's extravagant attacks on the reforms, his disregard of any intent to abide by them, and the machine's closed slating and continued electioneering. With these, the case began to be made and the realization set in that the machine ploys had failed: there would be a hearing and there was little the organization could do to prevent the available evidence from coming out.

Two full days of hearings (including one that pushed past midnight) had produced less than three hours of direct testimony. Nonetheless, the tide had turned. These two rowdy days were possibly the most significant of all those during the long months of the controversy. The national party had established its right, inferentially, to hold hearings and to adjudicate the dispute. The machine's attempt to prohibit totally any interference from the national party in the manner in which the local party had chosen and certified its delegation had failed.

Poole was clearly in charge as the hearings progressed. When next they resumed, eight days later, the organization was not in a mood to repeat the earlier performance. It had brought in its big guns—dramatically adjourning the City Council to ensure Keane, Holman, and the other aldermen would be there (precipitating a fight in the Council and prohibiting any business from being conducted in their absence)—all to little avail. Poole had mastered the onslaught. Meanwhile, much had happened in the days between meetings. The 160 delegates had convened in Springfield on the Friday following the first hearings to elect ten at-large members. They heard Daley, who assumed control of the group, castigate the reformers, claiming they were the same forces behind the riots at the 1968 national convention (an event he was never to forget). Daley again blamed the media ("the most lopsided reporting ever") and defended the police ("the police hit no one, but were attacked") before turning his oratorical and analytical skills to the substance of the challenge:

Now the same forces of the convention [1968] are at work, yelling about how we should select delegates by quotas. There can be no quotas in an election. The people establish these quotas by voting. [Daley's principal defense and a strong one.] I can only hope the people hoping for a confrontation hope as much for the party [sic]. And if they do, we'll elect the entire ticket.[22]

Daley's outburst had the unfortunate effect of buttressing many of the arguments his opponents were making. His proclamation, again, that no one dare put them out of the national convention placed his advocates—who were attempting to picture him as a man of reason who supported and fully applied the reform guarantees—in a difficult position.

On June 6th, two days before the hearing resumed, McGovern had virtually won the Democratic nomination by sweeping four primaries, including the all-important California test. The significance of these victories was that Daley would be facing a national convention presumably sympathetic to the reforms he had ridiculed. McGovern, with whom he had clashed on several occasions on reform questions and whom he inferentially blamed in part for the 1968 fiasco, now controlled the party convention. Finally, even if Daley won, his "uncommitted" delegates had lost their significance and his appeal at this stage could not entice other contenders (now seemingly out of the race) to come to his support. Matters did not turn out as simply as they appeared at this juncture—the California challenge launched by Humphrey again threw McGovern's nomination in doubt—but the atmosphere surrounding the third session had a finality not found in the others. All-out opposition by the machine stood to gain little.

The organization did revive their tactics of ridicule and veiled personal threats and they continued the paper blitz (motions, countermotions, affidavits, etc.), but their gusto was noticeably diminished. After several hours of renewed battle, their tactics had again failed to secure any material gains. Capitulating to the inevitable, the machine's lawyers sought the best deal they could. And they did not do badly. The challengers never did manage to present orally, for the television and the media, their full case. Too much time had been lost and the organization now wanted to speed up and complete the hearing, fighting their battle in some other location. Second, after having mercilessly badgered the early witnesses, they shrank from the spectacle of seeing some of their bigger names (Daley, for example) called upon to undergo similar treatment from the other side. They obtained agreement to avoid this unpleasantness by allowing the record for the case to be made and after one more lengthy day the hearing to be terminated.

The closing arguments, no less than the hearings more generally, demonstrated the inability of the combatants to agree on what precisely was at stake. Whalen, one of three lawyers for the challengers, accused the organization of showing "gross disregard," even "contempt," for the reforms. The results, he contended, ended in the "most flagrant violation of Democratic party rules in the nation."[23] The arguments of the challenged delegates failed to address these points. One of several lawyers speaking on their behalf, Ray Simon (later to appear before the Credentials Committee in a similar role), charged the Singer et al. group with wanting to take over power in Chicago, a theme that appeared repeatedly in their comments throughout the long struggle. He contended that national party rules cannot violate state law; that consequently, if Chicago delegates were challenged successfully, *all* delegates from Illinois would have to be unseated. Others on behalf of the "Daley 59" drew attention to the potential disenfranchising of Chicago voters (through voiding the primary decision), and one, Troy, warned that if the challenge carried it would represent "the death knell of the Democratic party as we know it."[24] All organization speakers hinted the party's presidential nominee would suffer if the challenge was sustained (a fact that must also have occurred to Mc-Govern and his advisors). On such a note did the climatic sessions in Chicago stagger to their close.

The Machine's Defense

The turn of events and the prospect of having their case decided on the national level forced the organization to develop its arguments more carefully. They chose two of their best lawyers to make the presentation before the Credentials Committee: Ray Simon, former city corporation counsel and a law partner of one of Daley's sons, whose manner was to affect a sincerity and reasonableness that contrasted with the shrill harangues of many of the others; and Jerome Torschin, an aggressive private attorney of independent legal reputation who represented Keane on other matters beside the challenge.

This defense of the Daleyites, the most serious they put forward, deserves attention. First, they argued that almost a million Chicago voters would be denied a voice in the national convention if they were unseated. Second, they maintained that any implicit quota system is impossible in a truly elective system. Third, they said any evidence of a machine-controlled primary was circumstantial, a not very convincing argument. Fourth, they attacked the manner in which the Singer delegates had been chosen and they questioned the representatives of the challengers' delegation, a most vulnerable aspect of the challenge, as will be shown, but one the Daley forces undercut through their own violent acts. Fifth, they denied the sincerity of the challengers, contending that they were not "good Democrats" and that they intended to destroy the party (i.e., oppose the Chicago organization).

If they had emphasized their stronger and more relevant arguments earlier (nos. 1, 2, and 4) rather than taking the blindly obstructionist approach they did, they would have given many people who were seeking it (in the name of political reality) grounds for supporting them or for arranging an attractive compromise on their behalf early in the proceedings and well before Daley's personal authority could be called into question. The Daleyites refused compromise; they offered little to those willing to take their side and they made no effort at coalition-building in support of their murky defense (until the full Credentials Committee hearing); they underestimated the strength of their opposition; they ignored the rules in effect and they chose to antagonize the national party, forcing them into the dispute on the side of their opponents; and they persisted in seeing the fight as a local squabble (a type of encounter they never lost) and fought it in this manner. In truth, the organization people did not appear to understand the nature of the controversy they were engaged in, consequently wasting a good deal of time in developing weak or extraneous positions. As things stood, their more relevant defenses were belatedly arrived at (consolidated after the well-publicized Chicago hearing) and they were not well received by the Credentials Committee, who now saw the issue differently: the total, arrogant, uncompromising defiance of the national party. Their tactical moves—court challenges, boasts as to the outcome, even continued defiance of the reform standards— were of greater importance at this stage of the controversy. These continued to be amateurish, initiated more from spite and anger than from any real effort to retain their convention seats. To understand the machine's response, it is necessary to appreciate the pressures the organization was under at this point in time. Within a broader context, the challenge to the fifty-nine delegates (which was to prove serious enough) was initially seen as one of many problems (and one of the least significant).

The Machine Has Its Problems

Unquestionably, it had been a tough year for the machine. A predawn raid over two years earlier (December 1969) by the state's attorney's office on a Black Panther apartment had resulted in the killing of two Panthers. The issues raised by the deaths and the police conduct in the raid had haunted the local party and the city administration over the intervening years. Events led in due course to a special investi-

gation by a court-appointed prosecutor and eventually to the indictment of the State's Attorney, Edward V. Hanrahan, a Daley favorite
and a machine "comer" (some believed the next mayor). Hanrahan
first received the machine's endorsement in the March primary. As
the case grew more ominous and the normally docile blacks organized
behind former machine lieutenant, U.S. Representative Ralph Metcalf,
to oppose Hanrahan and police practices more generally, the organization was split by a dispute. Many favored dropping Hanrahan while
others such as the aging but still influential Alderman Vito Marzullo
("Eddie's too tough!") wanted him retained as the party's candidate.
At the eleventh hour, Daley replaced Hanrahan as nominee with a
lackluster traffic court judge, publicized for his court reform and traffic
crackdowns (which later turned out to be nothing more than bookkeep-
ing changes combined with a publicity drive intended to make the
court's chief officer look good). Hanrahan won in a three-way race,
an outcome that led to mutterings about Daley's continuing political
judgment. (Hanrahan later lost the general election to a Republican
in an even bigger upset. He was acquitted of all charges in court just
prior to the November election, which, curiously, appeared to hurt
his candidacy.)

The scars from the intra-party war over Hanrahan did not heal
quickly. At the same time, the machine received another unexpected
jolt in the primary. It had endorsed a downstate Democrat, Lieutenant
Governor and later Congressman Paul Simon, for governor. Simon
lost a close race to Independent Democrat (and later Governor) Dan
Walker, an anti-machine candidate. Walker first gained prominence
as the author of a highly unfavorable official report into the conduct
of the city administration during the 1968 Democratic National Convention. Given these developments, the proposed Credentials challenge or the observance of the reform guidelines during the primary
election were not priority items on the organization's agenda.

The machine had been buffeted. And more was to come. Poole's
closing remarks as to how he was "deeply troubled"[25] by what he
had heard could not have been well received by the Chicago delegates.
This would have been a logical point for the machine to retrench,
soften its demands, and make the best of the situation. McGovern
was sympathetic and favored some type of compromise that would
seat the powerful Daley (a view he held until the final national convention vote on the issue) but he was not in a position to repudiate publicly
(thus weakening his candidacy) the reforms he helped father. The Daleyites appeared to demand nothing less. They were not open to compromise and they had yet to finish their assault on the new rules. In
fact, what followed amounted to the most frantic days of a demanding
election year for the Chicago party.

The State Convention

The day after Poole concluded his hearing the state convention met in Springfield, ostensibly to ratify the choice of the 10 at-large delegates selected a week earlier. The organization had other plans. Daley had been angered by the at-large vote of the 160 delegates which had rejected a number of old Chicago pros and two labor confidantes of the Mayor (although Daley's "uncommitted" slate had actually captured 6 of the 10 vacant slots). In fact, Daley had insisted on counting irregularly marked ballots which permitted "counting in" one more Chicago Democrat at the expense of a downstate party member. Nonetheless, the mayor was not placated. He proposed, and the State Democratic Convention ratified, a proposal to double the number of at-large delegates from 10 to 20 (giving each a one-half vote rather than a full vote) and the alternates from 9 to 18. Daley then appointed the newcomers. The move was another violation of national party rules and of the reform guidelines. It repudiated the national party's authority to set the size of state delegations and to authorize the division of the vote, it ignored the reform provision against split votes, and it violated both national party and reform standards as to how delegates were to be chosen. Daley simply assumed the power to appoint the new delegates. The state convention's delegates had not conferred such power on him nor did they vote on the appointees to the illegal vacancies. Daley no longer appeared to care.[26]

FIFTEEN

Chicago-Style Politics: The Machine Takes on the Reformers

A controversial series of developments came in the wake of the Chicago field hearing as both sides readied for the test to come before the national party. The events that followed provide a good insight into both the operations and concerns of the Chicago Democrats and the strengths, as well as weaknesses, of the reformers' position. They are recounted in detail and in the chronology in which they happened. As much as anything, the machine's heavy-handed response to the reformers' efforts to field a delegation was to adversely affect the case they were able to present to the national party's Credentials Committee.

Preparing for Battle: Two Hectic Weeks of Maneuvering

The first week opened with an irate Muskie delegate (the presidential candidate who lost the most when the at-large vote had been diluted) filing a challenge with the Credentials Committee. Said the delegate: "It is utterly disgusting to see how they [the party's state convention leadership] push things through, shout people down, not even attempt to make it [the proceedings] look legitimate. I now understand—not that I condone it—how people can be incited to violence."[1]

Under pressure, the machine often announces massive public-spirited projects: a new airport in the lake, a multi-storied bandshell over a sunken public garage, a new business complex constructed with the air rights over the railroad yards, a new civic auditorium, a new interstate highway to knife through the city, and the most persistent of all, a sports complex on the lake front with a new football stadium for the beloved Bears. Few of the projects ever come to pass, although they do divert public and press attention and they hold the promise of jobs for the faithful and contracts for the business community.

Tuesday. The Mayor launched an unusual part of his counterattack. He held a full-scale City Hall press conference to announce a "gigantic" (his word) new project, a "War on Litter." Surrounded by the streets and sanitations commissioner, the Chicago park district board president, the acting general superintendent of parks, the police and fire commissioners, and the president of the Chicago Federation of Labor, Daley indignantly told reporters that litter on the lakefront would not be tolerated. The Mayor assigned 1,000 additional workers (including 600 new people) to the battle, increased fines from the $5–$50 range to $50–$100, announced that a citizens' committee composed of businessmen and labor had been formed to fight litter, and asked the support of all Chicagoans in the battle. The Mayor vowed the cleanest 4th of July ever!

Daley also revealed the creation of a Citizen's Landmark Commission, to be appointed by the Mayor to help preserve architectural landmarks. Chicago already had such a commission (also appointed by the mayor) but the well-publicized action was taken after the demolition of the Old Stock Exchange Building, designed by Louis Sullivan, and the controversy it raised (including the death in the rubble of an architect scavenging for souvenirs).

Lost in the excitement was the rumor that U.S. Senator Adlai Stevenson might oppose Daley for the post of national convention delegation chair, a position Daley had held since 1956. Stevenson refused to deny the accounts. A Daley supporter put the reports in context: "If he [Stevenson] is taking on the Mayor, he's playing squash in White Sox Park."² The words, again, were prophetic.

Wednesday. The national party's legal counsel, Joseph Califano, responded to a request for a decision from an Illinois Muskie leader on the legality of the expanded delegation. Califano ruled that the number of delegates and their full votes had been set by the National Committee in its 1972 Call and could not be changed through the unilateral action of one state party. Daley's move was declared illegal.

Stevenson supporters claimed ninety votes (eighty-six were needed to win) for delegation chair "with more coming." Rather boldly, they inquired whether the Mayor would like to nominate Stevenson for the post "as a unity move."³ Stevenson and Daley met and assured each other they were in the contest to the end. The Mayor, continuing to emphasize his official duties, dedicated a controversial hotel built on public land at O'Hare Airport by private developers, including one city official and the owners of two local race tracks. The land has been leased with municipal financing. The Mayor described the hotel as a thirteen-year "vision."

Thursday. The Daley counteroffensive reached a crescendo. Stevenson's office began to hedge, claiming a "solid but slim" lead. The Mayor's supporters emphatically announced that Daley "has the votes, and will win."[4] Reports from various quarters circulated that the battle was "really bloody" and that the "screws are being turned." Supposedly, Daley was intent on being vindicated for 1968.

Daley, in turn, let it be known that he would fight any effort to cut Illinois' enlarged delegation. Taking their cue from Daley, state party officials spoke out. The vice-chair of the state party and the acting chair of the national convention delegation, John P. Touhy, referred to Califano's ruling as "just another lawyer's opinion." The state chair went on: "So what's the value of the opinion? . . . any question about the propriety of expanding the at-large delegation . . . [is] a matter for the Convention's committee to decide."[5]

State legislators continued to report threats against their party privileges and patronage allocations if they supported Stevenson. Touhy ruled that the expanded at-large delegates could participate in the vote for the state delegation's chair. A reporter asked Daley if he wanted to be chair: "That's a ridiculous question," an irate Daley answered and stormed off.[6] It was.

Friday. The June 16th meeting of the delegates turned out to be as explosive as anticipated. Several Daley supporters let it be known that they considered the enlargement of the delegation a violation of state law as well as party rules. Noting that the 59 delegates challenged partly rested their defense on the contention that they were properly elected under state law, one added: "But you can't say state law controls in the one case and not in the other."[7] Mrs. Dorothy V. Bush, secretary to the Democratic National Committee, announced that she would not issue credentials to the extra 10 delegates.

Stevenson people voiced fears of being counted out in the election for delegation chair. They admitted "some" delegates may have buckled under the political and economic pressure and abandoned Stevenson. To charges of pulling out all the stops, one Daley supporter replied: "Sure, this ain't no kids game you know."[8] Television commentators began to refer to the confrontation as an "alley fight," and remarked on the "unbelievable pressure" and "arm-twisting" by the pro-Daley forces. One delegate reported that Daley "called in all the political notes [due] of me and my father before me."[9] Sponsors of an equal rights amendment pending in the Illinois legislature reported that the bill was held up awaiting their actions on the chairmanship fight. Other legislators reported that support for their pet bills hinged on their backing Daley. Some feared that the budgets for popular programs would be held up or defeated, including that for the superintendent of public instruction, if widespread support for Stevenson surfaced. One attorney was notified that his business might suffer if he voted against Daley. A representative of another Chicago ward was warned that a wrong vote would result in all the patronage workers in his ward being fired. Bowing to the inevitable, Stevenson capitulated, stating that while he meant no disrespect for Daley, "I will not subject my friends to continued recriminations, nor my supporters to reprisals."[10] (Later post-mortems indicated that Stevenson had a likely 87 votes—one more than needed—with 5 more probable at his peak. Daley and Stevenson supporters both agreed that Daley had at least 100 votes when Stevenson withdrew.)

When the meeting to decide the delegation's chair began, a woman Muskie delegate was symbolically placed in nomination to oppose the mayor by a delegate who decried "the blatant arm-twisting, threats, coercion and force used on delegates" by the pro-Daley forces.[11] In turn, State Representative Clyde Choate (later rewarded with appointment as delegation vice-chair) yelled his brief nomination speech to a disorderly convention, marked by catcalls, noise, and general confusion. Choate did manage to praise Daley as a champion of free and open debate.

The uproar continued through Daley's easy victory (113½ votes to 25½ for his opponent with 11 undecided). Contrary to custom, the losing Muskie delegate refused to consent to make Daley's choice unanimous, saying, "I will not do it. . . . I represented a group of people disenfranchised by the tactics used."[12]

The convention was full of curiosities. Stevenson was absent from the room when his name was called, so the party regular presiding at the time cast the Senator's half-vote for Daley. Stevenson later returned and made it official. Twice Daley received standing ovations while the Senator, also on the stage, remained sitting and unclapping. When the roll call reached the eleventh of the 20 at-large votes added illegally a week earlier, shouts arose and cries of "Point of Order!" were heard. They were ignored. The presiding officer (Touhy) announced the delegates could do as they would but he was going to finish the roll. Later, he threatened that troublemakers would be forcibly removed if they persisted.

Daley, appearing impervious to what had happened, made an acceptance speech. Two themes predominated. First, and familiarly, he rehashed the 1968 Chicago convention. He said:

I have no apologies for what happened at the 1968 Convention. I was not responsible for what happened in the streets outside the Conrad Hilton Hotel.

The media and the press turned it around. No one wrote about what happened inside the Convention. In my 20 years, it was the most disorderly convention I've seen.

I hope to God that we don't have it again in 1972.[13]

Daley also warned the delegates, rather curiously, that the eyes of millions would be on them (the preceding scenes had already been captured by television cameras). He spoke of democracy in action and reminded his listeners that those who try to bend conventions (presumably at the national not the state level) to their own will must meet with failure.

The delegation elected its representatives to the national convention committees giving fair representation to each of the presidential contenders on all but the Credentials Committee, where the Daley people took 5 of the 6 seats. The delegation failed to divide the seats equally among men and women, however, as prescribed in party regulations, thus precipitating another fight with the national party. Anti-Daley dissidents marshalled their forces in an attempt to control one delegation office, that of secretary, but failed and settled for co-secretaries.

With that, the meeting ended. At the conclusion, commentators announced Daley's resurrection from the series of mishaps that had dogged the election year. They paid homage to his "clout" in critical tests, but they did observe that despite all he had less control of this delegation than any ever sent from Illinois while he had been in office.

Why indulge in such a blood-letting? Daley's need to reestablish his authority within the local party during a difficult election year is one explanation. A second involves the psychology of the machine. It does not like to be challenged, and once it is, it shows little restraint in attacking its adversaries. A third reason is suggested by an observer at the meeting who concluded: "It's vitally important to Daley, whose big moment was long ago when he got John Kennedy into the White House and who has been under heavy attack since the 1968 [National] Convention, that he end his career on top—vindicated, still the acknowledged leader."[14] If so, it was a curiously old-fashioned road to vindication, and one destined to grow curiouser.

Saturday and Sunday. Media attention returned to the anti-litter patrols which took to the Chicago beaches in force. Daley's "clout" was continually admired, and for the first time in months he appeared to have regained his former invincibility.

Monday, June 19th. Another bombshell—and another machine victory. A federal district judge in Washington, D.C., ruled in favor of Keane's suit contesting the constitutionality of the guidelines. In a confused decision that further muddled a bad situation, the judge voided three of the reform guidelines (and part of another), including the quotas provision, and upheld the rest. Prior to this ruling, Keane and his associates had already lost two cases in the federal courts and one in the state courts on the same or related issues. The new ruling was unprecedented.

Confusion reigned twenty-one days before the national convention. Forty-three percent of the elected delegates were under challenge at this point and 80 percent of the challenges were based on the quotas (now declared unconstitutional). The national committee's counsel (Califano) characterized the decision as a "major tragedy" and "a tremendous setback for the party's efforts on behalf of minority groups" as well as one that had "gutted" the reforms.[15] Challenger Singer noted that the federal judge did not issue the injunction against his group's appeal that had been sought by Keane and his associates. Thus, said Singer, both groups could claim "victory."[16] If so, the national party remained in an incredibly awkward position. Lawyer Torshen (counsel for Keane, Wigoda, et al.) indeed did claim "a tremendous victory for our side," but Keane, perhaps thinking the judge was a Chicago man, remarked: "He went much further than he needed to go for our purposes."[17] Daley, in New Orleans to address a meeting of the National Conference of Mayors, said that the "decision speaks for itself. It upholds everything that has been said in our petitions."[18] Singer declared that "the Chicago Challenge is alive and well and bound for Miami Beach."[19] Many wondered.

Later Daley met with National Chair O'Brien, reportedly to talk about their "families," although presumably other things were on their minds also.

Tuesday, June 20th. Daley, now back on top, met individually in New Orleans with presidential contenders Humphrey, Muskie, and McGovern.

Late in the day, a three-judge Federal Appeals Court overruled the lower court decision and declared the guidelines still in effect. Califano (speaking before the court) indicated how crucial the Chicago case was, declaring that it is "the hottest political issue facing the Democratic National Convention" outside of picking a presidential nominee.[20] The court in its ruling stated that Keane, Wigoda, et al. did not have the grounds for a case; they had not *yet* been denied anything. There was an implicit assumption that if the "Daley 59" did lose in the Credentials Committee they could then reopen their suit. The Credentials Committee hearings, scheduled to begin the following Monday in Washington, D.C., were further clouded.

Singer announced that congressional district caucuses, *not open to those chosen on the organizational slate* (the challengers, among other things, feared a takeover of their meetings by organizational people) would be held Thursday evening, June 22nd, in order to select alternative delegates. (Up to this point, the challengers had *no delega-*

tion to substitute for Daley's should it be removed from the national convention). A county convention was scheduled for Saturday, June 24th, to complete the process. Little noticed at the time, these meetings were about to produce another upheaval.

The anti-litter campaign receded from the headlines to be replaced by stories of an alleged "hit" (assassination) squad within the Police Department, composed of law officers (one of whom seven years earlier had been accused of killing two prostitutes, resulting in his transfer from one police district to another). The officers allegedly worked with dope traffickers and killed on contract (in at least one case reportedly executing the wrong man). The story continued in the headlines for days (and the case dragged on in the federal courts for over a year). National convention maneuvering was (only momentarily as it turned out) overshadowed by the rush of normal news events.

Wednesday, June 21st. The Mayor, still in New Orleans, took the floor at the conference to support President Richard Nixon's war policies: "In the name of God," pleaded Daley, "stand behind the President."[21] Many Democratic regulars appeared a little stunned.

Torshen announced that the Appeals Court decision "in no way undermines or detracts from our attack on the constitutionality of the guidelines."[22] The Credentials Committee admitted to being in a fog. A spokesman reported:

> The lower court said the guidelines dealing with adequate, proportionate representation for various groups was improper—but the appeals court has not set that aside, so the guidelines are still in force.
>
> But if we use them, then the courts may throw them out—and we'll have to start the whole credentials business all over again.[23]

This came with only 19 days to go before the national convention. Late in the day, a report from Washington said that the Democratic National Committee and the Credentials Committee might refuse to seat the Illinois representatives to the national convention committees because of the state delegation's failure to divide its seats equally between males and females. Seventy-seven percent of the Illinois nominees for the committees were men. A national party leader admitted he did not know what to do about the situation. The Illinois State Democratic Chair professed confusion also: "I haven't yet figured out what to do about it," he said.[24] Congressman James O'Hara, chair of the convention's Rules Committee, announced that the Illinois representatives to his committee definitely would not be seated when the group began its deliberations on Thursday.

Late in the day also, Daley returned to Chicago and met immediately with his local party leaders, including the president of the County Board, Aldermen Marzullo, Holman, Frost, Gabinski, Vrdrolyak, and Burke, the Cook County assessor, and County Commissioners Stroeger and Bieszczat (among others), many names familiar in the challenge, to discuss "voter registration." The meeting drew little public notice.

Thursday, June 22nd. Another unexpectedly climatic day. The leader of the Illinois delegation to the Rules Committee (a state senator and the Democrats' nominee for attorney-general) told O'Hara that the state would not abide by the provisions of the 1972 Call requiring an equal division of convention committee seats by sex: "I herewith declare that any rules having to do with balancing and quotas violate 150 years of history, traditions and principles of the Democratic Party," he said.[25] (Not true. The old rules also required an equal division by sex.) O'Hara refused to allow the Illinois delegation voting rights on his committee. The angered delegation leader told (as the machine representatives repeatedly did) a television interviewer that Illinois had "the most open delegate selection system in the nation" and he also threatened still another suit. Lawyer Torshen was rushed to Washington to guide the legal proceedings. The Illinois challenge of these points was serious and coincided with that of nine other states (Alaska, Arizona, Florida, Georgia, Hawaii, Kansas, Minnesota, Washington, and West Virginia), all of whom were refused national convention committee voting privileges (lessening the committee membership considerably).

Thursday evening. The Singer group held 8 congressional district caucuses to elect 51 delegates. The quota-conscious group selected 31 whites, 16 blacks, and 4 Latin Americans; 26 men and 25 women; and 23 people aged 30 or younger. This, however, was not the big story. The meetings were raided by Daley loyalists, who systematically proceeded to disrupt them. Some unusually nasty and unnecessary encounters took place. The confrontations would do little to help the "Daley 59"'s position once they became known to the national party (see below).

Friday, June 23rd. Illinois overnight capitulated to national party demands and evenly distributed its national convention committee representatives between men and women. Five men resigned and Mayor Daley appointed five women to replace them (pending confirmation from the full delegation), thus evening the split between the sexes. The leader of the Illinois delegation to the Rules Committee was unrepentant. He told the committee that there were "insuperable obstacles" to a court challenge at that time and he admitted to a belated realization that a court case might result in Illinois having no voice in any national convention committees. "The Democratic Party had always deplored quotas of any kind as basically un-American," he continued. "The free election process is sacrosanct."[26] (The sole holdout among the states, Florida, initiated a federal court suit on the matter, which it promptly lost.)

A hearing officer in a challenge in the Sixth Congressional District, a suburban area contiguous to Chicago (but a group not included in the "Daley 59" challenge), found that three delegates, all machine candidates (the county coroner, the assistant house minority leader and a sanitary district trustee), were improperly slated by the regular Democratic organization and that the machine had made no effort to include women on the delegation. He recommended that these officials be replaced by women.

Saturday, June 24th. The insurgents held a county convention to elect eight additional at-large delegates, thus completing their convention delegation. Daley supporters invaded the meeting and a shouting match preceded the session, but unlike Thursday night there was no violence (see below).

Monday, June 26th. The Credentials Committee hearings opened in Washington. The period roughly encompassed by the arrival of Louis Oberdorfer in Chicago on May 24th in an abortive bid to open the Chicago hearings and terminating with the selection of the completed delegation of challengers represented the most exciting and unpredictable month in the entire four-year reform effort. The Chicago dispute constituted only one of many—the Credentials Committee was scheduled to arbitrate a staggering seventy challenges from thirty states, involving 1,281 delegates or 41.2 percent of the total national convention membership—but by any test it was easily the most significant to come before the national convention. The events depicted parallel the close of the primary season, the ending generally of all delegate selection, the institution of the Humphrey challenge to McGovern's victory in California (based on the contention that "winner-take-all" primaries should not be allowed), the realization that McGovern had about won the nomination, and finally, the anticipated beginnings of the Rules and Credentials Committee sessions. In contrast, the credentials hearings, while exciting by any reasonable standard, proved something of a let down compared with the events that had preceded them. Before recording the highlights of these sessions, however, a few words on the matter of the events surrounding the choosing of the membership of the insurgents' delegation.

The Challengers Select an Alternative Delegation

The weakest part of the Singer group's challenge lay in the absence of a legally elected substitute delegation with which to replace Daley's should the challenge succeed. One of the curiosities of the contest was that it was brought not by defeated delegates (although there were some in the group of ten put together explicitly to institute the challenge) trying to unseat the victors in the primary but that it was based on the alleged violation of national party rules instituted for the conduct of party elections. After the challenge had been brought, the insurgents then faced the problem of choosing their alternative delegates. The job was not to be easy.

The ideal answer was to hold another primary. This, of course, was impossible. The most reasonable solution—and the one ultimately followed—was to convene caucuses in each of the congressional districts to select the district-level representatives and then to hold a county-level convention to select the remaining at-large delegates. Twice meetings were scheduled to accomplish these ends and twice they were postponed. One reason for the indecision was the pending court cases. Another and more pressing concern, however, was the fear that the meetings would be disrupted by the Daley regulars who would then either proceed to select their own representatives or make the conduct of any business impossible. With time running out, the insurgents gave into necessity and finally scheduled the necessary caucuses for the evening of June 22nd and the county-level meeting for two days later.

The selections were considered a formality. They were not expected to add substantially to the moral weight of the challengers' argument or to detract from the points being made by the machine delegates. The caucuses received little media attention, being lost in the drama of the more significant events then unfolding.

The challengers had devised an awkward set of rules for the congressional district sessions that they hoped would allow them to proceed with the first step in electing an alternative delegation while at the same time avoiding any takeover by the machine forces. Their plan was to schedule open meetings and to permit nominations from the floor but to restrict voting to those who had sought delegate status in the primary but had lost. These "electors" would cast a weighted vote equal to their support in the primary. The only people specifically barred from the proceedings were organization members already elected as delegates.

The plan was fragile. It had been devised to meet a unique set of circumstances. Undoubtedly, it could be challenged before the Credentials Committee and it would be hard to defend, especially before people who had no reason to sympathize with the seemingly unreasonable fears of the insurgents as to the machine reaction. Attention, however, quickly, and unexpectedly, shifted from the legitimacy of the selection process to the response of the organization to the meetings, behavior startling enough to nullify what might have been the last advantage of the Daley organization.

The meeting of Daley and his lieutenants the day before on "voter registration" had in reality been called to discuss and coordinate the organization's policy on the insurgents' caucuses. An overview of the fruits of their work on the night of the gatherings is provided by a local newspaper account (Chicago *Daily News*, June 23rd):

> Hundreds of Mayor Richard J. Daley's Regular Democratic ward organization backers, shouting curses and obscenities, stormed caucuses called by rival independent Democrats to elect an 'alternative delegation' to the Democratic National Convention.
>
> They disrupted seven of eight district caucuses held throughout the city and forced them into temporarily adjourning Thursday night.
>
> They beat two men, forcibly detained another for 10 minutes, pulled the hair of women challengers and overturned chairs and tables.
>
> Using battery-powered microphones, they 'elected' their own chairman and seized control of the podium at one of the caucuses. Independents trying to flee the violence were shoved back and terrorized.[27]

At the caucus in the Second Congressional District, when Wayne Whalen (a lawyer for the challengers) attempted to convene the meeting in a church, he reported being "rushed by Aldermen Vrdolyak and Aducci and fifteen to thirty others, who proceeded to punch him in the stomach and knock him to the floor. Vrdolyak, carrying a bullhorn, announced he had taken over the meeting. He addressed a crowd, many of whom had arrived with him, calling the challengers "the kind of people who are trying to destroy the Democratic Party."[28] The crowd, in turn, cursed, booed, and heckled the challengers as the church's pastor shouted for order. When Whalen succeeded in adjourning the meeting, witnesses reported that he and his group were forced to "run the gauntlet" through the crowd to the rear door of the church while they were "pushed, shoved, spat upon and had their hair pulled."[29]

In the Seventh Congressional District, when the presiding officer sought to open the caucus in the same room in which the Poole hearings had been held earlier, a city corporation counsel and a county commissioner stood across the table shouting at him through a bullhorn. Alderman Marzullo led five bus-loads of party regulars (brought in for the occasion) in shouting obscenities. When the Singer representative adjourned the meeting (hoping to reconvene later in a law office), Marzullo's yelling "We'll follow you to the grave!" apparently reflected the mood of many in the crowd who would not let the insurgents leave. As the moderator attempted to make his way through the 400 or so hecklers "he was accosted at the elevators and—while Marzullo shouted, 'Kill the mother——' —he was shoved back into the conference room and forcibly detained."[30] An associate was pulled from an elevator, knocked to the floor, and punched and kicked before escaping.

The Eighth Congressional District held its meeting in the basement of a parish hall. Here yet another alderman (Gabinski) took over the proceedings and passed several resolutions praising the Daley delegates. When he adjourned his session and the challengers again tried to conduct theirs "the regulars stormed on stage, switched off the lights, turned over the tables at which the independents were sitting, and began pulling the chairs from beneath them."[31] When the husband of the woman who was chairing the meeting objected, he was informed that he "would be beaten to a pulp" if he resisted.[32]

The Fifth Congressional District meeting, held in a Catholic church, found the oldest son of the mayor, Richard M. Daley, and still another alderman leading the troops (300 to 400 Daley loyalists who arrived just as the meeting began) in a fist-waving, shouting demonstration that had the intended effect of breaking up the gathering.

The insurgents in the Ninth Congressional District held out for an hour despite the yells, taunts, arguments, and threats from many in the crowd. To cries that the proceedings were "anti-democratic" and similar to ones "used in Russia," one spunky (or danger-loving) woman in the audience rose to ask the protestors, "How many of you were invited by the Regular Democratic Organization to take part in the selection of their slated candidates?"[33] The demonstrators were momentarily taken aback, although not enough to deter them from eventually shutting down the meeting.

The Daley supporters in the Third Congressional District arrived early, convened, and then adjourned their own meeting. When the insurgents' chair arrived (Singer's administrative assistant), the crowd alternately ridiculed ("Get a haircut!"; "Go home button shoes!") and cursed him. As he left, a Cook County deputy sheriff followed, screaming at him to show his credentials (whatever that meant).[34]

The only meeting not disrupted was held in a private home in the predominantly black First Congressional District. Presided over by an official of Jesse Jackson's "Operation Push," it listened to the objections voiced by the city administrator's representatives, Alderman Holman, and County Commissioner Stroeger, but then proceeded without undue incident to the business at hand, the selection of a substitute delegate slate.

The immediate response

Reactions to the night's events were quick in coming. Singer termed the onslaught "barbaric."[35] Jesse Jackson, reporting a number of personal threats against his life, wondered aloud if the Daley organization had gone "insane."[36] A lawyer (Stephen Schwab) for the insurgents' delegation who had conducted the meeting in the Ninth District attempted to put the attacks in a perspective relevant to the challenge: "The Daley organization, every step of the way, has been digging their grave a little deeper in this delegate challenge. They did it again tonight," he predicted.[37]

The Daley group, however, was hardly defensive about their actions. Two principals in the night's actions made this clear. The Mayor's son, for example, contended that the caucuses "made a mockery of the democratic process and were in flagrant disregard not only of the McGovern rules and party rules, but also of the spirit of democracy."[38] Young Daley concluded that the insurgents had "brought on themselves" the disruptions that occurred. Alderman Vrdolyak claimed to have now been elected twice to delegate status, the second time by the meeting he had invaded. As to the allegations of violent behavior, he responded that "any charges by Whalen [the moderator] that he was injured, or even touched, is a fraud." The alderman served notice that he had every intention of attending the insurgents' upcoming county convention and of "encouraging everyone I know to be there, too."[39]

Despite all, the challengers did manage to reconvene the seven disrupted caucuses in private homes, law offices, or church rectories and complete the business of choosing their fifty-one delegates. They also determined to proceed with Saturday's county-level session to complete the process of delegate selection. Apparently, another encounter was in the making.

Insurgents select their at-large delegates

The challengers needed to fill eight at-large vacancies in their delegation at their "county convention" held in a downtown hotel. Trouble was expected. The Daley people had let it be known they would be there in force. The Chicago police had declined a request to assign policemen to the meeting to prevent disruptions because, according to a police spokesman, it might inhibit "free speech."

As the moderator (again Whalen) attempted to open the meeting, young Daley; Aldermen Vrdolyak, Frost, Holman, and Burke; Commissioner Stroeger; and others crowded the podium, shouting loudly and repeatedly, "Point of Order!" "You're part of the Ogilvie [Republican governor seeking reelection] machine." "This isn't a democracy." "By what authority do you conduct this meeting?"[40] And whatever else occurred to them. A press report of the incident (Chicago *Sun-Times*, June 25th) noted that the meeting:

> . . . exploded in a wild vocal uproar . . . when ranking supporters of the mayor disrupted the gathering by chanting and yelling points of order and accusations.
>
> The uproar went unabated for 10 minutes and became so intense that Wayne Whalen, the meeting chairman, could not be heard over the public address system as he attempted to read an agenda and rules for the gathering. . . . Many of the hundreds of persons jammed into the meeting appeared stunned at the outburst.[41]

The situation could have resulted in some unfortunate incidents. The room was overly full and hot, the Daley supporters were packed into sections of the meeting hall, and the atmosphere was charged. Still, violence was averted and only minor scuffles and verbal abuse marked the day. Tiring of the shouting, and apparently pleased with their performance, Vrdolyak yelled that the meeting was adjourned and he, young Daley, and an estimated 300 machine regulars left. The insurgents then proceeded to complete their slate. With this done, the scene shifted to the opening of the Credentials Committee hearings in Washington, only days away.

Conclusion

What did the machine gain? Apparently, it had hoped to demonstrate that the challengers' procedures were neither open nor representative, points that could more easily have been made in the verbal presentations to the Credentials Committee. The insurgents' selection procedures would not bear up under close scrutiny. What the machine leaders succeeded in doing, however, was to make themselves the point of contention again. They demonstrated why the challengers had to be so circumspect in their manner of choosing an alternative delegation. The machine, once more, would be called on to explain, if it could, its behavior in the matter. It had, as the challengers' lawyer had predicted, dug its hole a little deeper.

SIXTEEN

The National Party Makes Its Decision

The Credentials Committee Hearing

An overloaded Credentials Committee expeditiously went about its business. It was expected to resolve in one manner or another the record eighty-two challenges before it. Quite early, the chairwoman, Patricia Roberts Harris, whose appointment nine months earlier had been the center of a bitter controversy between party regulars (pro-Harris) and reformers (anti-Harris), demonstrated her command of the deliberations and her unwillingness to tolerate delay. The committee members also appreciated the gravity of their task: In effect, it was up to them to decide if the new reform guidelines would, in the last analysis, be applied and the severity with which they would be enforced. As the days progressed, it became quite clear that the group had every intention of supporting the guidelines to the extent they felt they were relevant to the issues in dispute, settling once and for all their status as controlling party law.

The major controversy facing the committee prior to the Chicago dispute, and actually at this point far more crucial to the nomination race, was the challenge over California's "winner-take-all" primary. In actuality, the challenge did not involve the reform guidelines. The McGovern-Fraser Commission had considered the issue of a proportional vote distribution for each of the candidates receiving support in a primary or caucus, but had decided not to make any recommendations (the Mikulski Commission later did enact proportional representation). Humphrey, who had lost to McGovern in California, had first decided not to institute a challenge (to do so, he told Walter Cronkite on television, would be to become a "spoilsport") but then in a last desperate bid to win his party's presidential nomination he reversed himself.

His argument was that the "winner-take-all" primary (i.e., where the plurality victor receives all the primary votes rather than only his proportional share) violated the spirit of the new reforms as well as, for example, prohibitions as to the unit rule. The politics of the situation were clear. McGovern with 44.3 percent of the state's vote (as against Humphrey's 39.2%) had won all of California's 271 convention votes. If the primary were declared illegal at this late date and the votes redistributed on a proportional basis, McGovern would receive 120, Humphrey (who still would not have enough to claim the nomination himself) 106, with the rest scattered among a number of other contenders. The reduction of 151 votes in the McGovern total was believed sufficient to pull him below the majority needed to claim the nomination (although no other candidate at that point would have anything approaching a majority).

The hearing officer in the California case had declared for McGovern. The issue seemed clear enough. The significance for the Chicago organization (which controlled five of the six Credentials Committee seats awarded the Illinois delegation) was in whom they would support. A pro-McGovern vote would lay the groundwork for a possible compromise on the Chicago question (the challengers had little independent political support) or even, although it would be difficult to justify in light of the rules, a rejection of the insurgents' arguments. An anti-McGovern stand (unless based on pique) had better be sure that the stop-McGovern drive would succeed. Every vote in this contest was critical. Unfortunately for McGovern, he had less strength on this committee than on any other in the national convention. To compound his difficulties, ten California representatives to the Credentials Committee (those who would be affected if the challenge succeeded) were denied the right to vote on the matter. The situation was critical.

A serious effort—the most intensive despite the fact that the McGovern people were to try right up to the final national convention vote—was made to compromise the Chicago challenge. Conflicting reports emerged from the principals. Frank Mankiewicz, a McGovern strategist, met with both groups and emerged publicly optimistic. "No side," he reported, "has staked out a total win position."[1] Mayor Daley reported he was "always willing to compromise" and the Reverend Jesse Jackson found an even split of the delegation "reasonable" (although he was suspicious of Mankiewicz, whom he feared favored Daley).[2] Daley, in turn, let it be known that some type of split was conceivable ("depending on who he has to split with").[3] The fact that he refused to speak to or acknowledge the existence of the Singer group made the admonition more noteworthy. Even more troublesome, reports from Chicago indicated that Daley, who believed he had a strong case, intended to fight, alleging that the insurgents had shown a "gross disregard of party reforms" in the conduct of their caucuses.[4] Singer meanwhile was truculent. He let it be known that he was in Washington to argue his group's case: any compromise would have to come from Daley first (a concession, such as it was, to the McGovern camp's pressure to reach an accommodation).

The effort at compromise fizzled. In a stunning blow, the Credentials Committee voted 72 to 66 to strip McGovern of the 151 disputed California delegates (distributing this proportionately among Humphrey and the seven other contenders in the primary), thus effectively throwing the presidential nomination once more into doubt. McGovern reacted in shock and anger, uncharacteristically speaking of "crooked and unethical procedures" within the committee.[5] The five Chicago loyalists had voted the Humphrey position, exercising the balance of power in the dispute.

Poole's report

The next major test was the Chicago question. The Credentials Committee staff had released the hearing officer's findings. In it, Poole reported "gross violations" of the national party standards and he ruled in favor of the challengers.[6] The report was explicit. Concerning the alleged role of the machine in the primary, Poole wrote:

> From the mass of sharply conflicting evidence, there emerges a clear pattern of concerted action by the organization in the use of its influence and prestige in support of its regulars, encouraging their candidacies, agreements on numbers, cooperation in the preparation of sample ballots, their widespread distribution by party workers, their prominence at headquarters of ward officials, and the formidable array of party power in behalf of its preferred candidates.
>
> All of this compels the irrefragable conclusion . . . that Guidelines C-1, C-4, and C-6 have been violated in the nomination and election of the challenged delegates and alternates in Chicago.[7]

As to the quota issue, Poole added:

> The underrepresentation complained of was not the result of fortune, unaffected by the efforts of the organization, but was a continuation of the same conditions exposed in the Commission Report and came about because, although diligent in including its own regulars, the organization in Chicago expended no such resources on the segments of the population as required by Guidelines A-1 and A-2 [mandating the quotas].

The Hearing Officer accordingly finds that those Guidelines have been violated both in letter and spirit.[8]

Not much was left to be said. The wording of the report as well as its findings seemingly acted to undercut any lingering hopes the organization might harbor.

But the machine fought on, at times to dubious advantage. Simon, one of two lawyers in Washington to present the "Daley 59"'s side to the Credentials Committee (the other being Torshen), acknowledged that women, for example, were underrepresented on the delegation: "Some of the delegates would not be adverse to letting women on the delegation, perhaps their wives."[9] On the day of the Chicago vote, the Credentials Committee members awoke to find a full-page advertisement in the *Washington Post* pleading the case of the "uncommitted" delegates, a curiously expensive vehicle through which to reach its judges. An attorney for the regulars, in appearing before the committee, argued that the "Daley 59" should retain their seats regardless of national party rules because they had been elected by the people of Chicago. He went on to question the committee's power to enforce any ouster. Holman, speaking for the organization in the general debate that followed, accused the insurgents of "dissension, disorganization and venom," words not calculated to ease tensions. He went on to attack personally as a "big hero" a Muskie delegate who introduced a resolution to compromise the issue by dividing the seats between the contesting delegations, a proposal Holman rejected out-of-hand ("We will not share *our* seats with Jesse Jackson and William Singer") (italics added).[10]

The decision

One member of the Credentials Committee in addressing his colleagues remarked: "This is not a question of presidential preferences. . . . It's a question of whether our guidelines and rules apply to Mayor Daley and his delegates."[11] This statement about summed up the matter. On the vote that followed, the Credentials Committee—despite its previous stand against McGovern, despite the Mayor's preeminent position within the party, and despite the effect it might have on the November election—voted 71 to 61 to unseat the Daley regulars and replace them with the Singer delegation.

When Chairwoman Harris announced the results, the room exploded: cheers, applause, and even hugging, kissing, and dancing in the aisles followed. Possibly, it was just the release of tension built up over the preceding days of deliberations or, for some, reaching all the way back to the March primary. Perhaps others felt it balanced out the California challenge or struck a blow at a symbol of the disruptive Chicago convention of 1968. Given the implications for the party, a more sober reaction might have been appropriate.

One dimension of the "Daley 59" 's reponse quickly became apparent. Shocked by the Credentials Committee action, the regulars threatened through their lawyer, Torshen, to return to the federal courts to press their claim (which they did and lost) and to bring legal action to prevent the name of the national convention's nominee from appearing on the general election ballot in Illinois, an extreme action (used by some southern states in 1948 and 1960) that indicated the extent of the Chicago machine's displeasure. As it turned out, the Credentials Committee's actions on both the California and Chicago delegations were taken before the federal courts. In an accelerated series of hearings, the District Court upheld the Credentials Committee's action, the Circuit Court supported the Chicago decision but overturned the California outcome, and the Supreme Court, convened in an extraordinary summer session to rule on the cases, reaffirmed its historic role of traditional noninvolvement in party affairs (unless compelling constitutional issues arise), in effect accepting the Credentials Committee's and the national convention's resolution of the matters.

The National Convention

"We're going to get the old bastard today," one delegate reportedly told an organization supporter attempting to solicit his vote on behalf of the "Daley 59."[12] The day, of course, was the session in which the Chicago Challenge would come to the floor of the national convention. By the time the issue did arise, however, it was something of an anticlimax.

The opening night's session of the Miami Beach Convention was very long, lasting until almost 5 A.M. the next morning, but by the time it was over, all of the major issues to come before the assembly had been effectively resolved. The California dispute came up early and the McGovern forces won a decisive victory, overturning the Credentials Committee recommendation by a 1,618.28 to 1,238.22 vote. McGovern regained his delegates from the state, and more importantly, demonstrated his impregnable position within the convention. The nomination was assured and the bulk of the other presidential contenders quickly dropped out of the race.

Another effort was made to compromise the Chicago problem by a presidential candidate now looking forward to the November election, but too much had happened and too little time existed to lay the effective groundwork for such a move. An attempt to suspend the rules, despite the McGovern camp's best efforts to convince its followers—markedly unsympathetic to the mayor and his delegation—to support the move, narrowly failed, 1,411.05 in favor as against 1,-483.08 opposed. The Credentials Committee recommendation to seat the insurgents in place of the Daley regulars was upheld 1,486.05 to 1,371.55. The mayor and his delegates were relegated to the role of outsiders. The machine regulars gathered their belongings and quickly vacated Miami Beach. Daley, on vacation in Michigan (reportedly with his bags packed ready to come to the national convention on a moment's notice), reached another low point, possibly the worst, in a long and tumultuous election year. As fate would have it, meanwhile, it would fall to Illinois a few nights later to cast the 119 votes required to put McGovern over the 1,508 needed for the nomination, the tally announced by the same (downstate) party regular who had placed Daley's name in contention for the delegation chairmanship a few weeks earlier at the raucous Springfield meeting.

The Aftermath

As a long-time party loyalist, Mayor Daley did go on to support Mc-Govern in the general election despite his (and the organization's) threats to the contrary. He even invited McGovern to address gatherings of Cook County party regulars on several occasions and he went as far as financing a one-hour telecast in Chicago of a local rally featuring the senator (although the program unfortunately conflicted with one of McGovern's few nationally televised addresses and his most important). Not all of the machine lieutenants, ward captains, and precinct workers adjusted as quickly or forgave as readily. The aging and acerbic Vito Marzullo, ward boss and Daley confidante, to select one example, worked for Nixon (which prior to the events of the spring would have been unthinkable). The alderman still proclaimed himself a "Daley Democrat" and remained a principal organizational strategist. Marzullo failed to carry his ward for the Republicans although he did claim McGovern's margin of victory was down from what normally could have been expected. Illinois, along with forty-eight other states, went for Nixon but it would be difficult to blame the state's showing on a lackluster machine performance. McGovern's troubles far exceeded anything Chicago might contribute.

The mayor was considerably less forgiving toward his opponents, the insurgents who had prevailed at the national level. A local court had adjudged the Daley regulars the legitimate national convention delegates, and when the insurgents returned to Illinois, held them in contempt for taking their seats at the national convention. The judge, sympathetic to the machine (and quoted in the newspapers comparing Singer's actions to "Hitler in Germany and Mussolini in Italy"), threatened the former challengers with jail.[13] The case, with appeals, was to drag on for over two years, working its way—at great cost in time, money, and psychological uncertainty to the insurgents— up through the Illinois courts and finally again to the Supreme Court. The challenge to national party rules was not to end with the decisions of the Miami Beach Convention. The lawyers for the challengers, after petitioning to be relieved of the case in order to move on to other things, were castigated by the judge and forced to remain on the case. Individuals associated with the challengers appointed by the newly elected Independent Democratic Governor Walker were routinely turned down by a state legislature in which the Chicago regulars held the balance of power. The machine firmly believed in punishing its enemies whatever the cost. Ironically, when the Illinois national convention delegation was reconvened after the Miami Beach gathering to select national committee delegates from the state, it was the "Daley 59" who were represented and who made the choices.

The November election not only witnessed the election of the Independent Democrat Walker as governor and the loss of the state to the Republican presidential nominee but, and far more significant for the machine, a politically knowledgeable Republican prosecutor was elected to the office of the Cook County state's attorney. Combined with an active Republican U.S. attorney (appointed by the Nixon administration in late 1971), the organization began to experience a prosecutorial zeal it had not had to tolerate before. Within a three-year period, the federal prosecutor alone had managed to convict 75 public officials, many of them organization-related figures. Among those found guilty of various misdeeds relating to the abuse of public office for private gain were Keane and Wigoda (principals in the national convention drama from the beginning) as well as five other aldermen or former aldermen, Daley's long-time press secretary, and the Cook County clerk. The indictment of another Daley protégé, the influential clerk of the Circuit Court, a position noted for its control of patronage, indicated a previously unknown willingness to go after the organization leaders as well as the lowly canvassers.

This time around Daley himself did not escape unscathed. Not only were many of his closest associates in difficulty but it was revealed that one of Daley's sons had managed to gain a real estate license through a fixed exam and that an insurance firm associated with another of his sons had been awarded millions of dollars of public business in no-bid contracts. The mayor and his wife were revealed to be secret part-owners of a real estate holding company that did well. These incidents were the first evidence of private gain for Daley and his immediate family, previously believed to be removed from any taint of personal scandal.

Personally and politically, although matters quieted down, his problems continued. Singer announced early his intention to run for mayor in 1975. Death took its toll (Holman, for example) of an organization led primarily by old men. Daley himself suffered a stroke (the first major illness for the over-70 mayor) that disabled him for a good period of time although he did return to his duties. The usual police scandals (accusations, indictments, convictions) continued as did the annual school crisis (Would the teachers strike? Where would the budget funds come from?). The machine seemed bothered, maybe even threatened, by the continued unwillingness of blacks to return uncritically to the fold and the spot opposition offered by a somewhat rejuvenated (but still largely disorganized and inept) county Republican party.

Lest, however, one think things had changed markedly or before prematurely counting out the organization, some evidence from another miniconfrontation with the post-'72 national party may be relevant. The Democrats held a midterm national convention at the tail-end of the 1974 election year. The machine, with the national party's implicit blessing, managed the delegate selection. Working through processes controlled by the regulars, they selected an almost uniformly loyalist delegation to the off-year convocation. Still courting problems, machine regulars attempted to branch out and take control of the North Shore Cook County caucuses called by Independent Democrats in areas geographically well removed from the city. Their actions again ran afoul of national party intentions and a weak challenge was instituted. Many of the same people (Touhy and Simon, now chair of the state party's "Affirmative Action Council") presented some familiar arguments to the national party body convened to adjudicate the disputes. Specifically, the organization was accused of not equally representing women in the 108-member delegation (10% were female, by a considerable margin the lowest of any state delegation) to the midterm convention, and even more explicitly damaging, of nominating and electing in another of the now familiar Springfield conventions (the proceedings were rigged and were "like a scene out of Marat-Sade,"[14] one challenger testified) an at-large slate of seventeen, only two of whom were women. Simon contended it would have been "reprehensibly sexist" to elect a balanced delegation.[15] He admitted the machine slated and elected their nominees (thus accepting responsibility for the outcome), but while claiming to be "loaded with good faith," he added, an honorable electoral process is more important than a balanced delegation. "The delegates (at Springfield) put their faith in veteran politicians, people they know something about." "Are you going to tell popular Democratic office-holders they don't mean anything because they aren't female?" he asked.[16]

The national party committee, eager to avoid confrontations (the national headquarters had been very solicitous of Daley's organization since 1972), felt that the machine had used "questionable judgment" and that the "wise and prudent" course would have been to meet the standards.[17] The committee then proceeded by an 18 to 4 vote to deny the challenge and thus not force the state party to reconstruct its delegations.

As to the national party more generally, a follow-up committee (the Mikulski Commission) to the McGovern-Fraser Commission, convened in the post-'72 period, moderated (although without substantially diluting their overall effect) the guidelines in force for delegate selection to the Miami Beach Convention, including, significantly, the provisions as to slate-making and quotas, the two items that had caused the Chicago organization such great difficulty. The national party actively courted the party regulars and federated labor (the AFL–CIO leadership) angered by the events of 1972. Mostly, however, it sat back and watched as the series of far more significant scandals associated with "Watergate" engulfed the Nixon presidency and the Republican party.

Two Post-Convention Tests: The Local Level and the National Level

The local level

A legendary ward politician and bar-keeper, Paddy Bauer, once claimed that "Chicago ain't ready for reform!" The remark seems at times to serve as the city's motto. Bauer returned from his retirement in the southwestern United States to vote in the Chicago Democratic primary of February 25, 1975 (for all practical purposes, *the* election) to decide the party's mayoral nominee. The move was symbolic. The Daley forces had massed for a smashing victory. Daley, seeking his fifth term, was opposed by: Singer, who had campaigned hard for sixteen months; Edward Hanrahan, one-time Daley favorite and former state's attorney; and Richard Newhouse, the "black" candidate, a state senator with a good legislative record but little public visibility. The campaign was full of the hyperbole, countercharges, and the vaudeville that marks all such local efforts. The mayor, of course, did not campaign, choosing to appear at civic functions to extol the virtues of his administration or before carefully recruited (by city hall administrators) audiences of old people, blacks, and the like to tell them how good things were. The real work was done in the streets and in the precincts. Here the challengers had no hope of equaling the machine efforts.

Daley won a truly impressive victory, capturing 58 percent of the primary vote to Singer's 29 percent, Newhouse's 8 percent, and Hanrahan's 5 percent. Daley regulars actually increased their control of the City Council, taking over 90 percent of the seats (a few independents did survive). Adeline Keane, wife of the convicted former leader of the council, Tom Keane, won her husband's seat handily and did so with virtually no campaign appearances of any kind. This, as much as anything, tells the story of the election. The Daley forces, relying on strenuous efforts from park district employees, saturated the ward of the lone remaining Republican on the council and defeated him (although, as events would have it, a Republican newcomer did manage to survive the machine blitz). The Republican alderman had been Daley's token opposition in the April general election.

In a moment of triumph, the Mayor chose to be humble: "I shall embrace charity, and love mercy, and walk humbly with God."[18] The flurry of scandals—from Watergate-type assertions of illegal police spying on Daley opponents to the institution of a mid-decade congressional reapportionment designed to eliminate from the Congress one of the few Democratic representatives who did not endorse Daley—suggests that the Mayor's "humility" retained its characteristic Chicago flavor.

The national level

One other noteworthy occurrence took place. The U.S. Supreme Court in January 1975 sided with the Singer delegation and rejected the "Daley 59"'s arguments. Speaking for the Court, Justice William J. Brennan wrote that national parties "serve the pervasive national interest in the selection of candidates for national office, and this national interest is greater than any interest of an individual state."[19] The national convention, said the Court, is "the proper forum for determining intra-party disputes as to which delegates should be seated," and going even further, added that "the states themselves have no constitutional role in the great task of the selection of presidential and vice-presidential candidates."[20] The decision could be of immense historic importance. As Alderman Keane pointed out in another context, it goes further than it had to for the purposes at hand.

The impact in Chicago? Singer said the ruling would have little effect on the politics of the city because "it is not relevant to the issues facing Chicago."[21] He was correct. Chicago is Chicago and the machine is the machine. Obviously, this had not changed.

Conclusion

Chicago is certainly not typical of the nation as a whole or even of other major cities. Yet in every state and each urban area, the same process of uncertainty/rejection/hostility/and/acceptance (forced or otherwise) was played out with some degree of political emotion. The reforms had an enormous impact at all levels of presidential selection, and as a consequence, implications for the conduct of local (as well as national) politics. In all cases, some groups won and others lost. Given these conditions, it is not difficult to see why the opposition to reform has been prolonged and why, in many respects, the Democratic party is still groping toward some type of accommodation between reformers and regulars that sacrifices the vital interests of neither. It is, and has been, a long and hazardous passage. Not too far in the future, it may be that the party is going to have to make its ultimate commitment to one side or the other, with consequences for the long-run conduct of American politics which have yet to be anticipated.

PART FOUR

Reform in the Republican Party

SEVENTEEN

Reform and the Republican Party

One of Sir David Low's cartoons depicting the indestructible Colonel Blimp shows the good colonel discoursing on political change. The caption reads: "Gad, Sir, reform is alright as long as it doesn't change anything!" Many critics would contend that the Republican party's bow to reform would not have disturbed the colonel. Some would argue, with merit, that basic change was never truly entertained as an objective and that in truth the party backed into—and through— the period that brought such a pained metamorphosis to its sister party.

Be that as it may, in fairness it should be noted that there are several ways to approach an examination of the Republican reform attempt. The Republicans were not feeling the aftereffects of decades of indifference to and abuse of organizational forms that had come to plague the Democrats. Republican reform, to the extent that it existed, evolved from two quite different pressures: the party's historic concern with continually updating and reevaluating structural mechanisms; and pressures generated by the opposition. One major party cannot change within the American system without the other being profoundly affected. Whatever the rationale—the need to modernize; the desire to keep abreast of the opposition; a public relations attempt to capture press attention to appeal (superficially) to youth, newcomers, and independents; reassurance for members who watched what was happening in the other party; or more simply, the inability to ignore the electoral and statutory changes within the states meant to apply in the main to one party, but more often than not encompassing both— a mild (very mild) reform tremor did rattle through the party.

Background

The Republican exploration of reform differed markedly from that of the Democrats. Despite their deceptively similar governing forums,

national and local party structures, and even—to the unpracticed eye—
apparent unity on such matters as general policy, the two national
parties are distinctively separate entities, each with its own traditions,
social roots, and organizational and personal values. If the Democrats
can be described broadly as a loud, frantic, organizationally lax and
quarrelsome bunch, their style of politics nevertheless does not mask
a deep love of the game and an impressively relaxed practice of the
art. Organizational concerns hold a low priority for the bulk of the
personally oriented Democratic politicians. Organizational questions
are looked upon as a nuisance, given episodic attention, and then ignored. The Democrats, of course, pay a price for their lack of concern.
They are given to violent (and potentially creative) outbursts of activity
interspersed with long periods of inertia and neglect. That an accumu-
lation of convention procedure grievances over decades could result
in a Chicago convention should not be too surprising. Once suitably
warned, and no doubt to their own amazement, the Democrats moved
expeditiously to remedy some of their problems.

Republicans are quite different. Their approach to organizational
problems appears to reflect an innate restraint, a sense of order and
disciplined change, a quest for efficiency, and a belief in appearances.
Innumerable committees deal with and evaluate questions, recommendations are passed on to other committees and superiors, and out of
this over a period of time modest change in line with the party's values
is expected to emerge. The atmosphere is dignified and the entire
process decorous, not unlike the local gentry who view with alarm
the modification of traditions that have served them so well. Constructive, reasoned change moderately indulged in may have its place. Tempestuous excesses instituted on short notice are confined to their more
unruly counterparts in the Democratic party. In the felicitous phrasing
of the DO (Delegates and Organizations) Committee's chairwoman,
"reform without revolution" was the objective.[1]

It is good to recall the respective positions of the two parties before
entering a discussion of the differing reform strategies. During 1968,
the Republicans had no Chicago convention, no riots, no cries of police
state rule, no devisive war to rationalize, no mass demonstrations to
counter, no searing party breaches to mend, no raw emotions to placate, and no president to reject. They could concentrate on the politics
of normality and give their energies to an election campaign they
were destined to win (if narrowly). Whatever the extenuating circumstances, a minority party that wins the presidency has to be doing
something right. Such a party has relatively little to gain and a great
deal to lose from any effort to reopen discussion of the forms and
meaning of political representation within its ranks. A winning coali-

tion, like any work of genius, is best left undisturbed. That the Republican party chose to review some of its basic procedures reflected more a commitment to its continuing assessments of incremental modifications in its rules than it did any desire for full-scale reform. There was no major dissatisfaction within the Republican party with its practices.

A Distinctive Republican Experience

The late Nelson Rockefeller quipped on being asked why he had failed to win his party's top spot in 1968: "Did you ever see a Republican Convention?"[2] Rockefeller may have had something. The national conventions of the two major parties are far more different in form and substance than they may appear to the casual observer. The rules that structure convention representation are the products of contrasting traditions and assumptions that upon examination give way to far greater differentiation than one would reasonably expect. Combined with the social distinctions in group memberships, a discernible contrast in the approach to politics, and differing policy commitments, the parties and their national conventions have evolved not unexpectedly as singularly distinctive institutions with markedly dissimilar operations.

The first and most lasting impression of the differences between the two in the pre-reform era can be bluntly put: The Republicans had a body of generally accepted convention rules, and for all practical purposes the Democrats did not. While the Democrats blundered from one national gathering to the next with its "common law" emphasis and personalized management of each gathering until the fateful Chicago encounter, the Republicans had evolved an orderly set of written proposals to guide their deliberations. These provisions were reviewed by a committee of the Republican National Committee in each of the four-year intervals between conventions and any changes (normally, of course, modest recommendations of a procedural nature) that were endorsed, in turn, by the full national committee membership were presented to the Rules Committee of the convention for action. Any rules adopted by the full national convention membership would go into effect, under normal conditions, for the *next* presidential election year.

The process was long, sensible, colorless, and thorough. It ensured a workable set of printed rules, fashioned by the party leadership in response to the needs it perceived, and available for the conduct of business. It provided for the orderly execution of party decision-making and it appeared to insulate the party from the flash tides of resentment over arbitrary and discriminatory practices that characterized, as an example, the bitter fighting between reformers and regulars that consumed the Democrats during the long months prior to Chicago.

The panoply of rules crafted over the decades had one other unexpected outcome. A pride in their attainments led to a certain insensitivity in the party leadership as to the need for modification and improvement. The Republican national chair for much of the reform period, Senator Robert Dole of Kansas (as well as other Republican chieftains) dismissed the much-publicized Democratic reform efforts as belated attempts to emulate the Republicans. "We're still about forty years ahead of the Democrats as far as reform is concerned," the national chair was fond of declaring. According to him, the opposition was "just catching up!"[3] As a consequence, the significance and eventual impact of the proposed changes had a belated impact on a Republican party which had underestimated their potential.

Dole, of course, was not alone in his views. The Republican party, despite then President Richard M. Nixon's oft repeated proclamation of it as the party of the "open door" during this period, felt little need to apply any substantial effort to make its claim a reality or to amend in any meaningful sense any of its procedures. There was a problem developing here. The party did come under some self-generated pressure to acknowledge in some way the reform movement. One answer was to adopt some type of modified quota system for example, but one without teeth as to enforcement and to be used primarily as an incentive to state parties to recruit new members. It was hoped also that this approach would provide the party with a public relations coup of sorts. At a minimum, it would represent something the party could point to when put under pressure to compare its achievements with say that of the Democratic party's McGovern-Fraser Commission.

The easy road—and the one most often taken—was to back away with alacrity from any proposals that might be made to expand the party's membership. In a rightist version of the AFL-CIO line within the Democratic party, it became fashionable (even patriotic) to declare the rules in force the very best conceivable and to deride efforts at change. "You can't improve on the system we have of selecting our delegates" became a refrain echoed in various forms over the succeeding years. Even the supposed reform leader, National Committeewoman Rosemary Ginn of Missouri, could appear inordinately complacent: "One cannot," she said at one point late in her committee's deliberations, "tamper with so great an institution as the Republican party without being grateful for what we have."[4]

National Convention Operation

The apparent superiority of the Republican procedures was more ephemeral than first appearances indicated. The closer one examined their substance and their application both in state selection practices and within national conventions, the more they were found wanting. Republican conventions, for example, were at least as offensive as their Democratic counterparts as repositories for political "junk," the endless inanities and sanitized political shows that had come to mark the worst of the circus aspects associated with these meetings. These stage-managed productions were time-consuming. They emphasized entertainment. They were boring. And they substituted the illusion of participating in a matter of great consequence for the power associated with the real thing. While some political showmanship is inevitable, and even desirable, during what are often long and tedious convention sessions, too much wastes the delegates' and the public's time and can, in extreme cases (of which the Republican Convention of 1972 can serve as an example), permit and transform a forum designed for the transaction of serious party business into something much less. The national convention can become little more than a diversion intended to occupy painlessly the delegates while redirecting attention from the more basic concerns of a national political gathering. The Democrats had made an effort (through the O'Hara Commission) to restrict severely the more frivolous convention activities and had done so with some success.

The Republicans had not faced the problem. In part, this was because of the discretion in program control allowed national party leaders. Yet the difficulty was real enough. The 1968 national convention, held in a year when no incumbent sought renomination (and, therefore, one that could be expected to have some serious choices to make), provides an illustration of how encumbered party forms can become with these least consequential of activities. Benedictions, welcoming addresses, lengthy introductions of party functionaries by other functionaries, bland "addresses" by party stars and other candidates and officeholders of no particular distinction on topics of no great relevance ("The Revitalization of Our Urban Communities"), poems, "remarks" (by among others the eighteen-year-old winner of the American Legion's oratorical contest), awards and recognitions (the "Gold Convention Badge") for unknown organizational notables, commentaries, and songs continue indefinitely, threatening to replace by inundation the real work of the convention. Stage and film actors of past celebrity are invited to give "inspirational readings" from the works of great Americans with perhaps the highpoint reached in 1968 with the scheduled presentation to the delegates by then cowboy star John Wayne ("I'm as political as a Bengal tiger.") of a patriotic piece "Why I Am Proud to Be an American."[5] Such junior high school oratorical flourishes would not be missed in convention gatherings. They were staples of the pre-reform conventions. They can come to substitute for the work of choosing a candidate, determining party policy, and evaluating alternative courses for the national organization; at a minimum, they diverted time and attention from the real duties of the delegates.

To their credit, the Republicans (unlike the Democrats) did distribute written copies of their rules to convention participants and they did pioneer in such matters as the inclusion of state chairs on the national committee and in national party bodies, efforts to open party deliberations to the party's actual power base. Yet the Republican party for all of its commitment to order, clarity, and precision, did permit, as did the Democrats, a reliance on the rules of the House of Representatives, a factor that added layers of ambiguity to the proceedings and which served to further centralize discretionary power in the convention's leadership. The Republicans also continued to insist on the equal representation of all state delegations in committees of the convention, a rejection of any concept of proportionate representation. Their apportionment formula for the allocation of delegates among the states is equally regressive, compounding electoral votes with a set of bonus votes for party performance that serves to defy intelligible translation. Politically, it best serves the middle-sized and smaller states (geographically those in the midwest, south, and mountain states) with strong records of party support, among the more conservative in the party and least reflective of national political changes. The result is a bias to Republican conventions that helps reward its most conservative elements.

Attempts within the party to modify the distributions are strongly resisted as efforts to "liberalize" a conservatively biased apportionment. These thrusts are translated into potential candidate encounters (Rockefeller versus Goldwater, Percy versus Agnew, and even Ford versus Reagan), thus resurrecting the deep and apparently irreparable conservative against moderate-to-liberal division within the party. In any showdown along these lines, the less conservative forces stand to lose.

The continuing Republican concern over organizational matters has led to a de facto diminution of the convention's authority in some areas. The process is subtle. The convention's Platform Committee (Committee on Resolutions) is the *only* convention committee to meet before the Republican convention begins. The rationale is that this particular group needs the week before the convention to hold hearings and shape a party platform. Position papers are prepared by the staff of the national committee well in advance of the deliberations of the body. This is not unusual and roughly conforms to the Democratic practice. The principal difference between the parties appears to be that the Republican platform sessions are more carefully orchestrated than those of the Democrats, with less left open to chance occurrence and a more blatant exclusion of unwanted representatives of issue positions not favored by the party's leaders. Fewer policy matters are actually resolved by the group in its working sessions.

In other respects also, the Republican national conventions operate much as they have in the past. The Republican party (unlike the Democrats) retains its Committee on Permanent Organization. Its duties— "to act upon the recommendations made by the National Committee concerning the Officers of the Convention"[6]—leave no delusions as to authority and consequently may not create the difficulties experienced by the more fractious Democrats in earlier periods. The jurisdiction of the Committee on Rules and Order of Business generally parallels that of its Democratic counterpart. The principal differences— and these are significant—appear in operation. This committee entertains proposals made by the Committee on Rules of the National Committee, a separate group that has four years to consider prospective modifications. The convention committee meets only after the convention's initial session, a time sequence not permitting the in-depth hearings and research needed to instigate significant changes. De facto power in this situation gravitates to the national party's ongoing assessment committee.

Another practice in the Republican party is less apparent but still influential. The Democratic National Committee has no continuing convention office. Little effort is made to keep records pertaining to the convention's management, and there is no office or permanent professional staff charged with organizing the quadrennial conventions and supervising all activities relating to them in the four-year interim. New people are usually taken aboard every four years to create *de novo* a national convention, adding to the semi-chaos that seems to characterize the affair. Resolutions of the Democratic national convention are enforced by the national committee if appropriate or by agencies created explicitly to fulfill a given mandate. The McGovern-Fraser, O'Hara, Mikulski, Sanford (Charter), Hunt, and in its second coming, Winograd commissions typify these arrangements. The relationships between these newly created groups with specific missions to accomplish and the ongoing national committee is uncertain at best and frequently has been antagonistic.

The Republican party, on the other hand, does retain a well-managed and permanent convention office with a competent professional staff. Continuity is preserved over time in the position of a director, a position that has alternated between two people in three decades, a civil service type of arrangement for which the Democrats can offer no parallel. Continuity is also apparent in the supervision of the convention's business by this office in the interim between election years. The office maintains a close working relationship with the various committees and reform groups mandated by the national convention: a cooperative posture that can include providing the staff work for the group and supplying the centralizing focus and direction needed by such agencies. Further, the Republican party has instituted a quite different policy in choosing members to serve on the reform committees, tending to favor national committee members. A good argument can be made that this represents one of the major functions of the national committee and that in fact the practice constitutes an intelligent use of committeemembers.

The practical effect of such in-house reviews is to deprive the reform groups once established of independent figures of political stature comparable to those that appeared on the Democratic panels. The Democratic reform bodies have been able to cultivate a freedom in initiating unconventional proposals and an audience for their ideas that the Republicans cannot match. National committeemembers in either party are not often the best known or most influential people within their states. They are drawn disproportionately from the successful, economically secure, and older members of the party. Sources of discontent—or symbols of new constituencies and new ideas—do not find themselves included on such committees intended to assess party policies. The Republican approach serves the purposes of efficient and orderly review; it does not encourage a boldness in approaching party problems that the Democrats for better or worse have captured.

Finally, the procedures for reviewing credentials challenges (much like those for proposing new convention rules or advocating differing policy proposals) are far more torturous within the Republican party. On the plus side, the national party rules are, within reason, explicit and involve specific procedures of review not unlike those eventually adopted on a more ambitious scale by the O'Hara Commission. The party also allows the state party virtually total control over its delegate selection procedures, thus reaffirming its view of the confederate nature of the party structure and effectively minimizing any role the national party and its convention could be expected to play in supervising the process.

It is the Republican party's interpretation and application of the rules and the actual operation of the process for adjudicating challenges that is questionable. First, as indicated, the Republican party emphasizes its federal structure. Power resides in the state and local units rather than at the national level. The party invests a great deal of unfettered discretion in the state parties, clearly enuciating that state and local party practices take precedence over national demands (such as they are). The point is critical to an understanding of the Republican mentality. An approach that emphasizes the decentralized nature of the party system and the independence of state units has a certain ideological attractiveness: it also ensures a diversity of selection procedures, the retention of power in the hands of state-level party regulars, and the virtual impossibility of any serious grassroots reform. In short, such a policy while historically credible enshrines the status quo and protects a "politics-as-usual" approach. It is not simply a benign concession to past observances. It also diverges markedly from the Democratic struggle to institute some basic national guarantees as to representative and procedurally fair party practices, a move that came to full fruition with the compliance aspects of the McGovern-Fraser Commission.

Within this framework, the bulk of national party rules (outside of such things as delegate apportionment formulas, for example) and reform proposals are "recommendations" only with no enforcement authorization. Discretion as to the substance or application of state rules and procedures is retained by the state party leaders, a practice that led to much bitterness within the Democratic ranks. Conflicts over the interpretation of rules occur, expectedly, considerably less frequently in any formalized manner under such a system. As logic would dictate, credentials challenges are settled in the vast number of cases in the first instance by the state parties, meaning that in many situations the defendant in the action directly or indirectly also serves as judge. A credentials challenge would have to survive several different levels of review and clearly involve a national party matter before it could appear on the agenda of the national convention. Not many issues or challenges survive such pitfalls.

A Look at a Republican Credentials Challenge

The 1972 delegate selection involved an example of the practice. Three challenges—one from the Tenth Congressional District of Virginia (a D.C. suburb), one from the District of Columbia, and one involving a would-be (Congressman Pete) McClosky delegate from New Mexico—had national implications. In none of these cases were the litigants satisfied with permitting a state party entity the last word in the matter. The Virginia challenge focused on Rule 32 of the national party statutes requiring state parties to "take positive action to achieve the broadest possible participation in party affairs,"[7] a provision horrified Republicans began to suspect might represent a covert quota concept. As a consequence, and in line with the DO Committee's difficulties over the same issue, the Rules Committee and the national committee attempted to change the "take positive action" proviso to the weaker will "strive to achieve" broad representation. After initial successes, the move failed and in fact the national convention extended the provision to include alternates as well as delegates, specified "women, young people, minority and heritage groups and senior citizens" as the groups to be represented and opened all delegate selection to the "qualified" public.

The Virginia challenge cited procedural irregularities in the delegate selection process including lack of clarity in the Call to the Convention and its limited public distribution. The District of Columbia challenge involved Rule 32 also, although its main thrust was at what appeared to be gross procedural abuses in selecting the Nixon delegation. Finally, the New Mexico challenge questioned the propriety of a state convention (by a 621 to 612 vote) substituting a Nixon loyalist for the one McClosky delegate, ensuring no opposition delegate would have the opportunity to use the national convention as a forum to attack the president on his Vietnam war policies.

The validity of the challenges is not being weighed here. Two were rejected (Virginia and New Mexico) at each stage of appeal and one (D.C.) was compromised. The process the principals went through to attain a hearing though represents a commentary on the closed nature of the system. Information as to how the structures worked, what was expected of the challengers, and even such minor items as where and when the relevant groups would meet to hear the complaints was extremely hard to attain. Hearings were held, even by national committee groups, eventually in Miami Beach, maximizing the cost and inconvenience to the challengers and ensuring that at least one other challenge (from Washington state) would not be pursued. The rules defining the role of contestants were not closely enforced, allowing party regulars who were not members of the Credentials Committee to participate in the proceedings, permitting personal innuendo and allowing fact-finding bodies to make recommendations supposedly not within their jurisdiction. Selective reports (not embodying the full range of the testimony or a comprehensive recounting of the issues under question) were distributed.

Given these abuses, and they are not unfamiliar to Democrats, the process is as follows. First, a brief is filed with the national committee formally notifying it of the challenge. Second, a seven-member Contest Committee, a subgroup of the national committee, schedules a hearing and issues a report as to the party law in dispute and the facts of the case. This stage is crucial and determines the bounds for the contest. If objections are raised, the committee holds further hearings and issues a second report (all occurring within the week before the national convention). The Republican National Committee then rules on the challenge. This decision can be appealed to the Credentials Committee of the national convention once it is convened, and if sufficient support is generated here, to the floor of the national convention. The Credentials Committee does not have the time to conduct its own investigations or the desire to challenge the verdict of the national committee. Under all but the most compelling of circumstances, the finding of the national committee is accepted overwhelmingly by voice vote, thus avoiding embarrassing party squabbles, unwanted press attention, or, it could be added, a viable and independent adjudication process for convention challenges.

Previous Republican Party Challenges

The system employed by the Republicans institutionalizes conflict avoidance; it deflects and rechannels dissent before it can emerge ultimately at the national convention. When problems do boil over, not surprisingly, they can involve extraordinary abuses implicating the central party and the misuse of office. Historically, possibly the most controversial intra-party disputes over the abuse of party authority occurred during the fight for the 1912 Republican presidential nomination. The Republican National Committee, responding to the initiative of incumbent President William Howard Taft, managed to disqualify and ban from the national convention what the Progressive Republicans considered to be legally elected representatives whose one offense was their pledge to support the insurgent candidacy of Teddy Roosevelt. All regular party delegates on the list provided by the national committee, including those under challenge, were allowed to vote on organizational questions, denying Roosevelt a control over the proceedings he otherwise could have exercised. The furious Roosevelt supporters rejected the validity of the national convention's decisions, refused to be bound by them, and eventually put the former Rough Rider forward as a third-party nominee who ironically outpolled the regular party's candidate (Taft).

The 1912 convention ranks among the nastiest on record. The 1952 convention, involving another Taft (Senator Robert Taft, son of the 1912 candidate) and a similar split between the conservative and moderate wings of the party, bears some similarity but is devoid of the explosive personal and institutional overtones of the earlier meeting. Senator Taft, while not holding the presidency, did control a sympathetic national committee that again certified his delegates. The Eisenhower forces were in a position not unlike that of Roosevelt's supporters. However, the moderates this time managed to frame the issue in terms of a "fair play" resolution denying delegates under challenge the right to vote on convention matters, a focus clearly centering on the divisions within the body and one on which they could, and did, marshall broader support.

These two Republican conventions forty years apart mark the unusual occurrence of highly inclusive delegate challenges, and in fact, 1952 represented the last severe Republican credentials challenge. The more familiar case is similar to that of 1972, which found only one credentials challenge of any political significance (the New Mexico case) although the resolution of this situation may be as unwelcome as any that preceded it.

Conclusion

The Republican National Convention and presidential delegate selection rules then centralize an inordinate amount of power in party regulars and convention leaders. While more systematic and orderly in appearance, they rivaled those of the pre-reform Democrats in arbitrariness and in their potential for misuse. Grounds for improvement existed, but as noted, the mood of the party, the pride in its organizational accomplishments, the risk implicit in the serious analysis of accepted party procedures, and the lack of a perceived need or specific source of pressure pushing for reform militated against any substantial accomplishments. Another factor, a product in part of the party's own efficiency and sensitivity to some types of organizational shortcomings, worked against broader achievements. As will be shown, the Republican party had a reassessment of convention procedures ongoing through most of the sixties, a factor that would lessen any crisis aspect of the need for change.

Finally, the Republican time frame and their conception of what a national party can and should do contrasted markedly with those held by the Democratic reformers. In line with a sense of Burkean gradualism, the Republican reform process, even when instituted, worked slowly. The national convention would mandate a reform committee and its jurisdiction. During the four-year interval preceeding the next convention, the reform agency would proceed with its explorations and conceivably draft some reform proposals. It had no power to enforce these provisions. Rather, it would deliver its conclusions to the national committee and in turn the Rules Committee of the national convention (and the convention itself) for their consideration and proposed action. The reform groups in short were exploratory and advisory with clearly no implementation powers. The party regulars and the party leadership acting through the national committee and the convention retained uncontested power over what if any change would be instituted. Further, and most significantly, presuming that all these hurdles were successfully negotiated serious questions arose as to exactly what could have been accomplished. In line with their federal conception of party alliances, the "reforms" as they applied to the national convention, of course, could be implemented. As they pertained to presidential delegate selection within the states, the provisions amounted to nothing more than recommendations that the state parties were free to adopt, reject, modify, or implement as they saw fit. The national committee and any reform group that might exist perceived its role as one of quiet consultation intended to achieve objectives the national party might feel desirable but which it believed itself devoid of power to enforce.

This is exactly what happened. As an example, the 1968 Republican National Convention believed the potential need for improvement in an area great enough to justify the creation of a committee to explore alternatives and offer recommendations. It authorized the existence of such a committee and set its areas of concern. The national committee then implemented the mandate and appointed the reform committee members. For the next four years or so, the committee proceeded with its work and at some time prior to the 1972 national convention might authorize a separate and more intensive investigation into these problems with a report due to be presented to the 1976 national convention. Should this convention act favorably on the recommendations, they in turn would take effect for the next, or 1980, convention. The process is very lengthy. And to the extent the proposals dealt with matters traditionally reserved to state jurisdiction, they would only be advisory. Unlike the Democratic party, they chose not to give them the force of party law.

The conception, evolution, and impact of the reform movement within the Republican party then was quite different from that found in its sister party. The process was one of educating party members to certain goals commonly acceptable to all party elements. It would, of necessity, lack the bite of the Democratic proposals. The structural arrangement of the reform committees meant that these were a more traditional part of the operating party structure and their membership closer to the mainstream of party regulars than was the case with the Democrats. If these differences can be appreciated, attention can turn to delineating the actual efforts to achieve party change.

EIGHTEEN

The Republican Reform Groups and Their Impact: Three Examples

Republic Reform Movements

"The Republican approach to reform," Hubert Humphrey once told his fellow Democrats, reminded him "of George Bernard Shaw's attitude toward exercise—whenever he felt the urge to take some, he lay down until he got over it."[1] If such be the case, prior to the 1970s the Republicans had been "lying down" with considerably greater frequency than had their Democratic opponents. The Republican fondness for dabbling in organizational tinkering dots their history over the last five decades. With a greater consistency than Democrats, they have toyed with various types of policy committees in the inter-campaign period and they have shown a greater interest in evolving an efficient and manageable national party organization. Of particular concern to the efforts directed toward modernizing national conventions was the Committee on Convention Reforms created in reaction to the bitterness engendered by the 1964 San Francisco convention.

The "Eisenhower" Committee

The principal mover behind the establishment of the new committee was Dwight Eisenhower, although he gave precious little support to it once established or to its recommendations intended, as the committee put it, to create "the most confidence-inspiring atmosphere" for selecting presidential nominees possible.[2] The general had never been comfortable with nominating conventions. Not weaned as a politician, he found their noise, vulgarity, ubiquitous cigar smoke, and disorder unsettling. This strain which he commented on often merged with another more serious political problem to launch the first of the recent efforts at change. Eisenhower was offended by Barry Goldwater's extremism in the early 1960s but despite several ambivalent efforts proved extraordinarily ineffectual in mobilizing support behind a moderate alternative or in even clearly articulating his displeasure. Appalled by what he witnessed on television of the 1964 convention, the former president determined to bring about some changes.

Eisenhower announced his intentions in a speech to the Republican National Committee in June 1965. It was time, he said, the party did something constructive to impress upon viewers that delegates to national conventions are intelligent people fully aware of the seriousness of their mission. Responding to Ike's initiative and with his battle cry before them ("Let's reform the National Convention!"), the national committee authorized and Ray Bliss, the national chair, appointed in January 1966 a select eleven-member group composed of national committee members.

The committee's mandate was broad and vague—to review suggestions for reforming and modernizing convention arrangements and procedures—but its responsibilities were clear: It was to report back its findings to the national committee. It was not a creature of the convention and it had no enforcement powers.

The committee held substantive meetings in May, June, and September exploring the convention problems with representatives of the television networks, the written press, former national chairs, convention administrators, and academicians. After nine days of hearings divided among its meeting dates, the committee met with Eisenhower for an exchange of ideas. Thus fortified, they reconvened in November for two days to draft their report and one year after their appointment, in January 1967, made their recommendations to the semi-annual meeting of the Republican National Committee.

The committee report demonstrated a general uneasiness with the convention experience as transmitted into the home by television, a reaction conditioned by the ugly episodes that emanated from the 1964 national convention held in San Francisco. The reformers saw merit in the convention system, as the later reformers would, and tended to focus on the role of the electronic media, again as would be done a few years later. The group touched briefly on the obligations and problems posed by the media and went on to deal with their mandate as they envisioned it: "to make the Republican National Convention attractive to the eye, interesting in content and appealing to the ear and mind."[3] The approach was clearly cosmetic: Make national convention proceedings more attractive and interesting to the viewing public. No substantive changes of consequence in proceedings or representation were envisioned.

In line with its conception of its job, the group identified twelve problem areas and sets of solutions including: limits on the access to the convention floor granted individuals in order to reduce the confusion and overcrowding, a reduction in the number of entertainers and honorary speakers, an improved design for the convention's rostrum, a relocation of press seats or a redesign of the press section, a prohibition on participating in candidate demonstrations on the floor to all except delegates and alternates, better ticket security, more interesting means for presenting the party platform, cutting the "honorary assistant sergeants at arms" to 500, provisions for the removal of discourteous or rowdy people, a booklet on convention operations to be sent delegates prior to their arrival in the convention city, shortened sessions, and "special research" be undertaken into limiting the number of members attending future conventions (this from a convention body averaging 11,000 to 13,000 members at the time).[4]

The recommendations of the Committee on Convention Reform were superficial. They were not built on intensive investigation of convention practices nor did they reflect widespread dissatisfaction with the ways in which the national conventions operated. The committee, led by a Wisconsin businessman, Robert Pierce, and composed entirely of national committee members, did not represent all elements of the Republican party and it commanded little media, public, or party attention. The majority of proposals themselves were as vague as the group's mandate, indicating in essence potential areas of discomfort with the party's (or the national convention's) image which the party might concern itself. The committee's work had no appreciable effect on the 1968 or later national conventions.

The DO (Delegates and Organizations) Committee

The Republicans tried again after the 1968 election. Given their success in presidential elections, one might ask why. There are several reasons. The inability of the Republican party to broaden its base was one incentive. During the 1968 campaign year, and after his election as president, Richard Nixon spoke of the "party of the open door." The reference was to a party that would prove attractive to large numbers of voters dissatisfied with Democratic policies and appeals. Reform was to find ways to ease the entry of significant numbers of recruits into the party. It would not prove to be an easy task.

Second, the Republicans were envious of the publicity and media attention the Democratic reform effort attracted. Whether for good or bad, the debate over reform had begun to revitalize a moribund, and in 1968, highly dispirited party. The party had received extensive free television exposure that had brought the battles and problems of the Democrats into the home. The Democrats were making an honest effort to confront their problems. Reform helped stage an image of a party undergoing a progressive transformation at a time when the party could use any publicity it could attract. The Democrats seemed to be regaining their velocity and establishing an openness and receptivity to change refreshing to the American party system. By contrast, the Republican party was doing little to nothing and the implicit comparison between the parties hurt. Hence the Republican party's reform effort was born.

There were two principal Republican reform committees in the period paralleling the Democratic reform era, the DO (Delegates and Organizations) Committee and the Rule 29 Committee. As events were to show, neither was to have a substantial impact on the party.

Creating the DO Committee

The DO Committee was established in June 1969 in line with the wishes of the 1968 Republican National Convention. The convention had mandated that:

> The Chairman of the Republican National Committee shall appoint a Committee of the Republican National Committee to review and study the Rules adopted by the 1968 Republican National Convention and the relationship between the Republican National Committee, Republican State Committees, and other Republican organizations, and implementation of the provisions of Rule No. 32 which provides that participation in a Republican primary, caucus, any meeting or convention held for the purpose of selecting Delegates for a County or State or National Convention shall in no way be abridged for reasons of race, religion, color or national origin, and said Committee shall report with recommendations to the next Republican National Convention.[5]

The mandate appeared to be broad, rivaling in scope and authority that was given to the Democratic party's McGovern-Fraser Commission. In truth, however, the authorization gave the new reform committee authority only "to review and study" potential recommendations. It had no authority—and for that matter, no desire—to enforce change. It was a study group and little more. The contrast here with the McGovern-Fraser Committee and its efforts in reforming the Democratic party could not be more pronounced.

DO Committee membership was restricted to Republican National

Committee members. No outsiders—not congressmen, former presidential candidates, or governors or local leaders not already on the national committee—were included on the seventeen-member body. This assured a committee consisting of relatively established party leaders, content with the party system, basically conservative in orientation and with little predisposition to question a social order and a political system in which they had prospered.

The chairperson of the committee was the national committeewoman from Missouri, Rosemary Ginn. She was eminently reflective of the committee's membership and her credentials, with few alterations, could serve to introduce virtually interchangeably any other committee member.

They were: national committeewoman for Missouri, 1960—; member, Executive Committee of Republican National Committee, 1962–64; member, Task Force on Federal Fiscal and Monetary Policies of the Republican Coordinating Committee, 1965–68; member, Housing Committee of the Committee on Arrangements for 1964 and 1968 Republican National Conventions; member, 1968 Convention Committee on Rules and Order of Business; delegate at large, 1968 Republican National Convention; alternate delegate at large, 1956 Republican National Convention; state coordinator for Nixon Inauguration; state chairman for cultural and educational affairs for the 1968 campaign; member, National Women's Committee for Nixon, 1968; member, Appointments Advisory Committee for Missouri since 1968; president, Federation of Republican Women's Clubs of Missouri, 1959–61; member, Board of Directors of the Missouri Stores Company since 1937.[6]

Ginn had no national reputation or constituency to mobilize on behalf of reform (if she had wanted to). She was an unknown politically and had never served in elective public office. The contrast with Senator George McGovern, the Democratic leader of reform at this stage, again was pronounced.

The DO Committee had no independent staff. Rather, they relied on the services made available by the Republican National Committee. The committee's meetings were closed to the public and the press. In its own words, the committee worked "quietly" and "has not sought publicity for its work."[7] Yet, Republicans were later to complain vociferously about the media attention paid the ongoing Democratic reform efforts and as contrasted with the neglect shown their own. It was largely their own fault. They operated in secrecy and discouraged inquiries. Even as a public relations vehicle for the party, reform was to fail. The media, if they had any doubts, soon learned the party was not serious about reform. They had no intention to reshape party practices most party members—and certainly those represented on the DO Committee, on the national committee, and in the national conventions—could find little fault with. The committee made its position clear in the remarks accompanying its report. These explanatory comments also showed that the DO Committee conceived of "reform" as encompassing basically technical recommendations meant to expedite national convention business and provide more orderly and workable convention proceedings. "We have no problems that demand the entire system be discarded," the committee wrote.

> We have the privilege of showing our Party in action, and we will work to create the best ways for the American people to see and hear Republicans making history.
>   Around these basic elements, we will build and adapt rather than throw out the system or minimize an opportunity for the American people to observe and know that our presidential nominating procedure is evidence of greatness in our Republic.[8]

The committee had sent a preliminary questionnaire of five items ("Do you have any comments on the conduct of our national convention?") to national committeemembers; state chairpersons; and Republican members of congress, senators, and governors. The intent was to map the nature of party members' concerns. The responses were predictable, covering ground for the most part explored by the earlier Committee on Convention Reform: "Much too long. Much too much nonsense. Too many speeches no one listens to." "Our national convention needs to be streamlined. The speeches are too numerous, too lengthy and too useless. TV must be recognized as a tremendous factor—calls for more dash, color, glamour (even staged excitement)." "The floor was too crowded—too many people who had no credentials were on the floor—and the pressmen were awful!" "You've got to get better control over the *activities* of the press allowed on the floor . . . the press actually generated *politics*, as well as news, in Miami." Etc.[9]

Overall, the major complaints were over noise, the length and number of speeches, and overcrowding. Judging from these comments, the party membership were basically content with their institutions. The difficulties purported were minor complaints in comparison with the intensity and range of problems encountered by the Democrats. The fundamental satisfaction with its procedures is apparent throughout the Republican review. Only an unrepresentative off-comment, delivered without any particular emphasis ("The obvious lack of representation from minority groups is striking." ". . . with the microphones turned off for each state, it does reflect an undemocratic procedure, and I wonder if some method could be devised whereby a degree of recognition could be given to the individual state delegates when they have a point to make, rather than to almost totally deny them the right to participation."[10]) begins to suggest any representational or procedural shortcomings of the magnitude of those facing the Democratic reformers.

The DO Committee recommendations

Other inquiries and responses along these lines followed. In line with these and its "build and adapt" strategy, the DO Committee recommended in the first of its two reports that[11]:

- The convention system be retained for nominating presidents and vice-presidents.
- The national committee appoint a task force to hold public hearings and gather information for the national convention's platform committee.
- A committee be appointed to study ways to best present the platform to the national convention.
- A committee be appointed to study the use of "electronic equipment to assist the convention chairman and others in the conduct of the convention."
- Previous reform recommendations be reviewed to assess if they could be of help to future conventions.
- The committees of the national convention review all comments and recommendations sent to the DO Committee.
- Convention demonstrations be allowed only for presidential and vice-presidential candidates "who have substantial delegate support."
- National committee members be seated on the floor of the convention with their state delegates.
- *Robert's Rules of Order Revised* be used for national convention proceedings.
- The first state in the call of the roll for presidential and vice-presidential nominations be chosen by lot.
- Nominating speeches for presidential and vice-presidential candidates be confined to ten minutes.
- No more than two seconding speeches of two minutes' duration be allowed for any candidates.
- Nominating and seconding speeches for favorite son candidates not exceed a total time allotment of five minutes.
- A "serious" presidential candidate be only those with evidence of support in a minimum of five states.

These are extraordinarily mild and harmless suggestions. The contrast with, in effect, the demands made by the McGovern-Fraser Commission could not be greater.

The DO Committee did return in July 1971 with an additional set of recommendations. There is a little more substance and focus to these than the previous ones, but again they lack the force and direction of the comparable McGovern-Fraser "guidelines." The DO Committee recommended that[12]:

- All meetings relevant to presidential nominations be open to all qualified citizens.
- District conventions be held on different days and in a different community than the state convention (to attract more participants).
- Alternate delegates be chosen in the same manner as regular delegates.
- No delegates or alternates be required to pay any assessments.
- No proxy votes be allowed in meetings concerned with delegate selection and that alternates vote in place of the regular delegate if the latter is absent.
- No automatic (i.e., unelected or ex-officio) delegates be allowed at any level of delegate selection procedures (this conflicts with the thrust of the earlier recommendation that national committee members be seated in the national convention by virtue of their party office).
- State delegates to each national convention committee include one man, one woman, one person under twenty-five, and a member of a minority ethnic group, for a total of four (this did not carry in the national convention).
- Each state attempt to have an equal number of men and women in its delegations.
- Each state attempt to include youth (those under 25) in its delegation in numerical proportion to the population.
- The national committee assist the state parties in instructing people on how to participate in delegate selection.

Having made its recommendations and filed its report, the DO Committee went out of existence.

The rules in perspective

A number of things can be said about the recommendations. First, they are, for the most part, inoffensive. They lack the bite and urgency of the Democratic party's recommendations. The DO Committee was not interested in fundamental reform. Even more to the point, they were concerned with not ruffling any feathers. The recommendations reflect this. The closest the committee came to dealing with issues of the "open door" were the proposals to include proportional numbers of youth and women in state delegations and to have states appoint four representatives, including one minority or ethnic group member, to national convention committees. These suggestions were to have little impact and the issue was held over for another reform commission to deal with.

The second set of DO Committee recommendations do reflect those settled on in late 1969 by the McGovern-Fraser Commission. If the McGovern-Fraser guidelines could be generalized and watered down, and most importantly, be made nonmandatory, they would come to resemble those fixed on by the DO Committee.

Second, the DO Committee proposals were suggestions, nothing more. They did *not* have the force of party law. They were not required of the state parties or of the national committee or the national convention. Those bodies could act on them as they chose. As a consequence, the recommendations had little impact.

Third, the Republican party had a highly complex and technical set of procedures for the consideration and adoption of reform proposals. As indicated earlier, after a committee, such as the DO Committee, came in with its report, its recommendations went to the Rules Committee of the national committee. After further consideration, and modifications or deletions as the committee chose, the package was voted on. What passed was then sent to the full membership of the Republican National Committee for further consideration and amendment. The proposals approved by the national committee were sent as recommendations to the Rules Committee of the quadrennial Republican National Convention for further debate and review. When this committee acted, its report was presented to the membership of the Republican National Convention for debate, modification, rejection, or approval.

The process was long and torturous and it was controlled by the party regulars. It was most unlikely anything of consequence would survive such a review, and little did. To further debase the process, any recommendations adopted by the national convention could only apply to the next national convention, four years away.

Fourth, and this gets to a basic value dear to the Republican party and in direct opposition to that of the Democrats, the Republican national party firmly believes that the state parties are independent units. The national party, and its national committee and national conventions, are simply assemblages of the state party representatives.

The national party does not have the power to demand that the state parties conform to its rules. The national Republican party, in short, takes a states' rights view of its party units and their relationship to the national unit. This used to be the approach emphasized by the rival Democrats throughout their history and up, in recent times, to the 1950s. The Republicans were known for providing more centralized direction.

The Democrats changed in the mid to late sixties and seventies. The national party, in line with the social pressures being exerted on it, assumed the power to demand certain minimal standards from the state parties. At first, most of the demands grew out of the civil rights controversies of the sixties and centered on the need to include more blacks in state party deliberations. The reformers drew on this trend and assumed powers for the national party that covered almost all aspects of party affairs.

While these events were taking place in the Democratic party, the Republican party became even more firmly committed to its laissez-faire, states' rights approach. With the ascension of conservatives to the control of the national party apparatus in 1964—a control they have exercised since—the Republicans have stressed the independence and autonomy of the state party unit. They hold suspect national party direction and initiatives. Under these conditions, any recommendations emanating from a national party reform commission could only be advisory. They would have as much impact on state party procedures as the state parties chose to allow. Not surprisingly, this was minimal.

Finally, and perhaps most importantly, there was no constituency for reform within the Republican party. There was no major group within the party that felt left out of the party deliberations or ignored in party councils. There was no great social issue splitting the party (much as the Vietnam War had the Democrats) and demanding resolution. The moderates and conservatives within the party were satisfied with the status quo, and despite what might have seemed to be the desperate condition of the party to an outsider, Republicans saw little need to change their ways. No group of consequence within the Republican party was demanding change and none was likely to emerge. The Republicans, for better or worse, were content with their lot.

Ginn touched on this strain, possibly unwittingly, in explaining her committee's role and their contribution: "Our job was primarily one of evaluation. Any changes will have to come from within the states themselves. *We found there are no great problems with state structures. No basic structural changes are needed*" (italics added).[13] The contrast between the parties does not need further elaboration. Without a commitment to change, or even a perceived need for improvements, nothing is likely to be accomplished.

Nonetheless, there were pressures to deal with at least some of the issues implicit in reform. The issue of the "open door"—a party more representative of all demographic groups, and specifically blacks—would not conveniently disappear. It was a central concern in the ongoing debate over Democratic reform and the unsettled social conditions of the early seventies demanded that some action, however tentative, be taken to deal more effectively than the DO Committee had chosen to do with the problem of increasing the participation of blacks, youth (a concern of the early seventies), and women in party affairs. The result, the 1972 Republican National Committee decided, was to be a new reform body, the Rule 29 Committee.

The Rule 29 Committee

The Rule 29 Committee was a more serious attempt than the DO Committee to grapple with reform questions. Its fifty-eight members, while still dominated by a national committee membership, included Republican members of Congress, governors, state legislators, mayors, several youths, an academian, a good sprinkling of state party leaders, and so on. A more diversified membership and the designation of a concerned and accomplished committee leader, the late congressman William A. Steiger of Wisconsin, ensured more lively deliberations and a potentially more significant report.

The objectives of the committee, as stated in its final report of January 1975, were commendable:

Resolved, That the Republican Party is the party of the open door. Ours is the party of equality, of opportunity for all; favoritism for none.

It is the intent and purpose of these rules to encourage the broadest possible participation of all voters in the Republican Party activities at all levels; to assure that the Republican Party is open and accessible to all, answerable ultimately to the people in the true American fashion.[14]

Unfortunately, most of the endorsed rule changes fell considerably short of the challenge implicitly in the committee's own statement of its objectives. The bulk of the proposals are taken directly from the DO Committee and pertain to technical and obscure matters of concern primarily to lawyers and parliamentarians (e.g., the states called to lead roll calls should be chosen by lot; references to "states" in the rules shall include the District of Columbia, Guam, Puerto Rico, and the Virgin Islands unless otherwise indicated; press and staff personnel shall be admitted to sections of the convention hall authorized for them; national convention delegates and alternates shall be chosen in a manner consistent with national party rules unless in conflict with state party laws; that the term "chairman" in party rules be changed to "chair" wherever it appears, "unless the context in which it appears makes the change inappropriate" [actually a subject of heated controversy on the committee]; and so on).[15] The rules adopted by Steiger's committee are not as comprehensive as they might have been, but they do review the entirety of national convention and national party bylaws and make some modifications in these. Most of the changes are organizational and pertain to such things as the number of vice-chairpersons in the national party, the composition of the national party's executive committee, and who among party officials should be kept on retainers.

The Rule 29 Committee reports

Two issues did rise above the mundane and deserve comment. These speak to concerns that plague the Republican party.

The first was Watergate. In actuality, in the presently weak and decentralized system of national parties, there is little either party—through its formal organization—can do to stand up to a president of its own party, no matter how grievous the abuses entered into by the president. Nonetheless, the Republicans took a stab at it.

The deliberations of the Rule 29 Committee in the period 1973–1975 were not as much overshadowed by the work of the reformers within the Democratic party (much as the efforts of the DO Committee had been) as they were by the unfolding scandal of Watergate. A Republican president was battered by a continual series of revelations, from violations of civil rights and the criminal cover-up of illegal conspiracies and break-ins, to the illegal use of funds. As the spectacle ran its course, a president elected a few short years earlier by one of the greatest margins in history was forced under threat of impeachment to resign. The Republican party would like to have ensured that no such abuses could happen in the future. Their solution was to create a seven-member "Select Committee on Presidential Campaign Affairs":

> to receive from the Republican nominee for President his or her full plan of financial expenditures and periodic reports during the campaign for President in order to insure that all expenditures are in full accordance not only with the law, but with established ethical practices for political campaigns.

These provisions shall include all committees organized by the candidate above the state level.

All Republican candidates for President shall agree in writing to this rule prior to his or her nomination.[16]

If a presidential candidate chose to ignore the national committee's directive to submit his or her proposed expenditures to the Select Committee, what could the national party do? If the Select Committee disagreed with a budget authorization it found offensive, what leverage could it bring on a presidential candidate? Would a national party desire to embarrass its presidential nominee during a campaign by arguing that certain types of tactics or expenditures were unethical? If a presidential candidate had differences of opinion with a national chairperson, what would keep him from exercising his time-honored perogative of replacing the national chairperson with someone more to his liking? What would prevent the new chairperson from reinstituting the Select Committee (on grounds of political incompatibility, of course, not disagreement over ethical standards) with persons sympathetic to the presidential candidate's perspective?

Is it unlikely that matters would even get so far? The proposal was remarkable and was never put into effect. The national party has no effective sanctions over a presidential contender and the weakness of the proposed reform simply underscored the point.

The debates over, and resolution of, the issue of the "open door" demonstrated just how opposed to any fundamental reform the Republican party remained. The outcome of the controversy effectively illustrated who held dominant power within the party.

The wording of one DO Committee proposal of potential consequence was adopted by the 1972 Republican National Committee in revising Rule 32 of its bylaws. This provided that the Republican National Committee and the state committees should attempt to achieve the broadest participation by everyone in party affairs, including women, youth, minorities, ethnics, and senior citizens. The rule is a statement of principle, in no way binding on the state or national party. It set the stage for the debate in the Rule 29 Committee over the meaning of the vaguely worded proposal, and more significantly, how it could be implemented.

Led by Republican moderates, Steiger, Congresswoman Margaret Heckler of Massachusetts, Governor Christopher Bond of Missouri, and Senator Pete V. Domenici of New Mexico, the committee adopted an "Interpretation of Rule 32" that was intended "to assure greater and more equitable participation of women, young people, minority and heritage groups, and senior citizens in the political process" and specifically at the 1976 Republican National Convention.[17] The "Interpretation" included such proposals as publicizing in advance the time, place, and rules for party meetings concerned with delegate selection; that such meetings be held at reasonable times in accessible places; that "outreach" workshops and speakers be used to acquaint people with the workings of the Republican party at the state level; that "How to Become a Delegate" pamphlets be distributed to the public; and that wide participation in platform and rules committee hearings of the national convention be encouraged. The state parties were pushed to establish their own Rule 29 committees, broadly representative of Republicans in that state including women, young people, minority and heritage groups, and senior citizens. The purpose of the state-level Rule 29 committees was vague: They were to help the state parties "take positive action [left unspecified] to assist the development of a statewide out-reach program as it regards the delegate selection process and other party affairs."[18] In other sections of the "Interpretation," the committee asserts that a "special emphasis" should be made toward attracting the demographic groups it had targeted. Each state was to provide the Republican National Committee with "examples" (rather than the "plans" the moderates wanted) of their efforts to offer the opportunity to participate in all party activities, including delegate selection, to all people "regardless of race, creed, national origin, religion, sex, or age."[19] The committee did not go beyond this point. Nonetheless, it had gone far enough—too far—if the reactions of the party conservatives were to be believed.

It is important to understand that the "Interpretation" was prefaced by comments stressing that these were recommendations intended only to be of assistance to the state parties. The conservatives on the Rule 29 Committee, led by a perennial power within the party, Clarke Reed of Mississippi, reacted angrily. Upon their insistence, a further clarification was appended to the end that specified that the proposals were not to be construed as "any type of a quota system" and that furthermore they were not "binding upon any state organization."[20] In short, they had no enforcement power whatsoever. The deliberate absence of sanctions and the vagueness of the recommendations ensured that they would not seriously inconvenience the party; in fact, they would have little to no impact on the party's deliberations.

The Rule 29 Committee went out of existence calling for another reform committee to continue to study and update the party's bylaws. These duties were assigned to a subcommittee of the Republican National Committee after the 1976 election, ensuring once again a captive group totally unlikely to embarrass the party with any impertinent calls to reform. The Rule 29 Committee was as adventurous as the Republican party chose to get in the area of reform. The experience would not be repeated in the near future.

Conclusion

The Republican record on reform and its attempts to adapt to the challenges posed by contemporary society are not impressive. The psychology appears to be that of a party in ruins perhaps, but at least "the ruins are ours." The party's good showing in presidential elections obscures its real problems. In successive elections at the national level, contested seriously by only two candidates, Republicans do well. Faced with the two alternatives, voters are going to award a disproportionate (as measured by their strength in the electorate) number of votes, and victories, to the minority party. Much of the minority party's success can be traced to the factionalism and strife in the majority party or the unattractiveness of a given candidate or set of policy issues that splits the majority coalition. A minority party can capitalize on the majority party's troubles in a race in which it offers the only alternative. The Republican party, with reasonably attractive national candidates and relying on television as the medium of communication, has developed the art. Its success is illusionary.

The Republican party is inhospitable to reform. Worse even, it appears actively opposed to meaningful change. It has often been said that the Republican party has a death wish. Viewed in the perspective of fifty years of gradual but consistent decline in party strength, the party does appear to be dying. If it is, from all outward appearance, it is content with its fate.

CONCLUSION

Reform and the Future

The dapper little mayor of New York City during the 1920s, Jimmy Walker, used to say that "a reformer is a guy who rides through a sewer in a glass-bottomed boat."[1] Walker kept enough reformers busy to qualify as something of an expert on the subject. The basic question may be what to do about the sewer? Or the glass-bottomed boat? Republicans chose to look at the glass-bottomed boat.

Republican Reform

The Republicans have not been aggressive in seeking reform. The prospects are that the party's position will remain the same. Its major concern appears to be with packaging: how to better present its ideas, candidates and national conventions to the public. When reform moves into areas of more serious concern, it is quickly redirected. The conservative coalition that controls the party and represents the interests of its members has no intention of permitting its influence to be diluted by any changes designed to broaden the party's base.

In recent years, another point of view has emerged. Essentially, it is argued that the Republican party has "reformed without reforming." What is meant is that the party has developed its national party capabilities impressively since the mid-1970s, providing funds, candidate recruitment, campaign consultants, media expertise, and in general, resource contributions to party candidates and national, state, and local parties on a scale new to American politics. The Republican party nationally has made itself more relevant to the major concern of a party—winning elective office—than either party had ever done and more than many even thought possible a few years earlier. This is a new departure for the American parties and a welcome one. Still, it does not deal with the major problem facing the Republican party (and both parties for that matter): how to make the party more responsive to, and representative of, an electorate largely disaffected from politics and caught in a process of change.

> Too many Americans think that Republicans are elitists. Too many Americans feel alienated from us. Too many Americans believe that Republicans don't care about people problems, but only about such things as balanced budgets and big business, things without souls. As long as we are cast in that mold, we will languish outside the mainstream of American politics.[2]

These remarks were made by a Republican national chair to the Republican National Committee in 1977. Little has changed since. The Republican party's problems remain basically the same as they have been in the past.

Democratic Reform

The Democratic party's reform movement grew from different roots than that of the Republican party's. Walker's "sewer" analogy is strong, but for many early reformers it would not have been unthinkable for describing what they found in the Democratic party.

The Democratic reformers did bring about real change. Reform opened the presidential nominating process and involved more groups in party decision-making. It gave the primary voter and caucus participant a direct and decisive voice in presidential nominations. Power has been transferred from a select group of party and interest group leaders gathered in convention to a more representative cross-section of the party's grassroots membership. It has allowed for meaningful choices among candidate issue positions. These rank as the most important achievements of the reform movement.

On a different level, the reform of national convention procedures has introduced a sense of order and rationality into processes badly in need of such qualities. Reform did not address the concerns of the delegate or do much to clarify and strengthen his or her control over convention deliberations. The reform effort also did little to reduce the power of the presiding officer or the national party chair in setting the national convention agenda and in directing its operations. These constitute major areas of omission.

Reform of the national party structure has introduced the midterm policy conference into political life, a development that could help to update a party's appeal and keep it current with constituent needs. Beyond this, reform (and specifically the party charter) has had a limited effect in revitalizing a moribund party organization.

The Future

We may be witnessing the painful transition from one political system and political era to another, yet uncertain one. Future developments are unclear in these regards. Nonetheless, the challenges posed by an unsettled political environment and a failed party system must be met. Perfect knowledge does not exist. Profound cultural changes have taken place and will continue to take place. These developments, and the political concerns they generate, must be addressed. The relevance of the party system, and even conceivably, the type of representative arrangements familiar to generations of Americans, may hang in the balance. The reformers proposed one model of a party system, based on values of participation, openness, fairness, and a concern with policy, that they felt responsive to contemporary demands. Its adequacy, it can be said, has yet to be fully tested. The anti-reformers hold to a different conception of democratic performance, one based on indirect representation, closed (or quasi-closed) political processes and decision-making, and a limited public role. Its relevancy has been brought into question by the events of the last several decades. Still, for many it constitutes the ideal of what a party system should be and how the political system should operate.

Societies change and political institutions must respond. This much is clear. The fight over reform can be approached in this context. It is a battle for the survival of a party system and it is one in which all have a stake.

Notes

Chapter 2. A Party System under Siege

1. Avery Leiserson, *Parties and Politics* (New York: Knopf, 1958), p. 37.
2. E. E. Schattschneider, *Party Government* (New York: Holt, Rinehart and Winston, 1942), p. 4.
3. Ibid., pp. 2–3.
4. Ibid., p. 1.
5. V. O. Key, Jr., *Politics, Parties, and Pressure Groups*, 5th ed., (New York: Crowell, 1964), p. 10.
6. Walter Dean Burnham, "American Politics in the 1970's: Beyond Party?," in William Nisbet Chambers and Walter Dean Burnham, eds., *The American Party Systems: Stages of Political Development*, 2nd ed. (New York: Oxford University Press, 1975), p. 349.
7. Ibid., p. 354. See also: Burnham, *Critical Elections and the Mainsprings of American Politics* (New York: Norton, 1970), p. 192.
8. James Madison, "Paper No. 10: The Source and Control of Factions," in Ray P. Fairchild, ed., *The Federalist Papers*, 2nd ed. (Garden City, NY: Anchor Books, 1966), p. 16.
9. Alexis de Tocqueville, *Democracy in America* (New York: New American Library, 1956), p. 89
10. James Byrce, *The American Commonwealth* (New York: Putnam's, 1959), p. 151.
11. M. Ostrogorski, *Democracy and the Organization of Political Parties*, Vol. II (New York: Doubleday, 1964), p. 143.
12. Jack Dennis, "Support for the Party System by the Mass Public," *American Political Science Review*, 60 (1966), p. 608.
13. Ibid., p. 614.
14. Jack Dennis, "Changing Public Support for the American Party System," in W. Crotty, ed., *Paths to Political Reform* (Lexington, MA.: Lexington Books/D. C. Heath, 1980), pp. 35–6. See also: Dennis, "Trends in Public Support for the American Party System," *British Journal of Political Science*, 9 (1975), pp. 187–230.
15. Dennis, "Changing Public Support . . . ," ibid., p. 54.
16. William Crotty, *Political Reform and the American Experiment* (New York: Crowell, 1977); and Crotty, "Political Reform in the Late Twentieth Century," in Crotty, ed., *Paths to Political Reform*, op. cit., pp. xi–xxix.

236

Chapter 3. The Roots of Reform

1. Lewis Chester, Godfrey Hodgson, and Bruce Page, *An American Melodrama* (New York: Dell, 1969), p. 104.
2. *World Almanac* (New York: Doubleday, 1970), p. 37.
3. *Foster's Daily Democrat*, March 7, 1968, p. 1.
4. Transcript of radio announcement released by McCarthy for President Committee, March 11, 1968.
5. Chester et al., pp. 110–11, 87–112.
6. Ibid., p. 4.
7. Doris Kearns, *Lyndon Johnson and the American Dream* (New York: New American Library, 1976), pp. 356–7.
8. Chester et al., p. 162.
9. Congressional Quarterly, *The Presidential Nominating Conventions, 1968* (Washington, D.C.: Congressional Quarterly Press, 1968), p. 179.
10. Ibid., p. 154.
11. Ibid., p. 202.
12. Ibid. See also: *Rights in Conflict* (Washington, D.C.: Report of National Commission on the Causes and Prevention of Violence, 1969).
13. Hubert H. Humphrey, *The Education of a Public Man* (New York: Doubleday, 1976), p. 384.
14. Ibid., p. 385.
15. Ibid.
16. Ibid., p. 387.
17. Ibid., p. 386.

Chapter 4. The Opening Shots in the Battle for Control of a Party

1. Commission on Party Structure and Delegate Selection, *Mandate for Reform* (Washington, D.C.: Democratic National Committee, 1970), p. 30.
2. Ibid., p. 11.
3. See: Ibid.
4. Ibid., pp. 52–3.

Chapter 6. Presidential Selection I: The McGovern-Fraser Commission

1. William Crotty, *Decision for the Democrats* (Baltimore: Johns Hopkins Press, 1978), pp. 33–4.
2. Commission on Party Structure and Delegate Selection, *Mandate for Reform* (Washington, D.C.: Democratic National Committee, 1970), pp. 38–48.
3. Ibid., pp. 36–7, 52–3.
4. Transcript of Democratic National Committee Proceedings, Meetings of January, 1968, Democratic National Committee. Also reproduced in Ibid., p. 39.
5. Commission on Party Structure and Delegate Selection, *The Party Reformed*

(Washington, D.C.: Democratic National Committee, July 7, 1972), pp. 2–3.
6. Ibid.
7. Ibid., p. 2.

Chapter 7. Presidential Selection II: The Mikulski Commission

1. William Crotty, *Decision for the Democrats* (Baltimore: Johns Hopkins University Press, 1978), p. 224.
2. Commission on Delegate Selection and Party Structure, *Democrats All* (Washington, D.C.: Democratic National Committee, 1973), pp. 15–24.

Chapter 8. Presidential Selection III: Turning Back the Tide with the Winograd Commission

1. Commission on Presidential Nomination and Party Structure, *Openness, Participation, and Party Building: Reforming for a Stronger Democratic Party* (Washington, D.C.: Democratic National Committee, January 25, 1978).
2. Ibid., p. 91.
3. Ibid., p. 108
4. Ibid.
5. Records of the Commission on Presidential Nomination and Party Structure, Democratic National Committee.

Chapter 9. Presidential Selection IV: The Hunt Commission and Post-1980 Nomination Changes

1. Address of Governor James B. Hunt of North Carolina to the "Conference on the Future of American Political Parties," American Assembly, Arden House, Harriman, New York, April 17, 1982.
2. Commission on Presidential Nomination, *Report of the Commission on Presidential Nomination* (Washington, D.C.: Democratic National Committee, March 26, 1982), p. 60. Quotations and references to the commission's recommendations are taken from this report.
3. *Report of the Commission on Presidential Nomination,* Ibid.
4. Records of the Commission on Low and Moderate Income (1980–82), Democratic National Committee.
5. *Report of the Commission on Presidential Nomination,* op. cit., p. 36.
6. Records of the Commission on Presidential Nomination, Democratic National Committee (*Democratic Party of the United States of America* v. *La Follete,* Supreme Court, February 24, 1981).
7. Records of the Commission on Presidential Nomination, Democratic National Committee.
8. Ibid.
9. *Report of the Commission on Presidential Nomination,* op. cit., p. 15.

Chapter 10. Reform and the National Conventions

1. Commission on Rules, *Call to Order* . . . (Washington, D.C.: Democratic National Committee, June 14, 1972), p. 8.
2. Ibid.
3. *Call to Order* . . . , op. cit., esp. pp. 69–93.
4. "Platform Accountability Resolution," (Washington, D.C.: Mimeo, n.d.). Records of the Platform Accountability Commission and Transcript of the Proceedings of the 1980 Democratic National Committee, Democratic National Committee.
5. Ibid. The references to the resolution that follow are from this document.
6. "Charge to Platform Accountability Commission," (Washington, D.C.: Mimeo, n.d.). Records of the Platform Accountability Commission, Democratic National Committee.

Chapter 11. Reform and the National Party

1. Democratic Charter Commission, Draft Charter: *The Democratic Party of the United States* (Washington, D.C.: Democratic National Committee, 1974) and Democratic National Committee, *The Charter and the By-Laws of the Democratic Party of the United States* (Washington, D.C.: Democratic National Committee, n.d.)
2. Quoted in William Crotty, "The National Committees as Grass-Roots Vehicles of Representation," in W. Crotty, ed., *The Party Symbol* (San Francisco: W. H. Freeman, 1980), pp. 40–1.

Chapter 12. Issues in the Reform Debate: Who Gets Represented?

1. Langston Hughes, "Democracy," in *Selected Poems of Langston Hughes* (New York: Alfred A. Knopf, 1948).
2. Testimony of Frankie M. Freeman, U.S. Commission on Civil Rights, before Subcommittee on Constitutional Rights, Committee on the Judiciary, U.S. Senate, July 9, 1969, p. 8.
3. Commission on Party Structure and Delegate Selection, *Mandate for Reform* (Washington, D.C.: Democratic National Committee, 1970). See also the staff reports on discrimination prepared for the McGovern-Fraser Commission in the Records of the Commission, Democratic National Committee.
4. Transcript of meeting of Commission on Party Structure and Delegate Selection, September and November 1969, records of the Democratic National Committee.
5. Ibid.
6. Ibid.
7. Ibid.
8. *Mandate for Reform*, op. cit., p. 40.
9. Ibid.
10. Transcript of meeting of Commission . . . , op. cit.

11. "It Will Take Figuring for the Democrats in 1972," Wichita *Eagle & Beacon,* editorial page, November 26, 1969.
12. Basil Talbot, Jr., "Illinois Democrats 'Honor' the Woman," Chicago *Sun-Times,* September 8, 1978, p. 14.
13. Ibid.
14. Andrew J. Glass and Jonathan Cottin, "Democratic Reform Drive Falters as Spotlight Shifts to Presidential Races," *National Journal* (Washington, D.C.: Center for Political Research, June 19, 1971), p. 1304.
15. R. W. Apple, Jr., "Labor's Vote May Be Split at Democratic Convention," *New York Times,* February 6, 1972, p. 1.
16. Philip Shabecoff, "Labor Turning from Lobbying to New Political Tactics in Growing Struggle for Influence on Legislation," *New York Times,* June 23, 1977, p. 31.
17. Ibid.
18. Records of the Commission on Presidential Nomination (1980–82), Democratic National Committee.
19. Commission on Presidential Nomination, *Report of the Commission on Presidential Nomination* (Washington, D.C.: Democratic National Committee, 1982), p. 16.

Chapter 13. What Kind of Political Party?

1. Remarks of Congressman Donald M. Fraser before the Commission on Rules, January 15, 1970, records of the Commission on Rules, Democratic National Committee, Washington, D.C.
2. Jeane M. Kirkpatrick, *Dictatorships and Double Standards* (New York: Simon & Schuster, 1982).
3. The quotes are reprinted in the review of the Kirkpatrick book by Theodore Draper, "The Ambassador's Theories" in *The New York Times Book Review,* July 25, 1982, p. 111. On the anticipated consequences of reform, see Kenneth Janda, "Primrose Paths to Political Reform: 'Reforming' versus Strengthening American Parties," in William Crotty, *Paths to Political Reform* (Lexington, Mass.: D.C. Heath/Lexington Books, 1980), pp. 309–407.
4. Jeane M. Kirkpatrick, *Dismantling the Parties* (Washington, D.C.: American Enterprise Institute, 1978).
5. Joseph A. Schumpeter, *Capitalism, Socialism, and Democracy* (New York: Harper & Row, 1950), p. 291.
6. Ibid., p. 283.
7. Ibid., p. 295.
8. E. E. Schattschneider, *Party Government* (New York: Holt, Rinehart, and Winston, 1942), p. 60.
9. Transcripts of field hearings, Commission on Party Structure and Delegate Selection (McGovern-Fraser Commission), files of commission, Democratic National Committee, Washington, D.C.
10. Ibid.
11. Quoted in Austin Ranney, "Changing the Rules of the Nominating Game," in James David Barber, ed., *Choosing the President* (Englewood Cliffs, NJ: Prentice-Hall, 1974), p. 76.

12. Jeane M. Kirkpatrick, *The New Presidential Elite* (New York: Russell Sage Foundation and The Twentieth Century Fund, 1976), p. 375 (italics omitted).
13. Ibid., p. 353 (italics omitted). For a different perspective see William Crotty, "In Favor of the Status Quo," in Franklin J. Havelick, ed., *Presidential Selection* (Washington, D.C.: American Bar Association, 1982), pp. 15–20; and W. Crotty, "Two Cheers for the Presidential Primaries," in Thomas E. Cronin, ed., *Rethinking the Presidency* (Boston: Little, Brown, 1982), pp. 65–71.
14. Jeane M. Kirkpatrick, "Representation in American National Conventions: The Case of 1972," *British Journal of Political Science* 5, (July 1975), pp. 265–322, as reproduced and distributed by the Coalition for a Democratic Majority (Washington, D.C.: Mimeo, n.d.), p. 24.

Chapter 14. Chicago: An Unlikely Setting for "Reform"

1. The section on Chicago appeared in modified form in William Crotty, "Anatomy of a Challenge: The Chicago Delegation to the Democratic National Convention," in Robert L. Peabody, ed., *Cases in American Politics* (New York: Praeger, 1976), pp. 111–158.
2. Transcript of 1972 Credentials Committee Hearing, Records of the 1972 Democratic National Convention, Democratic National Committee, Washington, D.C.
3. Peter Yessne, ed., *Quotations from Mayor Daley* (New York: Pocket Books, 1969), p. 125.
4. Jerome Watson, "Convention Unable to Oust Us—Daley," Chicago *Sun-Times,* June 3, 1972, p. 3. See also: Joel Weisman, "Daley Hears '68 Echo," Chicago *Today,* June 2, 1968, p. 3.
5. Watson, op. cit.
6. Watson, op. cit.
7. See the editorial, "Fratricide at Miami Beach," Chicago *Sun-Times,* July 9, 1972, p. 15 and Arthur Siddon, "Dems Face Reforms," Chicago *Tribune,* July 9, 1972, p. 18.
8. Jerome Watson, "Full War Daley Delegates This Week," Chicago *Sun-Times,* May 21, 1972, p. 52.
9. Chicago Credentials Challengers, *Statement of Grounds of Challenge,* April 5, 1972, p. 1. Records of the Credentials Committee, 1972 Democratic National Convention, Democratic National Committee, Washington, D.C.
10. Ibid., p. 17. See also: Judge Hubert Will, *Memorandum Opinion,* 72C1001, U.S. District Court, Northern Division of Illinois, 1972, p. 4, in Records of the Credentials Committee, 1972 Democratic National Convention, Democratic National Committee, Washington, D.C.
11. Chicago *Daily News,* March 6, 1972, p. 21.
12. Ibid.
13. Chicago Credentials Challengers, *Statement of Grounds of Challenge,* op. cit.
14. Testimony Before Chicago Field Hearing of Credentials Committee, March 25, 1972, Records of the 1972 Democratic National Convention, Democratic National Committee, Washington, D.C.

15. Ibid.
16. Ibid.
17. *Congressional Quarterly,* April 25, 1972, p. 942 and ibid.
18. *Rules of Procedure of the Credentials Committee of the 1972 Democratic National Convention,* Appendix A, p. 4, Records of the 1972 Democratic National Convention, Democratic National Committee, Washington, D.C.
19. Chicago Field Hearing of Credentials Committee, Records of the 1972 Democratic National Convention, Democratic National Committee, Washington, D.C.
20. Ibid.
21. Ibid.
22. Weisman, op. cit. See also: Watson, op. cit.
23. Chicago Field Hearing of Credentials Committee, Records of the 1972 Democratic National Convention, Democratic National Committee, Washington, D.C.
24. Ibid.
25. Ibid. and Charles Nicodemus, "Democratic Referee Limits Daley Bloc Criticisms," Chicago *Daily News,* June 9, 1972, p. 13.
26. Joel Weisman, "Top Dems Out as Delegates," Chicago *Today,* June 3, 1972, p. 4; John Camper, "Muskie Adds, Three Delegates to His Illinois Total," Chicago *Daily News,* June 3, 1972, p. 3; "Arvey in Delegate Defeat, Surprised but not Angry," Chicago *Sun-Times,* June 4, 1972, p. 26; Weisman, "The Last Hurrah for Daley Machine," Chicago *Today,* June 11, 1972, p. 31; Ralph Whitehead, "Circulated Marked Ballot, Keane Says," Chicago *Today,* June 8, 1972, p. 7; Nicodemus, "Daley Delegates Offer a Network of Defense," Chicago *Daily News,* June 3, 1972, p. 3; Nicodemus, "Daley Slate Foes Have Win Downstate," Chicago *Daily News,* June 8, 1972, p. 2; and Watson, "Twenty-Four Downstate Delegate Challenges Are Upheld," Chicago *Sun-Times,* June 8, 1972, p. 4.

Chapter 15. Chicago-Style Politics: The Machine Takes on the Reformers

1. Jerome Watson, "Adlai-Daley Clash Looms," Chicago *Sun-Times,* June 13, 1972, p. 1.
2. Jerome Watson, "Adlai Feels He Can Beat Daley," Chicago *Sun-Times,* June 14, 1972, p. 5. On the litter campaign, see: Harry Golden, Jr., "Daley Asks Cleanup, Litter Fines," Chicago *Sun-Times,* June 14, 1972, p. 3; and Jay McMullen, "Daley Orders Littering Crackdown," Chicago *Daily News,* June 14, 1972, p. 1.
3. Charles Nicodemus, "Ask Daley to Tap Adlai," Chicago *Daily News,* June 14, 1972, p. 3.
4. Jerome Watson, "Reject Daley At-Large Delegates," Chicago *Sun-Times,* June 15, 1972, p. 1.
5. Charles Nicodemus, "Daley Will Fight Cut in Delegation," Chicago *Daily News,* June 15, 1972, p. 1.
6. Ibid.

7. Records of the Credentials Committee, 1972 Democratic National Convention, Democratic National Committee, Washington, D.C. See also: Watson, "Reject Daley At-Large Delegates," op. cit.
8. Jerome Watson and Burnell Heinecke, "Adlai Challenge Crushed; Daley Voted Chairman," Chicago *Sun-Times*, June 17, 1972, p. 3. See also: Charles Nicodemus and Henry Hanson, "Daley Rolls Over Adlai," Chicago *Daily News*, June 16, 1972, p. 1; Jerome Watson, "Richard J. Daley—That's Who," Chicago *Sun-Times*, June 18, 1972, p. 5; and John Camper, "Women's Rights Vote Linked to Dem Feud," Chicago *Daily News*, June 16, 1972, p. 2.
9. Watson and Heinecke, op. cit.
10. Nicodemus and Hanson, op. cit.
11. Records of the Credentials Committee, 1972 Democratic National Convention, Democratic National Committee, Washington, D.C. and Watson and Heinecke, op. cit.
12. Watson and Heinecke, op. cit.
13. Records of the Credentials Committee, 1972 Democratic National Convention, Democratic National Committee, Washington, D.C. See also: Watson and Heinecke, op. cit.; Nicodemus and Hanson, op. cit.; and Watson, "Richard J. Daley—That's Who," op. cit.
14. Watson, "Richard J. Daley—That's Who," op. cit.
15. Morton Krondracke, "Bars Democratic Reform Practices," Chicago *Sun-Times*, June 20, 1972, p. 3.
16. Ibid.
17. Ibid.
18. Charles Nicodemus, "Delegate Challenge Still Alive, Says Singer," Chicago *Daily News*, June 20, 1972, p. 15.
19. Ibid.
20. Ibid.
21. Chicago *Tribune*, June 22, 1972, p. 2. For one account of the police controversy, see: Chicago *Daily News*, June 20, 1972, p. 1.
22. Chicago *Daily News*, June 21, 1972, p. 6.
23. Ibid.
24. Chicago *Sun-Times*, June 23, 1972, p. 36.
25. Ibid.
26. Chicago *Sun-Times*, June 24, 1972, p. 20.
27. Charles Nicodemus and Larry S. Finley, "Slugfest Scatter Daley Foes," Chicago *Daily News*, (Blue Streak Edition), June 23, 1972, p. 1.
28. Chicago *Tribune*, June 23, 1972, p. 1.
29. Nicodemus and Finley, op. cit.
30. Nicodemus and Finley, op. cit. See also: Chicago *Sun-Times*, June 23, 1972, p. 1; and Chicago *Today*, June 23, 1972, p. 2.
31. Nicodemus and Finley, op. cit.
32. Ibid.
33. Ibid.
34. Chicago *Tribune*, June 22, 1972, p. 1.
35. Chicago *Tribune*, June 23, 1972, p. 1.
36. Chicago *Sun-Times*, June 23, 1972, p. 4.

37. Ibid.
38. Chicago *Sun-Times,* June 24, 1972, p. 2.
39. Chicago *Daily News,* June 24, 1972, p. 3.
40. Jerome Watson and Michael Minery, "Uproar Disrupts Final Anti-Daley Caucus," Chicago *Sun-Times,* June 25, 1972, p. 1. See also: "Challengers Denied Police Protection," Chicago *Sun-Times,* June 24, 1972, p. 2; Joel Weisman, "Daley Dems Again Halt Rebel Caucus, Chicago *Today,* June 25, 1972, p. 5; and William Jones and Frank Blanchford, "Daley Raiders Again Raise Voices at Rump Caucuses," Chicago *Tribune,* June 25, 1972, p. 7.
41. Watson and Minery, op. cit.

Chapter 16. The National Party Makes Its Decision

1. Washington *Star,* June 29, 1972, p. 1.
2. Washington *Post,* June 29, 1972, p. 1.
3. Ibid.
4. Ibid.
5. Washington *Post,* June 20, 1972, p. 1.
6. Report of the Credentials Committee, *The Chicago Credentials Challenge,* June 30, 1972, Records of the 1972 Democratic National Convention, Democratic National Committee, Washington, D.C., p. 16.
7. Ibid., pp. 13–14.
8. Ibid, p. 17.
9. Washington *Star,* June 30, 1972, p. 1.
10. Credentials Committee Hearing on the Chicago Challenge, Records of the Credentials Committee, 1972 Democratic National Convention, Democratic National Committee, Washington, D.C.; and Washington *Post,* July 4, 1972, p. 1.
11. Washington *Post,* July 1, 1972, p. 1.
12. Chicago *Tribune,* July 12, 1972, p. 7.
13. Chicago *Daily News,* July 11, 1972, p. 6. See also: Chicago *Sun-Times,* July 21, 1972, p. 4 and Chicago *Tribune,* July 21, 1974, p. 1.
14. Records of the 1974 Democratic Midterm Conference, Democratic National Committee, Washington, D.C.
15. Ibid.
16. Ibid.
17. Ibid.
18. Chicago *Tribune,* February 26, 1975, p. 7.
19. Supreme Court of the United States, *Cousins et al.* v. *Wigoda et al.,* No. 73–1106, decided January 15, 1975, pp. 12–13.
20. Ibid., p. 12.
21. Chicago *Sun-Times,* January 16, 1975, p. 43.

Chapter 17. Reform and the Republican Party

1. Tom Littlewood, "GOP Won't Alter Guidelines for Selection of Delegates," Chicago *Sun-Times,* May 30, 1971, p. 8. For various accounts of Republican reform and the reaction to it, see: Warren Weaver, Jr., "Half of Republican

Delegates in '72 May Be Women," *New York Times,* July 23, 1971, p. 21; Weaver, "GOP Convention Goes to San Diego," *New York Times,* July 24, 1971, p. 22; "GOP Reformers Drop Plans for Youth, Minority Quotas," Washington *Star,* August 9, 1972, p. 12; Weaver, " '76 Party Reform Draws GOP Fire, *New York Times,* August 10, 1972, p. 1; Weaver, "GOP Liberals Seek Convention Reform," *New York Times,* July 26, 1972, p. 20; Robert Walters, "Accord is Drafted on Formula for Delegate Seating," Washington *Star,* August 15, 1972, p. 8; Roy McGhee, "GOP Senators Ask Convention Reform," Washington *Post,* August 9, 1972, p. 9; Rowland Evans and Robert Novak, "Reform: A GOP Dilemma," Washington *Post,* July 21, 1972, p. 25; Jerome Watson, "Railsback Sees Reform Effect on GOP in '76," Chicago *Sun-Times,* August 21, 1972, p. 5; Lou Cannon, "Delegate Fight Stirs Old Animosities, Hints New Ones," Washington *Post,* August 20, 1972, p. 4; Weaver, "Rules Panel Announces '76 Delegate Plan Retaining Small State Advantage Intact," *New York Times,* August 22, 1972, p. 34; and Charles Bartlett, "Repairing the Damage of Rule 30," Chicago *Sun-Times,* December 10, 1972, p. 52.

2. Quoted in Theodore H. White, *The Making of the President 1968* (New York: Pocket Books, 1970), p. 304.

3. Walter R. Mears, "GOP Unit Delays Ruling on Ratio of Minority Delegates," Washington *Star,* July 25, 1971, p. 10.

4. Comments of February 19, 1971.

5. Transcript of proceedings of the 1968 Republican National Convention, Republican National Committee, Washington, D.C.

6. *Rules,* as adopted by the 1976 (and 1980) Republican National Convention and distributed by the Republican National Committee, Washington, D.C.

7. Ibid.

Chapter 18. The Republican Reform Groups and Their Impact: Three Examples

1. Remarks of Hubert H. Humphrey to O'Hara Commission Hearing, Minneapolis, Minnesota, January 15, 1970, files of the Commission on Rules, Democratic National Committee, Washington, D.C.

2. Committee on Convention Reforms, *Report of the Committee on Convention Reforms* (Washington, D.C.: January 23, 1967). For the background of the various reform efforts in both parties relevant to national conventions up through the mid-1960s, see: Republican Coordinating Committee, *The Development of National Party Policy between Conventions* (Washington, D.C.: Republican National Committee, 1966).

3. Committee on Convention Reforms, op. cit.

4. Ibid.

5. DO (Delegates and Organizations) Committee, *Programming for the Party Future, Part I: Progress Report (of the) DO Committee* (Washington, D.C.: Republican National Committee, January 15–16, 1971), p. 4; and Proceedings of the 1968 Republican National Convention, Republican National Committee, Washington, D.C.

6. Ibid., p. 25.

7. Ibid., p. 2.
8. Ibid., p. 5.
9. Ibid., pp. 9–24, and files of the DO (Delegates and Organizations) Committee, Republican National Committee, Washington, D.C.
10. Answers to DO Committee Survey Questionnaire (1970), files of the DO (Delegates and Organizations) Committee, Republican National Committee, Washington, D.C.
11. DO Committee, *Programming for the Party Future . . .* , op. cit., pp. 5–8.
12. DO Committee, *The Delegate Selection Procedures for the Republican Party II: Progress Report (of the) DO Committee* (Washington, D.C.: Republican National Committee, July 23, 1971), pp. 5–9.
13. Tom Littlewood, "GOP Won't Alter Guidelines for Selection of Delegates," Chicago *Sun-Times*, May 30, 1971, p. 8.
14. The Rule 29 Committee, *Report of the Rule 29 Committee as Received and Acted Upon by the Republican National Committee* [Washington, D.C.: n.d. (1974)], p. 1. For the Committee's report, see: The Rule 29 Committee, "Proposed New Rules," Files of the Rule 29 Committee, Republican National Committee, Washington, D.C., December 20, 1974.
15. The Rule 29 Committee, *Report of the Rule 29 Committee . . .* , op. cit., p. 22, pp. 1–31.
16. Ibid., pp. 6–7.
17. The Rule 29 Committee, *Report of the Rule 29 Committee . . .* , op. cit., pp. 19–20.
18. Ibid., p. 20.
19. Ibid.
20. Ibid.

Conclusion. Reform and the Future

1. Martin F. Nolan, " 'Reform:' The Catchword of Politicians Chasing Solutions," Boston *Globe*, June 5, 1977, p. A5.
2. Mary Louise Smith, remarks before Republican National Committee, January 14, 1977, transcript of meeting, records of the Republican National Committee, Washington, D.C.

Index